AUNG SAN SUU KYI

Related Titles from Potomac Books

Fragments of Grace: My Search for Meaning in the Strife of South Asia
—Pamela Constable

Iraq in Transition: The Legacy of Dictatorship and the Prospects for Democracy
—Peter J. Munson

Searching for a King: Muslim Nonviolence and the Future of Islam
—Jeffry R. Halverson

Simple Gestures: A Cultural Journey into the Middle East
—Andrea B. Rugh

AUNG SAN SUU KYI
A Biography

JESPER BENGTSSON

Potomac Books
Washington, D.C.

Published in the United States by Potomac Books, Inc. All rights reserved. No part of this book may be reproduced in any manner whatsoever without written permission from the publisher, except in the case of brief quotations embodied in critical articles and reviews.

Originally published in Swedish in 2010 by Norstedts (Stockholm) as *En kamp för frihet: Aung San Suu Kyi—Biografi*. This English-language edition was translated by Margaret Myers. Published by agreement with Norstedts Agency.

The author reserves the moral right to be identified as the author of this work in all countries where moral rights exist in law.

Library of Congress Cataloging-in-Publication Data
Bengtsson, Jesper, 1968–
  [Kamp för frihet. English]
  Aung San Suu Kyi : a biography / Jesper Bengtsson.—1st ed.
    p. cm.
  Includes bibliographical references.
  ISBN 978-1-61234-159-0 (hardcover)
  ISBN 978-1-61234-160-6 (electronic edition)
  1. Aung San Suu Kyi. 2. Women political activists—Burma—Biography. 3. Burma—Politics and government—1948– 4. Democracy—Burma. I. Title.
  DS530.53.A85B46 2012
  959.105'3092—dc23
  [B]
                    2011045398

Printed in the United States of America on acid-free paper that meets the American National Standards Institute Z39-48 Standard.

Potomac Books
22841 Quicksilver Drive
Dulles, Virginia 20166

First Edition

10 9 8 7 6 5 4 3 2 1

"The greatest sacrifice as a mother was to do without my sons, but I knew that there were those who had had to make even greater sacrifices. Clearly I did not make this choice light-heartedly, but I made it without reservations and without any hesitation. But still I wish that I had not had to miss out on those years in my children's lives. I would much rather have shared a life with them."

—AUNG SAN SUU KYI IN CHEE SOON JUAN'S *TO BE FREE*

CONTENTS

ILLUSTRATIONS

"I Have Always Felt Free"

It's been fifteen years since I first visited Burma. Looking back I realize that I made the trip almost by coincidence. My girlfriend at the time had arrived there one year earlier, and she had talked about the trip constantly for twelve months. She praised the beauty of the country and condemned the poverty and the ruthless military dictatorship. Back then I was a freelancing journalist and decided to go there myself to see what all the fuss was about.

I was hooked from the first second. Talking to democracy activists—Burmese students living in exile, regular people in the streets who approached you to give their view on the situation in Burma—and meeting people from the various ethnic groups made me understand the importance of Burma. Not only for its own sake, though that's reason enough, but also for its relevance on a more universal level. Study Burma and you'll find links to some of the most fundamental questions in politics today. How can we support democratic development in nondemocratic states? How does a state that once had a bright future become such a failure? How should we deal with ethnic conflicts in a postcolonial world? What does the rise of Chinese power mean to international relations and peace building?

What struck me most on my first visit to Burma in the 1990s was, of course, none of these theoretical questions. It was the immense poverty.

And when I returned again in early February 2011, little had changed. The cracks in the streets in downtown Rangoon are the same, the town's houses as battered as ever, and the children begging for a few kyats even more persistent than I remember them.

One thing is different, though: the luxury is more evident. From that point of view the military regime has succeeded. Since the regime started to privatize the economy twenty years ago in an attempt to emulate China (liberalizing the economy while continuing to suppress political dissent), a few have become filthy rich, but most people still live in extreme poverty. Foreign investors can be seen in the streets of Rangoon and Mandalay, mainly Chinese and Thai businessmen, but also a few Americans and Europeans. Burmese families with close ties to the military elite live in extreme wealth in old colonial mansions on the outskirts of the big cities.

Traveling by taxi from downtown to the headquarters of Aung San Suu Kyi and her party, the National League for Democracy (NLD), gives you a glimpse of all this: the beggars, the women cooking in the streets, the workers trying to fix façades of the old colonial buildings, recently renovated villas around Swedagon, and some of the fancy hotels for Westerners.

Compared to the hotels, the headquarters of NLD is so unappealing that you almost miss it. The office is located over a furniture shop. It has one small room where Aung San Suu Kyi works and a slightly bigger room where meetings with party officials are held. A narrow stair connects the office section with a public space next to the furniture shop. Here, anyone can enter to meet with other party members, organize local party groups, ask for legal advice, or just stop by for a cup of green tea or a rice and curry.

Paying the cab driver I notice two serious-looking guys sitting outside a teahouse on the other side of the street. They wear sunglasses and white shirts; seeing me, they raise their cameras and shoot a couple of pictures. A friend of mine who was at the headquarters a couple of weeks before had warned me about the intelligence officers; they have been there, watching the NLD office from the tea shop, since the day Aung San Suu Kyi was released in November 2010. They try to snap a photo of every Westerner who's meeting her, to make sure the visitors never again get a visa to Burma. That's the risk I take in seeking a meeting with her. Some journalists have even tried to mask themselves with sunglasses and a hat to avoid being recognized, but I simply don't care. If they manage to pick me out from one of their pictures and use it against me the next time I try to visit Burma, so be it.

I enter the public area in the office. It's full of life, very different from the previous times I've been here. But during those times, Suu Kyi had been under house arrest and her party under severe pressure from the regime. The pressure is still there, but her release has given the democracy movement a lot of new energy.

I grab a cup of tea, take a seat on one of the rickety plastic chairs, and wait for my appointment, which was quite a challenge to secure. Before leaving Sweden I was in contact with a friend in the Burmese exile movement based in Thailand. He arranged for me to meet Aung San Suu Kyi on a Friday. But when I got to Rangoon I realized it was all a misunderstanding. "Sorry," the young woman in the reception area said, "but you have to wait for at least two weeks. The Lady [as she is respectfully referred to in Burma] has been sick for a week, and now she is very busy."

My plane back to Bangkok and Stockholm was to depart a week later, so I couldn't wait that long.

I had made plans with this risk in mind and I had several other interesting appointments scheduled, but when I tried to convince myself that the cancellation didn't matter I felt like Cinderella in the Disney movie, standing in her tower, telling herself that a ball at the royal palace would be dreary and boring. To be honest, it felt like someone had hit me with a jackhammer. The first edition of this book had already been published in Sweden, based on interviews with colleagues and friends of Aung San Suu Kyi and written material, both by herself and by journalists and authors. But I hadn't met her myself. She had been under house arrest for many years without any chance for anyone to see her. Now I wanted to get her own perspective on the situation in Burma and her life after her release.

My optimism mounted again when I had the opportunity to engage in a long and interesting interview with U Win Tin, the eighty-one-year-old author and activist who up until recently spent twenty years in prison for his involvement with the democracy movement. He told me about his life in prison, the poetry he wrote on the walls during periods of solitary confinement, the use of civil disobedience, and how he and some cell mates had made a small "prison magazine" on tiny pieces of paper and secretly distributed it to other prisoners. And finally, after an hour, he promised to help me set up a meeting with the Lady.

Now it's Monday, and after a while in the public area, with the intelligence officers raising their cameras every time I look out through the main door, a staff member takes me upstairs. I sit down in a tiny waiting area with the blue paint peeling from the walls. Suddenly the wooden door to the office flings open and I stand face-to-face with one of the world's most famous and admired women.

Most journalists who meet Aung San Suu Kyi make comments about her looks and I had decided to avoid that (somehow male politicians never get such comments), but it is impossible not to notice her striking appearance. She is wearing a purple *longyi* (a Burmese sarong) and a pink shirt, and she has the trademark jasmine flowers in her hair. She celebrated her sixty-fifth birthday last summer and had been under house arrest for fifteen of the past twenty-one years. Still, she looks more like a woman of forty-five, and she has the energy of someone even younger. The hundreds, maybe even thousands, of people who saw her first public appearance after her release in November, during which she gave a speech in front of the headquarters building, made the same observation.

"She has experienced more challenges than most people do in a lifetime, and still she looked as if she was back from a two-week vacation," said an international observer who followed the event in Rangoon.

We sit down on a sofa, a few feet away from each other. She seems relaxed and perfectly composed. I ask her about her energy and apparently good mood. "It's not strange at all," she says with an ironic glint in her eyes. "The military gave me seven years of rest, so now I'm full of energy to continue my work."

Someone with a less optimistic view of life would define those seven years as "wasted," but not this Nobel Prize laureate and democratic icon. She has survived all these years of isolation by embracing it and choosing to see the benefits rather than the obvious downsides.

"I have always felt free," she says, laughing. "When my lawyers came to see me during the house arrest I was perfectly free to talk about anything I wanted."

She notices a skeptical expression on my face and continues: "I think freedom has two aspects. The first is your own state of mind. If you feel free, you *are* free. I think sometimes if you are alone, your time is your own and therefore you are more free. The other one is the environmental aspect. Is your environment free? And mine is certainly not because I don't think Burma is really a free country."

I meet her at a time when revolutions and popular uprisings are changing the political structure in much of the Arab world. The Burmese regime tries to block information about these developments from reaching the people, scared that the turmoil could spill over to Burma, but everyone knows about it anyway.

"They are not allowed to publish anything about it in the newspapers here," says Aung San Suu Kyi, "but a lot of people have heard about it. On the radio and through the Internet. However totalitarian a government is, people do get to know what's going on. That's very different from when I was arrested the first time, in 1989. As a matter of fact it's very different even from seven years ago when I was arrested the latest time."

Obviously the regime is so eager to control the news about the Arab uprisings because there are similarities to the revolt in Burma in 1988—the events that finally made Aung San Suu Kyi step forward and become the leading figure of the democracy movement. But she also sees some differences.

"Everywhere, all over the world, people do get tired of oppression and dictatorship. This kind of thing always happens in one way or the other. But I think people have to remember that it has taken years for this kind of development. For example, Egypt has been under military rule since the early fifties. And to some extent it's the same with Tunisia. The demonstrations seem to have changed things rather quickly, but you have to consider the long years it has taken for these countries to arrive at this point. But the military in Egypt decided not to shoot at the people. That's very different from what happened in Burma."

The last time Aung San Suu Kyi was free, for almost two years in 2002 and 2003, she was allowed to continue her political work. NLD organized a number of tours in the country and tens of thousands of people came to listen to her speeches, though the junta officially claimed, falsely, that her star was falling and that interest in her politics was diminishing. This time she says that no restrictions are placed upon her. She is supposed to be free to do whatever she wants and to travel freely around the country. But the junta has stated this before, without showing any obvious indications of a guilty conscience when the generals failed to live up to it. When I met her in February 2011 she still hadn't tested the limits.

"My schedule has been full with meetings and appointments in Rangoon and my office," she says, "so there has simply not been enough time to travel around the country."

She has met an almost endless string of party members, diplomats, foreign politicians, and journalists. Her face has been on the cover, or her name in the headlines, of the *Times*, *Financial Times*, Al Jazeera, BBC, and several other international media outlets. She has also met with many other political groups in Burma, both other parties and representatives from the country's major ethnic minorities.

From her first comments and interviews it was clear that Aung San Suu Kyi was more searching, less sure about the political environment than she had been seven years ago. As she's done so many times before, she talked about the importance of dialogue. "I want to hear the voice of the people," she said in her first speech. "After that we will decide what we want to do. I want to work with all democratic forces."

The last comment was a direct reference to the fact that the democracy movement in Burma split over the junta-controlled elections held only days before her release. A few democratic parties decided to field candidates in the elections, among them the National Democratic Front (NDF), a group founded by former members of her own NLD, which, together with several of the ethnic minority groups, had decided to boycott the elections. Suu Kyi tells me that she has met with people from the NDF as well but only on "a personal level," not as representatives from the party.

After her release she also proposed a new "Panglong conference" among the junta, the democratic movement, and the ethnic minorities. Back in 1940 her father, Aung San, held a conference in the town of Panglong, where he convinced several of the minorities to join the new Union of Burma and accept a federal constitution with great respect for the minorities' rights to self-determination. Many groups have called for a new meeting like that to deal with Burma's present problems.

With her trademark capacity for forgiveness, Aung San Suu Kyi has stated that she doesn't bear any grudges nor feel any hatred for her oppressors, despite her long house arrest. She wants to talk with the generals, not get back at them, and she has repeatedly said that she respects them as human beings though she "is critical of some of their actions." The junta leader and the state propaganda in Burma have spent the past twenty-one years trying to portray Suu Kyi as a dogmatic Western-influenced troublemaker. Her plea for reconciliation and for a dialogue including all ethnic groups stands in almost amusing contradiction to this.

So far her release has brought at least one major change to Burma: the democratic movement has been rejuvenated. It's obvious when you see the slightly chaotic activity on the ground floor of the headquarters as well as Aung San Suu Kyi's own agenda. Right after my interview with her, she would meet with two hundred young activists from all around Burma. After the meeting they will go back home and start organizing youth groups.

"Obviously I wasn't here during my arrest so I can't compare," she says, "but I think it's more energetic now. The day after my release I said I wanted to build up a new network and that has taken off. Not that everyone is joining NLD, but we have found that there are small groups in the civil society all over the place and they connect to us. They want to be a part of our network, and that's very refreshing to see."

She's hopeful but very wary of predicting any specific outcomes. That's a lesson every Burmese learns. Over the years there have been so many hopeful moments and so many crushed dreams—the students' revolt in 1974, the uprising in 1988, the saffron revolution in 2007, and the many times Aung San Suu Kyi has been released, only to be put under house arrest again when she becomes a threat to the military rulers of Burma.

"My hope for the short-term future is that we can continue to rebuild our organization and change more than we have done so far," she says. "But the only thing I can predict is that we will continue to work very hard. What I hope for is that the rest of the world continues to give us their strong support. That you don't let yourself be fooled by superficial changes on the political scene in Burma."

The last comment is aimed at those forces in the international community who have argued that the Burma strategy has to change. Before the elections in November 2010 some foreign diplomats and businessmen active in Rangoon claimed that the elections should be, if not respected, at least accepted by the rest of the world. Further, they argued that anyone who wanted change in Burma had to play along with the junta's strategy and work more with the parties that participated in the elections than with the NLD and Aung San Suu Kyi. The same argument was used against the sanctions championed by the United States and European Union.

During our conversation it becomes clear that Aung San Suu Kyi finds this debate futile. A new parliament has been elected and a supposedly civil government is in place instead of the military junta. But the flawed election process gave 80 percent of the seats in the parliament to the junta-controlled party, Union Solidarity and Development Party (USDP). Only four out of thirty ministers in the cabinet do not have a background as high-ranking officers in the military. And many experts on Burmese politics think that the former junta leader Than Shwe is running the show from behind the scenes.

"I don't exclude the possibility that some positive things may come out of this process," Suu Kyi says, "but it's far too early to change any policies. They can put anyone under arrest in Burma. At any time. So when people talk as if there has been progress in Burma I want them to think about this. We don't know who will be arrested and for what reasons. That is not the kind of situation you expect to find in a democracy."

Since then there have been signs of greater openness in Burma. The draconian media laws have been at least slightly lightened, a number of new magazines and papers has started, and Aung San Suu Kyi has several times met with the new president Thein Sein to discuss a possible way forward. She has, even if with great caution and a handful of objections, described it as the most promising change in a Southeast Asian country since the '80s.

As I write this, the regime has also released around two hundred political prisoners and there has been talk about the release of at least four hundred more. Aung San Suu Kyi's party, NLD, has also been allowed to re-register and run for some seats in the parliament, after being disbanded before the elections in 2010. An adviser to the president even hinted that she herself might be able to run for a political position, something that so far has been a complete no-go for the regime.

"I'm a skeptical optimist," says Aung Zaw, editor in chief for *The Irrawaddy* magazine, who for fifteen years has covered Burma issues from the northern Thai city of Chiang Mai. Aung Zaw has lived in exile for twenty-three years since the uprising in 1988, and for the first time he felt that there might be an opportunity to go back to his homeland. Not now, but if the speed of change continues, hopefully he will in a few years' time.

So, even if there are thousands of scenarios in which the future for Burma is black, there are still some signs that things are moving in the right direction.

Aung San Suu Kyi is of course aware of the risks. Every time she has been free or partly free, the military has put her back in house arrest before she has become too powerful for their taste.

"I'm not fearful," she said in an interview with BBC after her latest release. "Not in the sense that I think to myself that I won't do this or I won't do that because they'll put me under arrest again. But I know that there's always the possibility that I might be re-arrested. It's not something that I particularly wish for, because if you're placed under arrest, you can't work as much as you can when you're not under arrest."

House arrest or not, the only thing one can state with any certainty is that the junta will never be able to get rid of her. She will remain a unifying power for those who desire to see a different Burma, and the junta fears her more than anything else. Thanks to her ability to unite the many political and ethnic groups in Burma, she is and will remain the foremost threat against their prolonged monopoly of power. This is the reason they have kept her under house arrest for fifteen of the last twenty-one years. Her person is so charged with political meaning nowadays that it has even become taboo to say her name. In the streets in Rangoon she is called the Lady. In the state-controlled newspapers she has had several less flattering names over the years and has often been referred to as Miss Michael Aris or "the woman who was married to a foreigner." This also changed when the dialogue started with the new president. It is still forbidden to publish anything about her that has not been cleared by the Ministry of Information, but she is not being calumnied in the same way.

Aung San Suu Kyi's symbolic, almost iconic significance stretches far beyond the borders of Burma. She was imprisoned for the first time in 1989, only a few months after the fall of the Berlin Wall and the collapse of Soviet communism. She received the Nobel Peace Prize in 1991 and has since then been a symbol for the worldwide international struggle for democracy and human rights.

She has attained the same status as Nelson Mandela did during the apartheid regime in South Africa, and the similarities between them are many. Both are the most brightly shining political stars in their respective countries. Both have spent a great part of their lives in captivity. Both have also been forced to make enormous personal sacrifices in the struggle for freedom. When Aung San Suu Kyi was first confined to house arrest, her sons Alexander and Kim were sixteen and twelve years old, respectively. Since then they have only met their mother for brief periods of time. During the latest house arrest, they did not see her at all. Her husband, Michael Aris, died of cancer in 1999 without their being able to say farewell to each other. Aung San Suu Kyi has several times been offered the opportunity to leave the country but she has refused, fully aware that she would never be able to return as long as the junta are in power. She would be compelled to live her life in exile, which would mean abandoning her people.

At the same time activists all over the world have become involved in her cause. Artists and musical groups such as Madonna, U2, and REM have dedicated songs to her. Nobel Prize winners such as Václav Havel and Desmond Tutu have supported her in their writings and political campaigns.

Despite all the attention, campaigns, newspaper articles, and television programs, Aung San Suu Kyi has for most people remained just a symbol, a mirror that can reflect almost any dream or hope. So who in reality is the woman behind the image? Which are Aung San Suu Kyi's driving forces and what is it that makes her so interesting to the world at large? In what way is she significant when it comes to the possibility of Burma's breaking free from the grasp of the dictatorship? What is it that makes her continue the struggle against the junta, year after year, despite the enormous strain?

When I finally left the NLD head office, I realized I had been very lucky. Since Aung San Suu Kyi has been under house arrest during most of the years I have followed the developments in Burma, a meeting with her seemed unlikely. This time, however, it wasn't. It felt strange to meet someone I seemed to know so well, but only from my interviews with her friends and colleagues and her own writing. I'm not the right person to judge but I think it worked out pretty well: much of what people have told me over the years was confirmed, not contradicted, by my personal interaction with the Lady.

This is not a complete biography of Aung San Suu Kyi. Such a project would have required her own participation from the start. The major part of this book was written during her house arrest. My interview with her in 2011 was a way to learn her views of the situation in Burma and her own plans for the future. As a matter of fact she has not talked much about her background after her release. Her schedule has been full of more urgent events, and her focus is on the politics of Burma and the democracy movement.

Aung San Suu Kyi is of course sixty-five years old now, but in all probability she has many years left as an active politician. If the military power falls, she will be of decisive significance for a free and democratic Burma. Hopefully, that chapter in her life remains to be written.

This is a story about Aung San Suu Kyi and about Burma, though it doesn't start with either of them. It starts in May 2009 with a fifty-three-year-old American man who decided to take a swim in Lake Inya.

2

The Swimmer

God had appeared to him in a dream and given him a mission. Visions of great clarity had streamed through John's head. He had seen himself swimming across a dark lake and clambering ashore near a house of white stone. Sheltered by the darkness, he had stood by a door. Behind it there was a woman whom he was to save from being murdered.

The dream was easy to interpret. He had been at that spot only a few months earlier but had been turned away, so now he was compelled to make a new attempt. If he refrained, he would never be able to live with himself. Only two years earlier he had dreamed that his son Clint would die in a motorcycle accident. On that occasion he had not paid any attention to the warning, and when Clint perished in precisely such an accident a few weeks later, his grief was exacerbated by the fact that he could have prevented the tragedy.

The period after the accident had been dark and dismal, and he was not intending to make the same mistake again. That was why he now lay on his stomach in a drainage pipe on the outskirts of Rangoon. His clothes were covered with clay and water. A couple of minutes earlier there had been a close call. Two armed guards in green uniforms had walked by on the track leading around the lake. They passed him just at the opening of the drainage pipe so he had flung himself flat out into the muck and crawled forward in the way he had learned in the army more than thirty years ago. The pipe was around fifteen feet long and it gently sloped downward. The water level rose the closer he got to the mouth. It only took a couple of minutes, and then he was immersed in the cool waters of Lake Inya. There was a sudden splash when his two fully packed plastic bags broke the surface of the water; otherwise, there was silence.

He started to swim, but realizing that he could touch bottom, he took a couple of steps forward instead. He felt impeded by the clumsy flippers made out of hard corrugated cardboard that he had taped around his sandals a few minutes earlier.

Just then both soldiers caught sight of him. Or rather they caught sight of the plastic bags that bobbed up and down on the waves, hiding his head. One of the soldiers picked up a stone and chucked it toward him. It hit the surface a few centimeters in front of his face. Then there was another stone, and yet another. They were aiming at the target, as though they were trying to sink the plastic bags, and they seemed not to understand that a middle-aged Westerner was behind the floating objects. Slowly he tried to move the bags in time with the waves, and then suddenly the soldiers appeared to get bored. They turned and went away. He had pulled it off.

It took him a good while to reach his goal. Sometimes the water got deeper and he had to swim. When he saw the house with its white stone façade stained by damp, he knew that he had made it. He waded the last few yards with the plastic bags hanging loosely by his sides. He was tired and thought to himself that he was making terrible noise. But the darkness was impenetrable and none of the guards in front of the building could see him. Some steps led up to a veranda. On the last occasion when he had been there the house staff had turned him away. He had not been allowed to enter and therefore not been able to deliver his important message. All he had done was to hand over some books about the Mormon Church. He wondered sometimes whether the woman in the house had read them and whether she had understood anything of the message.

It was as he had assumed: the veranda door was unlocked. He opened it slowly, carefully, and then suddenly he was standing inside the house. In the dark room he could see two women staring at him. They looked astonished, almost shocked.

The time was five o'clock in the evening on May 4, 2009, and John Yettaw had just realized his dream. He had made his way into Aung San Suu Kyi's house by Lake Inya in Rangoon.

It is still unclear what John Yettaw, a fifty-three-year-old Mormon from the state of Missouri, hoped to achieve by his visit to one of the world's most famous and respected political prisoners. When he clambered out of the waters of Lake Inya that night in May, Aung San Suu Kyi had been under house arrest for fourteen of the last twenty years, and during the past six years she had been almost totally isolated from the outside world. Only a few people had met her: two domestic servants (they were the women who had met John Yettaw at the door of the veranda), her doctor, a contact person in the democratic movement, and, on rare occasions, representatives from the international community.

It is possible that Yettaw saw himself as the hero in a drama in which Aung San Suu Kyi would regain her freedom. In the two black plastic bags he was carrying among other items two black chadors—Muslim headdresses that cover the body from head to knee. Yettaw seems to have been planning on disguising himself and Aung San Suu Kyi in this garb, and then leaving the house via the main entrance. He does not seem to have reflected on exactly why the guards would accept two Muslim women from nowhere suddenly coming out of the house where Burma's most well-guarded political prisoner was to be found.

He was allowed a few hours' sleep on the floor in the hall, and as soon as darkness had fallen, he was transported away and let go, only to be seized the day after outside a shopping center in central Rangoon. The security services had clearly been keeping a watch on him and had only been waiting for the right moment. Shortly afterward Aung San Suu Kyi and her two domestic servants were also arrested.

To the military junta, Yettaw's little swim was like a gift from the gods. Aung San Suu Kyi's latest house arrest had begun in May 2003 and was due to expire only a few days later. According to Burmese law, the junta would be unable to detain her without first having her sentenced in a court of law. Releasing her was unthinkable. Burma found itself in far too sensitive a situation and the military junta's entire possession of power was at stake.

Barely two years earlier, in the autumn of 2007, the demonstrations of the Buddhist monks known collectively as the saffron revolution had focused the eyes of the world on the junta's violations of power. These huge public protests broke out after the junta had scrapped petrol, gas, and other fuel subsidies, which doubled fuel prices overnight. People suddenly had to invest their entire monthly income in fuel. However, at that point the unrest had been seething just below the surface for several years. Despite the efforts of the junta to open up the economy to the world at large, significant sectors had remained under the iron control of the state. All exports and imports require licenses, which entail masses of paperwork and corruption. The rice market is totally in the hands of companies that are directly or indirectly controlled by the junta. Trade with neighboring countries is rendered more difficult by the wretched state of the roads and railways, and many of the most vital everyday commodities are in shortage.

In other words, there were strong breeding grounds for the protests of September 2007. For several weeks the whole world followed the tens of thousands of monks who went out in the streets in protest against decades of power abuse, and the whole world was appalled when the junta quickly and efficiently crushed the revolt. The violence led to massive international protests. Both the United States and the European Union increased their sanctions against the country, and for the first time ever the crisis in Burma was placed on the agenda of the United Nations Security Council. Up until then China and Russia had blocked all attempts to put more intense pressure on the military junta. The Security Council demanded that a stop be put to the violence and that a dialogue be initiated between the junta and the opposition.

But even if the junta seemed superficially prepared to have talks with Suu Kyi, nothing happened in practice. The demands of the United Nations were principally met with arrogance and silence, and the world organization had no chance of carrying the question any further.

Barely a year later, on May 2, 2008, Hurricane Nargis slammed the Burmese coast. Vast areas of the densely populated Irrawaddy Delta were inundated by the waters. In retrospect, it is almost touching to read the Western media's reporting on what would later turn out to be an extreme natural disaster.

Even in Rangoon, which was far from the most severely hit regions, trees had been dragged up by their roots. Whole blocks had been on the point of collapse. Even 54 University Avenue, Suu Kyi's home by Lake Inya, had had its roof torn off by the storm gusts.

Nonetheless, both the Burmese authorities and Western media played down the damage. On May 5, the UK newspaper *Daily Mail* reported that "at least 350 people" had been killed by the hurricane. Three days later, Western mass media reproduced the junta's own figures, which stated that about 8,000 people had perished. Some weeks later the truth leaked out. The toll had risen to at least 145,000 dead, and more than 2 million people had been made homeless.

The military junta realized that a natural disaster of this magnitude might result in significant political consequences, and they did all they could to conceal the extent of the catastrophe. First, they refused to accept international assistance in the rescue work, then they accepted assistance but did not admit any foreign rescue workers. The military appropriated a great portion of the aid for its own use and handed out food and money as "loans" to the suffering population. Other portions of the aid were used as propaganda by the junta, which tried to steal the credit for supplying food, tents, and medical equipment. They finally admitted that their own resources were inadequate and allowed aid organizations into the country. By that time the death toll had mounted even higher, and yet even then the aid workers were not given access to the worst hit regions. The junta were scared to death that the need for foreign aid might be construed as weakness. The population must be given the impression that the junta had provided the aid, they believed; otherwise, the disaster might lead to a popular revolt.

Right in the middle of the disaster effort, while millions of Burmese were breaking their backs to keep body and soul together, a referendum was held about a new constitution. The junta had worked on the issue for years and asserted that it would lead to the democratization of Burma. Their suggestion was, however, a parody of democracy. The military was to be guaranteed 25 percent of the seats in parliament on a permanent basis, and persons who were or had been married to foreigners were not to be permitted to stand as candidates for any political positions. This stipulation was aimed straight at Aung San Suu Kyi, who in 1972 had married Englishman Michael Aris. The constitution did not have the federal stamp that the ethnic minorities in Burma demanded either. They wanted a large degree of self-government, but the junta suggested that several of the most important political spheres should end up under the central government's control.

When the referendum results had been counted, the junta asserted in all seriousness that 99 percent of the Burmese had voted and that more than 90 percent had voted in favor of the new constitution. The entire world laughed scornfully, but the generals did not even show a ghost of a smile. Thereafter the junta gave notification that an election was to be held in Burma—or Myanmar, as they call the country. The population was to be given the opportunity of voting for a parliament, yet the generals had rigged the election process in order to be able to retain their power. Aung San Suu Kyi was a threat to their entire carefully worked-out plan. She was just too popular. The junta realized that the election would be out of their hands if she were to be released. That was what had happened on the previous occasion, in 1990, when Aung San Suu Kyi's NLD won over 80 percent of the seats in parliament.

For this reason the junta made an issue of Yettaw's little swim. They accused Aung San Suu Kyi of two things. First, she had broken the house arrest rules by letting John Yettaw into her house, and second, she had broken the law stating that one had to apply for special permission if anyone apart from the family were to spend a night in one's home.

The matter was decided in one of the junta's military courts. The junta wanted at all costs to avoid extensive popular protests so they used a courtroom in the notorious Insein Prison. The room had a filthy stone floor and a roof but no walls. The two judges sat at the front on chairs with two-yard-high ornamented backs. It looked as though each of them was sitting on a royal throne. To the left of them sat Yettaw and his lawyer, and to the right, Aung San Suu Kyi's lawyers. There was no sign anywhere in the courtroom of a tape recorder, a court secretary, any books, or other indications of what was to take place. Aung San Suu Kyi arrived just before the trial began.

"Everyone says that she has such personal charm that I had really expected to be slightly disappointed," said the Swedish diplomat Liselott Martynenko Agerlid, who was there to cover the trial. "But when she stepped out onto that cement floor, she was 100 percent charisma." She talked and laughed with her lawyers and then she turned to the public. She spoke in a calm, quiet voice, and the audience had to closely gather around her in order to shut out the cackle of hens, the traffic noise from the street, and the patter of rain on the metal roof. She thanked them for coming and asked them to convey her gratitude to their governments. The presence of other countries was important, quite apart from whatever the outcome of the trial might be.

Both Aung San Suu Kyi and her two domestic servants were sentenced to three years in prison. By direct order of the junta leader, Than Shwe, however, the punishment was lowered to eighteen months' continued house arrest. Yettaw was sentenced to seven years' hard labor for, among other things, "illegal swimming." As a Westerner and an American citizen he did not need to worry, however. He was released after U.S. senator Jim Webb traveled to Rangoon and held negotiations to free him. John Yettaw was able to travel home to his wife and children in Falcon, Missouri.

Now the junta had the opportunity to fix the elections the following year. With Suu Kyi safely locked up in her home at Lake Inya, nothing could stop them from finalizing their plan to give power to a civil government and still keep the military in charge. A long process was about to end—a process the junta had been forced to start in the late 1980s when Aung San Suu Kyi had returned to Burma.

3

The Homecoming

Late in the evening on March 31, 1988, Aung San Suu Kyi and her husband, Michael Aris, were at their home in Oxford. It was a Friday. Michael had one or two matters on hand at the university the following day but otherwise they were looking forward to a quiet family weekend.

They had been living in Oxford for some time now, after having lived in different places for long periods of time, often separated from each other by the continents as well as the oceans of the world. Kim and Alexander, their two sons, had fallen asleep, and the parents had just made themselves comfortable in their armchairs for an evening of reading when some jangling telephone rings broke the silence. The call came from Rangoon. A close friend of the family told them that Aung San Suu Kyi's mother, Khin Kyi, had had a stroke. Her condition was critical and the doctors did not know whether or for how long she would stay alive.

If a person's life can be defined through separate moments, an occurrence or an opportunity that fundamentally changes his or her choice of path and priorities, then this was without doubt such a moment for Aung San Suu Kyi. "She put the phone down and at once started to pack. I had a premonition that our lives would change forever," wrote Michael Aris several years later in the book *Freedom from Fear*.

When Aung San Suu Kyi arrived in Burma to stand watch at her mother's bedside at Rangoon General Hospital, she had not lived in the country for more than twenty-five years. At the age of fifteen she had moved to New Delhi with her mother, who had been appointed as Burma's first female ambassador. When she was old enough to go to university, she was sent to Oxford, where she met Michael Aris. At the time of their wedding in 1972, Suu Kyi had already been working for several years as an employee of the United Nations in New York. She became pregnant with their first child, Alexander, when they were living in Bhutan, and from there they moved to Simla, a town in the Indian mountains. After that they returned to Oxford, leading a cosmopolitan life in a country that was a far cry from the isolated nation Burma had become under the military dictatorship.

Her mother, on the other hand, had returned to Burma after her years as ambassador and Aung San Suu Kyi had been to visit her practically every year in the 1970s and '80s. During these visits, friends and relatives updated her on what was happening in the country. They told her about the junta, about the human rights violations of the military, the wretched economy, and the wars against the ethnic minorities in the border regions of the country. "Sooner or later the discussions were always about politics," she said in an interview with Alan Clements in the 1990s, published in his book *Voice of Hope*. Those visits to Burma were, however, just visits and nothing else. There was nothing to indicate that she was seriously planning to live in her old home country, even less that she would shortly be one of the most talked-about political leaders.

One could of course assert that it was not her mother's illness at all, nor that telephone call, that decided the matter. As the daughter of Aung San, Burma's freedom hero, Aung San Suu Kyi had a heritage to live up to, people expected her to take a leading role, and it was perhaps the case that fate quite simply caught up with her.

Her father had freed Burma from British colonial dominion and drawn up the country's first democratic constitution in the 1940s. He was a person with strong charisma who also had support from most of the country's ethnic groups. Most Burmese and almost all the ethnic minorities counted on Aung San to become the first prime minister in an independent Burma, but a few months before the official independence he was murdered by a rival group within the nationalist movement. Soldiers burst into the government's meeting rooms in central Rangoon and opened fire with their automatic carbines. Several ministers were killed at the same time as Aung San. Many people are of the opinion that this led to the military's takeover of progressively more power, which finally resulted in the overthrow of the popularly elected government in a 1962 coup d'état.

Aung San is still held in high regard in Burma. His portrait is seen hanging on walls everywhere, from the smallest teahouse to the barracks of the military and the offices of the democratic movement. Everyone wants to bask in the glory of the mythical Bogyoke (General) Aung San.

Aung San Suu Kyi was only two years old when her father was murdered, and even though she had never had any concrete plans before 1988 of living a life in the public eye, she has been constantly aware of the significance of her heritage. During a period of time in the early 1970s, when she was working in New York and Michael Aris found himself in the little mountain principality of Bhutan on the other side of the globe, the two, who had only recently fallen in love, were able to communicate solely by means of letters. Over the enormous distance in time and space they carried on a conversation about their common future. In one of her letters Aung San Suu Kyi wrote,

> I only ask one thing, that should my people need me, you would help me to do my duty by them. Would you mind very much should such a situation ever arise? How probable it is I do not know, but the possibility is there.
>
> Sometimes I am beset by fears that circumstances and national considerations might tear us apart just when we are so happy in each other that separation would be a torment. And yet such fears are so futile and inconsequential: if we love and cherish each other as much as we can while we can, I am sure love and compassion will triumph in the end.

She knew that a time might come when Burma would demand her undivided attention. "She wanted me to promise not to stop her if her nation ever needed her. I made that promise to her," said Michael Aris later, in an interview with the *New York Times*.

But despite her social and political heritage, Aung San Suu Kyi totally refrained from getting involved in her home country's political game until 1988. In *The Voice of Hope*, she describes how the fate of her father; his exhausting, self-sacrificing work during the fight for freedom; as well as his ultimate sacrifice made her choose to turn away from a public role. She did not want it. And when she had now returned she had no plans for remaining there permanently. The only idea she had, apart from looking after her mother, was to start a library in the name of her father, as she herself has said.

The most likely scenario was thus that Aung San Suu Kyi would return to Oxford and continue the modest academic career she had started after the years raising her two small children. The world would then—at best— have gotten to know her as an author and researcher in the field of Burmese literature.

But history does not always choose the most likely path.

Her mother's illness coincided with a time of political upheaval in Burma. In the mid-1980s, the United Nations classified the country as one of the ten poorest in the world. The classification was made according to the wishes of Burma itself. If one landed on the list of the poorest countries, then one was actually given more advantageous terms by the World Bank and the International Monetary Fund, and Burma needed money.

In the twenty-six years that had passed since the military junta took power in 1962, the country had been transformed from one of the most promising in Southeast Asia into a total economic and political failure. Unemployment had reached an all-time high and inflation had eaten up people's savings. The price of rice could rise by 20 to 30 percent in a month. In parts of the country famine was rife, and in the border regions a seemingly never-ending civil war raged between the central government and the ethnic minorities. In the autumn of 1987 Ne Win, the leader of the junta, made the situation much worse in a single blow by annulling all existing banknotes. His daughter later declared that it was his astrologer who had recommended this measure to gain control over the economic development. From one day to another the old banknotes were replaced by new ones with new denominations, all of which were divisible by nine, that being Ne Win's lucky number. Suddenly the bazaars and teahouses were flooded with new and not terribly rational forty-five- and ninety-kyat banknotes. At this time most Burmese—and with good reason—did not trust the country's banks. They had their savings stowed away in their mattresses, and the decision to do away with the old banknote denominations, coming as it did with no warning, meant that millions of people lost all their savings overnight.

The day after this decision, the students at Rangoon's Technical University started a public protest. They left their dormitories in the northern parts of the city and went out onto the streets, throwing stones at public buildings, smashing up cars belonging to government officials, and destroying a few traffic lights while they were at it. The police intervened with violence and pushed the students back, but that did not quell their desire for revolt. A few weeks later the students in the state of Arakan (now Rakhine), situated in the east, went out in similar demonstrations, as was also the case in the little town of Pyinmana in central Burma. Since they had no political leaders of their own, several of the students were carrying placards with pictures of Aung San, which they continued to carry even when the police were shooting at them. At about the same time, a small number of bombs exploded in Mandalay and Rangoon. One of them partially destroyed the Czech Embassy, for reasons unknown.

It was far from the first time that social unrest had broken out in Burma. Students and activists have in principle always gone out onto the streets at the first possible opportunity. They protested after the military coup in 1962. They did it again when the former secretary general to the United Nations, U Thant, was to be buried in Rangoon in 1974. The junta had struck back with violence every time, quickly and effectively. All the same, the junta must have understood that this time they were faced with something that was qualitatively new. The students never seemed to give up, and under the surface the whole country seemed to be seething with anger. All that was needed was an igniting spark. And as was so often the case in Burma's history, it was the students at Rangoon University who started the fire.

Three weeks before the arrival of Aung San Suu Kyi, three young students went into a teahouse in the vicinity of the university. With an earthen floor and bamboo poles as walls, it was small and shabby but popular among the students because the prices were reasonable. And then there was a tape recorder and several cassette tapes with the latest artists. When these three students arrived the tape recorder was occupied by a group of local citizens

who were listening to traditional Burmese music. The young people had
brought a cassette featuring the artist Sai Hti Hseng, a kind of Burmese Bob
Dylan. After a while they asked the owner of the teahouse if he could change
the cassette, but then the older men started protesting loudly. The quarrel
developed into a scuffle, and one of the men hit one of the students, Win
Myint, on the head with a chair. He had to be taken to the hospital. The
police intervened, but it turned out that the man who had struck Win Myint
was the son of one of the local powers-that-be, and he was released almost
immediately from custody. The students became incensed and they went
out onto the streets yet again to protest. Now they were several hundred,
and on their way to the police station they were met by a force from the
Lon Htein riot police, who opened fire on the totally defenseless students.
A young man called Maung Phone Maw was shot and killed, and the fury
of the students grew even fiercer. The day after, the Lon Htein surrounded
the whole campus area at the Rangoon Institute of Technology (RIT). The
students responded by carrying out new demonstrations within the campus
area. After twenty-four hours, the gates of the area were forced by military
vehicles, and soldiers went in with batons and guns and indiscriminately
hit anything that moved.

Meanwhile, the authorities activated the state propaganda apparatus in
order to stop the protests from spreading. The state radio put out the information that the students inside the RIT had refused to negotiate and that
military action had therefore been necessary. And the government newspaper *Working People's Daily* reported that Maung Phone Maw had not been
killed by the soldiers at all but in a brawl between civilians.

No Burmese in their right mind believed these reports. After twenty-six
years of military government, they had learned that the newspapers and the
radio were full of lies and that the truth must be sought elsewhere. Rumors
about the bloody scenes that had occurred at the RIT spread like wildfire
through the city, and at that point even the students at the larger Rangoon
University woke up. A demonstration with a few hundred participants was
quickly organized to march to the RIT, which was quite close by. After only
half a mile or so, at the shore of Lake Inya, when the sun was at its zenith
in the skies, the demonstration was blocked by the army. Thick layers of
barbed wire had been rolled out, and when the students turned around they

were met by the Lon Htein, which blocked the road in the other direction. The students were caught in a bloody vise, and this time the junta had decided to make an example of their prey: they went in with the intention of killing. Young women were knocked unconscious and raped, others were left to drown at the water's edge. Over forty students were locked up in military vehicles where they suffocated to death in the oppressive midday heat.

This was the starting point for a summer of popular protests and violent riots, which were joined by more and more Burmese. Buddhist monks went out onto the streets in the thousands and workers left their factories. Green Islamic flags mingled with nationalist Bamar Kingdom (ancient kingdom of ethnic Burmese) symbols and flags with the peacock motif, which was a symbol for the ever stronger student movement. Pastors from the ethnic minorities carried around signs saying "Jesus loves democracy." Even journalists from the country's newspapers, previously under such iron control, broke free and now wrote what they understood as the truth about the country's development. The guidelines from the Ministry of Information, which landed by fax every morning and which had previously ruled the entire system of news reporting, were now thrown in the wastebasket. The situation was so chaotic that nobody stopped them.

"We had a month of freedom before the regime took control of the situation again. It was a strange experience to be able to write at last about what was really happening in the streets," said one ex-journalist when I met him several years later in Rangoon. He had been convicted and sentenced to five years' imprisonment after that brief period of freedom.

Aung San Suu Kyi kept her distance from the huge demonstrations. During the first months after her arrival in Burma, she more or less lived in the same ward as her mother and returned to 54 University Avenue only to bathe, launder clothes, and tend to practical matters. But even if she had not had her mother to take care of, it is doubtful whether Aung San Suu Kyi would have involved herself as early as that. The streets were not her arena. "I am simply not the kind of person who joins demonstrations," she said a few years afterward. "I admired the ones who did what they did, but it was a world I knew nothing about. I belonged to the silent majority who supported them."

On the other hand, she witnessed the effects of the junta's brutality when mishandled and severely injured young people were admitted to the hospital.

At the same time she often received visits from elderly politicians who had known her father and who were now sounding her out to see what the possibilities were of engaging her in the struggle against the junta. As early as the late 1970s, when she visited Burma to collect books for a library project in Oxford, U Tin Moe, professor of literature at the University in Rangoon, had asked whether she would consider doing anything to break the power of the military. "Yes, of course, uncle," she had replied. "But what?" At that time no answer had existed. Now the older politicians had realized that the protest movement needed an ideological center, something or somebody that all groups—students, ethnic minorities, religious associations, and union organizations—could be united around. For decades the junta had divided and ruled, playing out the many groups against one another in order to keep the power to themselves. A unifying force was required if the revolt were to succeed.

Revolt is the time for rumor, and for several weeks a rumor circulated that Aung San Suu Kyi's older brother Aung San Oo was on his way from the United States, at the head of a vast army, in the same way their father had invaded Burma together with the Japanese in the 1940s. But Aung San Oo had never shown any political ambitions. He had been an American citizen for years and he had been educated as an engineer. During the 1990s it also became apparent that he didn't sympathize with the democratic movement.

Aung San Suu Kyi was already in the country and she shared to the greatest possible degree the same values as the democratic movement. Who then could be better suited for the task than the daughter of the man who had freed Burma and then united the country after the colonial era? In other words—was there anything that Aung San Suu Kyi could contribute? She received the question on several occasions and deliberated on the possibility, but she gave no clear answer during the spring and summer.

At this point in time she was not a well-known person among the population in Burma either. Since she had left the country in 1960, the government newspapers had regularly published small notices about her, but always very sparingly, and when she appeared in public, it was always on account of the fact that she was the daughter of Aung San.

After three months in the hospital, it was clear that her mother was not going to survive. Her condition steadily worsened, and Aung San Suu Kyi saw to it that she was able to live at home during her last days. In July the school term had come to an end in Oxford, so Michael and the boys were able to travel to Burma to visit her and also take a final farewell of Khin Kyi. For the first time in almost four months the whole family gathered together under one roof.

The day after their arrival, on July 23, the junta leader, Ne Win, resigned. The pressure from the popular protests and the brutal violence in the streets had been too much in the end. It was a historic moment. Ne Win had run the country since the military coup in 1962, and poverty, the international isolation, and the military oppression were to a great degree his personal creation. Now he spoke regretfully about his "mistakes" and promised that a referendum would soon be held about the future of the country. It was slightly unclear what he meant but still a hopeful piece of information for the masses in the streets. The dictator's resignation was celebrated like a victory. Although the price had been high, since most people who had taken part in the demonstration knew somebody who had been imprisoned, mishandled, or killed, now a change seemed possible.

When Aung San Suu Kyi saw Ne Win's farewell speech on the government TV channel it was as though something fell into place inside her. "She, like the whole country, was electrified," wrote Michael Aris in *Freedom from Fear*. "The people at last had a chance to take control of their own destinies. I think it was at this moment that Suu made up her mind to step forward."

However, their hopes of a rapid transition to civil rule were almost immediately quashed. After Ne Win's defection, Gen. Sein Lwin was appointed as prime minister. It was Sein Lwin who had led the bloodbath against the students in the spring of the same year and he was commonly known by the nickname "the butcher from Rangoon." He was not exactly a politician whom the people would ever trust.

Sein Lwin initiated a state of emergency in the whole of Burma, and people in the streets became incensed. On the morning of August 8 at eight minutes past eight the greatest popular manifestation of unrest in the history of Burma started. Peter Conrad, a Buddhist theologian living in Bangkok, happened to be in Rangoon on that day. His eyewitness account is included in Bertil Lintner's book *Burma in Revolt*:

I was standing on the balcony of my hotel room just before 9 a.m. when I spotted some masked youths on bicycles racing down the almost empty road outside, calling out something in Burmese. Apparently they were announcing that the demonstrators were coming. A few minutes later, some students came and formed human chains around the soldiers who were posted at the main intersections. I was told that the students intended to protect the soldiers from possible, violent attacks from the demonstrators. And then they came in a massive column across the railway bridge at the Sule Pagoda Road with flags and banners, heading for the city centre. There were thousands of them, clenching their fists and chanting anti-government slogans.

Thousands was an understatement. Actually millions of people went out onto the streets in Burma that day. In at least 200 of Burma's 314 "townships," vast demonstrations were carried out. In Taunggyi alone, the capital of the mountainous Shan state in eastern Burma, over a hundred thousand people demonstrated.

Sein Lwin let them have their way until late in the evening on August 8. Then he sent in the military to clean up. During that night and the five or six following days, several thousand people were killed and even more imprisoned. There are brutal, almost indescribable stories from those who were there when the killing started. On my first journey to Burma in the mid-1990s, I met a tour guide who had been a student in 1988. He had marched in one of the front ranks in Rangoon when the military opened fire. A girl behind him had been hit by a bullet in the throat and died immediately. His best friend, walking beside him, had been shot in the leg and was then dragged away by his terrified friends along the filthy streets. The tour guide was arrested during the night and sentenced to a year in prison, after a summary trial.

"I hate this regime," he said, glancing nervously over his shoulder, afraid that one of his countrymen might hear him and report him to the authorities.

It was in this heated political environment that Aung San Suu Kyi chose to make a public appearance. Together with U Tin Oo and some others from the political opposition she wrote a letter to the junta in which they suggested a transitional solution in order to resolve the political deadlock. A committee without any connections to the military would take over the work of government and help guide the country toward democracy. The letter was basically about the need for dialogue, a theme that has returned time and again through the years in Aung San Suu Kyi's rhetoric. But the generals chose to understand the letter as pure provocation. One could say that this was the start of several decades of conflict between Suu Kyi and the military.

In that situation Aung San Suu Kyi did not yet see herself as the leader of the democratic movement. A few days after August 8, Aung San Suu Kyi met a group from a union organization that had been formed by teachers at the University of Rangoon. They had read the letter she had written to the junta and urged her to take on the role as leader of the opposition.

"She was very doubtful," said one of those who had been at the meeting. "She explained that she was not a politician. On the other hand, she could consider mediating between the demonstrators in the streets and the military junta."

However, the shabby white stone house by Lake Inya quickly became a central meeting place for the young and growing democratic movement. Activists, journalists, and student leaders flocked around Aung San Suu Kyi, as well as a group of older statesmen, defectors from the junta who had for a long time wished for a different development for their country. Former minister of defense U Tin Oo and U Kyi Maung, who had fought with Aung San against the British in the 1940s, were among the most prominent of those previously in power who now stood up for the democratic movement. Both had joined the army and made careers as officers during the democratic period in the 1940s. U Kyi Maung resigned as an officer in 1963, one year after the military coup, while U Tin Oo left the junta during the repercussions in connection with U Thant's funeral in 1974. Both became critics of Ne Win and spent several years in prison. For both it was a great development that Gen. Aung San's daughter now stood on the side of the opposition. "I knew her father," said U Tin Oo in an interview, "and she resembled him. The way she talked, her features, the way she smiled and moved her head. All her gestures were similar to her father's."

And living amid all this, in the middle of the tropical heat during the rainy period, the violence in the streets, and the more and more crowded housing on University Avenue, was Suu Kyi's family. Those months in Rangoon are described with tenderness by Michael Aris a few years later in his book *Freedom from Fear*:

> Despite all the frenetic activity in her house, it never really lost the sense of being a haven of love and care. Suu is an astonishing person by any standards, and I think I can say I know her after twenty years of marriage, but I shall never quite understand how she managed to divide her efforts so equally between the devoted care of her incapacitated, dying mother and all the activity which brought her the leadership of the struggle for human rights and democracy in her country. It has something to do with her inflexible sense of duty and her sure grasp of what is right and wrong—qualities which can sit as dead weight on some shoulders but which she carries with such eminent grace.

The bloodbath on August 8 did not stop people from continuing to demonstrate. They defied the machine guns and went out once again onto the streets, and in the end the junta realized that they had to change their strategy. Sein Lwin was dismissed from office as president and leader of the junta and was replaced by the well-known historian Maung Maung, who had written, among other things, an ingratiating biography of the dictator Ne Win. For the first time since the coup in 1962, there was a civilian at the head of the country's political leadership. The state of emergency was annulled, and Maung Maung repeated Ne Win's promise that a referendum would be held about the political future of the country.

On August 26, Aung San Suu Kyi gave a major public speech at the Shwedagon Pagoda. A few days earlier she had made a minor public appearance outside the Rangoon General Hospital, but that had chiefly been a dress rehearsal. This was the real thing. The place had been chosen with great care so that nobody would miss the symbolism. Shwedagon, with its two-hundred-foot-high completely golden *stupa* (the "tower" and center of the Buddhist temple) is one of Buddhism's holiest places. For the Burmese the pagoda has served for a long time as a symbol of the struggle against British colonial power. Aung San had besides given one of his most important political speeches at the same place in 1946, when Burma stood on the verge of independence.

Information varies concerning the numbers who came to listen to her on this occasion, but it was probably over half a million people. They poured in from the whole region around Rangoon. Several thousand had made their way there as early as the previous evening and spent the night in front of the pagoda, and others had gotten up early in the morning and walked several kilometers in order to arrive on time.

The propaganda apparatus of the junta was also active. They had understood that they were being confronted by a threat that was out of the ordinary. A small truck drove around distributing great piles of leaflets. When the spectators picked up the leaflets, they read the brutal attacks against Aung San Suu Kyi and her husband, from "call you bastard foreigner and buzz off" to "genocidal prostitute." Several of the drawings on the leaflets were downright obscene.

Aung San Suu Kyi arrived at the meeting a few minutes late. She was, as always, wearing traditional Burmese clothes: a short-sleeved white blouse; a colorful Burmese sarong, known as a longyi; and a white flower in her hair. Her ever greater band of followers had heard rumors that the junta was planning to murder her, and therefore she was surrounded by a dozen young women who were all dressed identically so that it would be difficult to distinguish her from the group.

Suu Kyi felt calm and sure that her voice would carry out to the vast public, but she grew nervous when her party was barely able to make its way through the mass of people. She realized that the meeting was going to be well and truly delayed. She finally climbed up on the temporary podium in front of the pagoda despite all. Behind her the organizers had suspended a large portrait of Aung San and placed a flag from the 1940s freedom movement beside it. Once again: nobody could miss the symbolism.

The inadequate sound system and all of the people meant that most of them did not even hear what she said. But Aung San's daughter had come to give them support in the struggle against the junta, and that was enough. It was just the kind of support they needed. In all the dark times the people of Burma had been through since the military had escalated its violence, she herself acted as an arrow of light and life. "Such was the mood of yearning and anticipation that she could have recited a laundry list and still her every word would have been applauded," wrote Justin Wintle in his book *Perfect Hostage*.

"We couldn't really picture her before the speech at Shwedagon," says Maung, who was later to become a leading member of the democratic movement's youth league. "Many of us were pretty skeptical. She had lived her whole life abroad. What could she know about our problems? Could she even speak Burmese? But she convinced us."

She gave her speech in almost perfect Burmese, and many of those who remembered her father were astonished too by the great resemblance between them. They looked alike, with the same slim figure and stately deportment, the same intelligent dark eyes, and the same clean facial features. They both had the same way of speaking as well. Aung San had been a more vociferous and agitating leader, more of a troublemaker, some might certainly say, but they had the same way of going straight to the core of a problem, without any circumlocution, and they used the same brief sentences and striking expressions.

She began her speech with a tribute to the students and other activists who had walked in the vanguard of the popular uprising, and she commanded there to be a minute of silence in homage to all those who had sacrificed their lives for a better future of their country. It must have been a magic moment, when half a million people turned from a noisy, seething mass into one that stood still and totally silent. After that Aung San Suu Kyi declared her reasons for choosing to get involved with the democratic movement:

> A number of people are saying that since I have spent most of my time abroad and am married to a foreigner I could not be familiar with this nation's politics. . . . The trouble is that I know too much. My family knows best how complicated and tricky Burmese politics can be and how much my father had to suffer on this account.

She talked about her father's doubts about actually taking upon himself the role of prime minister after the independence. He had realized that the road forward after the liberation would be complicated and that great personal sacrifices would be required of those who stood at the head of the new nation. He had spoken about withdrawing and becoming an author instead.

Since my father had such a desire I too have always wanted to place myself at a distance from this kind of politics. . . . So someone might ask why should I now be involved in this movement. The answer is that the present crisis is the concern of the entire nation. I could not as my father's daughter remain indifferent to all that was going on. This national crisis could in fact be called the second struggle for national independence.

That final expression is utterly central for the mission Aung San Suu Kyi now took upon herself. She intended to carry on her father's work. The Burmese had been robbed of their independence through the military coup in 1962 and the oppression that followed it. Now she spoke persuasively for the transition to a multiparty system with democratic elections. On one point, though, it was clear that she differed radically from her father. Aung San never hesitated to use violent methods in the struggle for independence. In fact, he agitated actively to get the young nationalists in the 1930s to arm themselves. On the contrary, Aung San Suu Kyi was of the opinion that the new democratic movement must be a nonviolent movement. Violent protests would only give the junta an excuse to reciprocate. But despite her pacifist convictions, deeply rooted in Buddhism and Mahatma Gandhi's ideas, she asserted anyway that the army must have a function to fill even in the future democratic Burma.

I do not wish to see any split and struggles between the army which my father built up and the people who love my father so much. May I also from this platform ask the personnel of the armed forces to reciprocate this kind of understanding and sympathy?

Michael Aris and their sons, Alexander and Kim, stood behind her on the podium, and Nyo Ohn Myint, one of the young activists in the democratic movement, relates that Michael Aris was proud but also full of doubt: "He had an expression in his face, kind of like: I'm going to lose my wife and my family and my privacy." On their way from the meeting, Nyo Ohn Myint traveled in the same car as Michael Aris. Aung San Suu Kyi had decided that she and her husband should travel in different cars so that

Michael would not have to be exposed to danger in the case of an attempt on her life.

"Everyone in the car was talking at once," says Nyo Ohn Myint when I talk to him more than twenty years later. "But Michael Aris sat silent, looking out of the side window, deeply sunk in thought."

Another one of those who listened to Aung San Suu Kyi that day was then twenty-year-old university student Khin (last name withheld). She had become involved in the demonstrations back in the spring. She had confronted the violence of the soldiers, and several of her friends had been mistreated and thrown into prison.

"When I heard Aung San Suu Kyi speak, tears were streaming down my cheeks," she said later, after having been compelled to go into exile. "I wept. I knew at once that she was the person we had been searching for. She would be able to lead the democratic movement."

The weeks after Aung San Suu Kyi's speech were tumultuous. After the massacres in August, it was no longer possible to control the masses of people, and the student groups that had led the demonstrations were not numerous enough to keep the most violent elements away. At least fifty security agents got in the way of aggravated mobs, who hanged them from the nearest lamppost or chopped off their heads with homemade machetes.

Aung San Suu Kyi did what she could to cool the heated mood and repeated time after time the significance of nonviolent methods. But it did not help. The mob continued rampaging, and now the military had been given all the excuse it needed in order to retake control again. On September 18, when the rest of the world had its attention focused on the first events at the Olympic Games in Seoul, Gen. Saw Maung sent out a bulletin that the military had once again taken control. (The date was not selected randomly: $1 + 8 = 9$, and September is the ninth month. Ne Win and his astrologer still ruled from the wings.) The civilian Maung Maung was removed from office as prime minister and returned to his role as historian. The group who were now to govern the country called itself the State Law and Order Restoration Committee (SLORC). For the second time in a short while, a state of emergency was declared throughout the country, and for the second time the population responded by carrying out massive protests.

Hundreds more lives were claimed yet again when the soldiers opened fire against defenseless civilians.

This time the military was considerably more structured and better organized than when it had crushed the demonstrations on August 8. The aim was to create an example as a lesson to others, once and for all.

The coup and the violence that followed it resulted in a wave of refugees who crossed the border to Thailand. Thousands of young students—activists who had been at the head of the protest movement—made contact with the guerrilla troops belonging to the ethnic minorities and joined the armed battle against the junta.

Amid this chaos, General Maung sent out information that the country was to change its name from Burma to Myanmar. Burma was a colonial name, which apart from anything else had not included the country's ethnic minorities, he asserted. The only problem was that the ethnic minorities considered just the opposite to be true. Myanmar was the name of the ancient Bamar kingdom, and the change of name was understood by most of the ethnic minorities to be an expression of the junta's ambitions to be the supreme rulers. Burma was the name given by the British, but it was also a state of which the minorities could see themselves as being a part. The democratic movement in its turn saw the name change as a cheap attempt on the part of the junta to launder their dirty reputation. This is the explanation as to why the democratic movement in exile, like most of the mass media in the world, uses "Burma" nowadays, whereas diplomats within the United Nations and other more formal institutions use the name "Myanmar."

Saw Maung also sent out a bulletin—somewhat surprisingly—that the junta was planning to carry out a democratic election. This information was a direct reaction to the popular protests. He realized that something had to be done to prevent the revolt from becoming a full-scale revolution.

Aung San Suu Kyi received the news via the radio in her mother's bedroom on the second floor of the house on University Avenue. "My strongest feeling was doubt," she said long afterward. "I doubted the sincerity of the junta, doubted that they really had the intention to have a free and fair election."

This doubt was justified. Behind Saw Maung stood a number of unscrupulous types, like head of the security service Khin Nyunt and Gen. Than

Shwe, who was later to maneuver himself to the position as leader of the junta. They were coldly counting on the election leading to a split parliament. Ethnic and political groups would fight against one another just as much as against the military. In that situation the generals would in practice be able to continue running the country. The junta also possibly had an exaggerated and flawed view of public opinion. In Burma there were no independent sources of information. All the newspapers, radio stations, and TV channels were under the intransigent control of the censorship authority. Everything, even down to the most minute funeral notice, was examined in advance and adapted to be of advantage to the interests of the military junta.

In most such national systems with iron control, the population knows that the media lie. They often do not bother about what is in the newspaper since there are other underground channels for finding out what is really happening in the country. This insight does not necessarily reach those at the top. The members of the junta are fed with information by subordinates who want to ingratiate themselves and make a career for themselves, and who therefore adapt the information, wash it clean of all unpleasant truths, and say what the generals want to hear. In that situation it seems as though SLORC leaders had understood that they enjoyed a popular support that in fact had never existed. They actually believed that they would win the election. They believed that the millions who had protested in the streets represented, despite everything, a minority. An unparalleled blindness.

The generals first chose to ignore the power of the protests. They then did not see what was specifically new in the democratic movement that had grown up during the year. Never before had all of Burma's ethnic groups joined forces in the same demonstration procession. Never before had they been so united in their criticism of the junta's misrule. Apart from this, Aung San Suu Kyi had made her entrance onto the political stage. She gradually adapted to the thought of not only mediating in the political crisis but also leading the opposition. The combination of a special moment in history and fate had carried her to her homeland just when she was most needed. For the first time in more than forty years, the critics of the regime had a person they could all unite behind. Her name was Aung San Suu Kyi. For the first time since independence, the path forward was once again wide open.

4

The Heritage

It is easy to start a conversation with people in Burma. Despite years of re-pression and the network of informers maintained by the security police throughout the country, people still want to talk about their daily lives and their contempt for the country's rulers.

During a trip to Burma a couple of years ago, I visited a Christian organ-ization whose main location was in Rangoon. One of the pastors told me about the resistance of the ethnic minorities against the junta and their struggle to be allowed to keep their own language and their own traditions.

After this meeting I crossed the road and went into a teahouse. It was the middle of the day and the heat was ridiculously oppressive. I ordered a Star Cola—Burma's equivalent of a Pepsi—and sat down to go through my notes. After a short while a man at the neighboring table started talking to me. It was only then that I noticed that he was wearing a military shirt. A worn-out green shirt without any officer's tabs. He may perhaps have been a soldier once, or he was possibly on leave.

The man, who was about twenty-five, asked what I thought about Burma, and since I was formally there as a tourist, I said all the usual things about beautiful pagodas and historical monuments.

"And what do you think about the economy?" he asked.

I looked up in surprise. Economy is a code word. When people ask about that, it is usually an invitation to a conversation on politics. After that we carried on a whispered conversation about the regime, poverty, and the lack of development. We were not able to speak about Aung San Suu Kyi. I did not dare to go that far. But when the conversation had almost come to an end, I pointed to a picture on the wall depicting her father, Gen. Aung San.

"He understood Burma's problem," said the man quietly. "He would have been able to stop the disruption."

This comment is typical. One hears it all the time.

Despite the passing of over sixty years since he was murdered, Aung San is still one of the most significant figures in Burma. Independence has been ascribed to him, and both the military and the democratic movement use the political heritage from him to legitimate their own politics. To put it simply, one could say that he is Burma's equivalent of George Washington, or perhaps the Swedish king Gustav Vasa. A man who chucked out the colonial rulers and established a nation.

Aung San was born in 1915 in Natmauk, a sleepy town in the dry central regions of Burma. He was the youngest of nine children. They and their parents belonged to the lower middle class—to the extent that one can speak of a middle class in the Burma of those days. Their father, U Pha, had grown up in a farming family but left the country and was educated as a lawyer. During Aung San's youth, U Pha ran a small legal office, but in a town like Natmauk the client base was limited and the firm earned just enough to pay its costs. It seems to have been their mother, Daw Suu, who stood for economic stability instead. She had inherited some land outside the town, and at the same time as she brought up the children and took care of the household, she also saw to it that the yield from the fields was sufficient for the family to get by on.

During the last years of the Bamar Kingdom in the nineteenth century, her family had belonged to the Bamar gentry. Her mother's cousin, U Min Yaung, had been one of the most stubborn guerrilla leaders during the first years of the British occupation in the 1880s. Aung San grew up with the stories about his famous relative, and he dreamed even as a child of standing at the head of a large army against the British colonial power.

The British had occupied Burma in three stages during the nineteenth century. In the 1820s they had taken the provinces Arakan and Tenasserim

on the coast. On that occasion the aim had really been only to push back
the Bamar Kingdom, which had its own plans of becoming a major power.
During the rule of King Bodawpaya the Bamar had invaded Arakan in 1784
and in principle made slaves out of the population. The effect was that a
wave of refugees fled over the border to India, where the British had already
taken power. In 1817 the Bamar invaded Assam in northeastern India, and
two years later they made a violent raid into Manipur and later also into
Cachar, where the previous rulers sought support from the British against
the Bamar attack. However, it was not until 1823, when the Bamar attacked
the British outpost on the island of Shapura, that the conflict with the British
led to a full-scale war. The British sent in an enormous armed force that
almost perished from disease when it was confronted by the Burmese rainy
season. Fifteen thousand soldiers died and the war cost the British five million pounds.

However, the British won the war, and thanks to this, they were able to
take power over some of the most strategically important sections along
Burma's coast. One of the deciding battles took place at Danubyu, roughly
fifteen miles northwest of Rangoon. Up until then the Bamar had been the
most victorious army, but at Danubyu the British succeeded in killing the
Bamar supreme commander, General Bandula, a military genius who had
personally drawn up the strategy during the war.

The Bamar court signed a peace treaty with the British (the Treaty of
Yandabo) that provided advantageous trading terms for the British East India
Company. Some years later, the British merchants started yet another war,
and in just a few days Rangoon was also occupied, along with parts of the
Irrawaddy Delta.

Now the British were in control of the entire coast and the fertile farming
country in the south, and for all intents and purposes the power lay in the
hands of the British East India Company. A trading company had been
accorded the status of a colonial power—even though it had a symbiotic
relationship with the English government.

What was left of the Bamar Kingdom became totally dependent on the
goodwill of the British for its survival. However, the merchants of the British
East India Company were still not satisfied. They wanted to construct a trade
route between the Indian Ocean and China, and they were of the opinion

that the mountains of northern Burma provided the best alternative. The
French were simultaneously expanding their sphere of interest in Indo-
China, and the British grew nervous about the competition. In a letter to
the governor-general of India in 1867, England's foreign minister, Lord
Cranborne, wrote,

> It is of primary importance to allow no other European power to insert
> itself between British Burmah and China. Our influence in that coun-
> try must be paramount. The country itself is of no great importance.
> But an easy communication with the multitudes who inhabit Western
> China is an object of national importance.

In the Bamar capital of Mandalay, King Thibaw later came to power via
a complicated web of intrigues. In order to get rid of all conceivable com-
petitors to the throne, he had had more than eighty of his closest relatives
executed. Men, women, and children had been stuffed into white sacks and
carted out to the palace courtyard where they all were clubbed to death by
Thibaw's bodyguards. The British had been looking for a good moral excuse
to occupy the northern parts of the country as well, and when this brutality
continued they were provided with one. When they actually attacked in the
autumn of 1885, the Bamar army had no means of defending itself against
the well-armed, disciplined English troops, and the war was over in two
weeks. Mandalay was captured and plundered and Thibaw was sent into
exile on the eastern coast of India.

Just before the British attack, Thibaw had made Aung San's relative U
Min Yaung commander of the town of Myolulin, situated near Natmauk,
Aung San's own birthplace. When the British had overthrown Thibaw, they
immediately destroyed the entire Bamar system of nobility and all the local
rulers were ordered to swear loyalty to the occupying powers. U Min Yaung
refused, however. He declared that he would rather die than give way to
the British, and he gathered together a guerrilla army under his command.
The British knew that he was a popular leader in central Burma, and they
did all they could to get him on their side. When they did not succeed, they
started a military operation to crush the opposition. After a time of playing
cat and mouse with each other, U Min Yaung was captured and beheaded.

Even so, in practice it took over ten years for the colonial powers to gain control over Burma. The red-clad soldiers met resistance everywhere, partly from ex-officers in the Bamar army and partly from the ethnic minorities.

The Bamar are the largest group of people in Burma. They constitute around 60 percent of the total population and they live mainly in the central parts of the country, in the vicinity of the Irrawaddy River with its six hundred miles. When using the word "Bamar," one thus means the majority group. The word "Burmese" is used to describe all the ethnic groups living within the mapped-out borders that constitute Burma.

Apart from the Bamar, there are several dozen ethnic minorities, of which the smallest consists of not more than a couple thousand people. The larger of these groups, however, are easy to distinguish as distinct and separate. They have had control over their own territory for a long time and built up their own social and political structures. They have their own languages, their own culture, and their own stories about their people's history. The largest groups are the Karen, Karenni, Mon, Chin, Shan, Kachin, and Rakhine. They live mainly in the mountainous, jungle-clad border regions of the country, and historically they have actually never been subjugated to the Bamar central rule. The country that is today called Burma/Myanmar and that nowadays is to be seen on the maps of the world has, in other words, never existed. The various groups of people have lived in their own societies, and the mountains have protected them from occupation and given them a certain degree of independence.

The border peoples have often been in conflict with the Bamar kings, and when the British attacked they did not intend to defend the Bamar monarchy. However, they also feared that the British would be more effective in their ambition to conquer the mountainous regions, and therefore several of the ethnic groups went out into battle to fight against the occupation.

In the end, the British chose to exploit the ethnic conflict for their own ends. In central Burma, among the Bamar, they established a regime that was as hard as nails and must be described for all intents and purposes as a military dictatorship. In the mountainous regions the ethnic minorities were given the formal self-government that they had always striven for. The British called these regions the Border Areas. The Kachin, Shan, Karen, and other groups were thus able to use the colonial period as a lever in their efforts to build their own nations. Men from the ethnic minorities, not least the Karen and the Karenni, were given posts in the army, police, and administration. Cheap labor was imported from India, and at the beginning of the twentieth century there were more Indians than Bamar living in the capital, Rangoon.

For the Bamar this development meant cultural, political, and economic degradation. They had been at the top of the social hierarchy and now they had suddenly ended up at the bottom.

Aung San grew up in a society that had left behind the old days. The kingdom no longer existed. The country was run by a brutal British regime that exploited the natural resources and let a large portion of the population remain in a state of poverty. A well-developed network of informers and a feared security police saw to it that the population was kept in check, and every attempt at armed resistance was beaten down with brutal violence. However, the new rulers had also developed the infrastructure, constructing railways lines from north to south and building bridges and roads. Industries had also grown up around the big cities. A system of education was introduced, partly to modernize the country and partly to compete with the Buddhist monastery schools, which were understood as being pockets of anticolonial resistance.

The final revolt, characterized by a conservative longing for the past and the old kingdom, was the so-called Saya San revolt at the beginning of the 1930s. Saya San had been a monk but left his monastery and joined the nationalist movement. In protest against the poverty in the rural areas, he gathered together a rebel army of peasants to confront the well-trained British forces with sticks and bows and arrows as their only weapons. The troops that the British put in the field to meet the rebels consisted to a great extent of soldiers from the Karen people in eastern Burma. Over three thousand rebels were slaughtered by the British; many killed had marched straight toward the British fire in the belief that the amulets they were wearing would make them immune to the bullets. Saya San was captured and executed in November 1931.

At that time the nationalist movement mainly thought of itself as anticolonial, and there were in reality no significant divisions or ideological differences between the different sections of the movement. However, at the beginning of the 1930s a breach occurred. The movement now came to be dominated by young men who had been educated at schools introduced by the British. They were nationalists to their fingertips, but they did not want to re-create the old monarchy. Instead they were influenced by Plato, Mill, Marx, and Lenin, but also by the new fascist ideas from Germany, Italy, and Japan.

On the other hand, they were still part of the Buddhist tradition. Burma was and is one of the countries most influenced by Buddhism. About 80 percent of the population are faithful Buddhists. The rest are Christian or Muslim, and the absolute majority, irrespective of belief, combine these religions with an ancient belief in so-called *nats*, a kind of mixture of pixies and spirits.

Buddhism became the dominant religion as early as a thousand years ago, when the first Bamar Kingdom was established. It is said that Anawratha, the first king, was visited by a monk immediately after he had taken power, and that the monk convinced him that it would be simpler to keep a kingdom together if there were a religion to link the people.

Most Bamar are active believers who spend some part of their lives in monasteries, as novices for a brief period during their teens or later in life in order to meditate and retire from the world. It is estimated that there are about 400,000 monks in Burma today. The monasteries offer an opportunity for children from poor homes to gain a basic education, since the state schools charge high fees. Thanks to its strong position among the population, the *sanghan*, or monk order, has always been a dominant power in civil society. The monasteries have offered an arena for debate and political action that no ruler has dared to set himself over. They have stood outside the jurisdiction of the state, even when the state has been at its most totalitarian. They have carried on social enterprises, giving support to the most vulnerable and formulating political, almost revolutionary theories when the men in power have gone too far. In other words, it was not just a matter of chance that the monasteries were a center of nationalism and resistance against the British colonial power.

Aung San was both a Marxist and a socialist, but he was also influenced by the Buddhist monk Thakin Kodaw Hmaing. As a child in the 1880s, Kodaw Hmaing had seen with his own eyes how the British invaded Mandalay and sent King Thibaw into exile in India. He is often viewed as the most tangible link between the precolonial Burma and the revolution that took place during the years at the time of the Second World War. Kodaw Hmaing blended socialist ideological goods with Buddhist beliefs. He wrote about an imaginary prehistoric era, a kind of nirvana, in which people lived in freedom and harmony with one another. But like all gardens of paradise, it was lost on account of greed and worldly desires and required a Buddha to lead the people lost in the perdition of reality. Similarities with the stories about Jesus in the Bible are obvious, but Kodaw Hmaing's mythological world was also well suited to the socialist ideology concerning common ownership and criticism of the class differences in a capitalist economy.

Aung San came to the university a year after the Saya San revolt. He was only eighteen years old and had sprinted through the school system with top marks in all subjects—a remarkable achievement considering his background and his mother's refusal for a long time to permit her youngest son to leave home, which meant starting primary school two years after his peers.

For a young Burmese from a rural area, Rangoon at that time must have meant the equivalent of moving from a place like Augusta in Montana, or Owensboro in Kentucky, to Los Angeles or New York. The city was marked by its multicultural identity. Indians, British, French, and Chinese walked the streets alongside those of Burmese descent. European cars drove along the straight streets in the blocks around the area of the port. Rows of bookstores were available to those who were interested in literature, both English and Burmese.

Englishmen dominated the university. The indigenous students were few, and the first professor with a Burmese background had been appointed only a few years previous. English and Burmese were compulsory subjects. However, all the course literature and all the lectures as well as discussions during the lessons were carried on in the language of the colonial power, even if some of the teachers were Burmese. The students had the right to dress in longyis, the Burmese sarongs worn by men and women alike, but the teachers were dressed in a strict European style, often a suit, shirt with cufflinks, and bow tie. For many of the students, it was a bizarre experience to sit through lessons in which the teacher barely mastered the language he was expected to speak.

In retrospect, Aung San does not appear to be an obvious candidate for the role of national hero. He seems to have been an oddity at university—a person who at a less dramatic time would have had difficulty in asserting himself as a leader. "He could sit by himself for hours, far away in his own thoughts," wrote Bo Let Ya, one of his closest friends during his years as a student. "He didn't reply when you spoke with him." Others described how Aung San was completely unaware of his own appearance. He dressed badly and always wore his clothes until they were so dirty that nobody could bear him any longer. And when he was going to change clothes, he always borrowed from friends, since he never had any of his own that were clean enough to wear. The anticolonial struggle was his whole world. "He was a political animal and politics was his sole existence," wrote the author Dagon Taya many years later. "Nothing else mattered for him. No social obligations, not manners, not art, and not music. Politics was a consuming passion with him, and it made him crude, rude, and raw."

When Aung San participated in debates he could take the floor and then talk until he was shut up by the boos and protests of the audience. "Aung San, you fool, sit down!" they would yell at him. His English was grammatically correct but his pronunciation was terrible, and since both teaching and public discussions were carried on in English, there were many who did not even understand what he was saying. On other occasions his friends discovered him holding long speeches for the bushes behind his student lodgings. When they asked what he was doing, he said that he was giving a speech to the bushes in the same way as the British politician Edmund Burke had held speeches to the sea, to train his rhetorical ability.

I suppose that even this type of personality can find its place in history, and perhaps Burma in the 1930s was such an opportunity for Aung San. It is clear that he became a leading representative of the young nationalist movement within a period of a few years, along with individuals like U Nu, Let Ya, and Rashid.

Their first platform was the student union at Rangoon University, and Aung San was nominated as the editor of the student magazine *Oway*, or "The Peacock." In one issue Aung San published the article "Hell Hound at Large," which accused one of the English teachers at the university of going to prostitutes. It was with all certainty a correct accusation since most of the British males living in Burma at that time more or less regularly visited the brothels. When the head of the university demanded that Aung San reveal who had written the article, he refused and was therefore dismissed from the university. This led to a major strike among the students. The head of the university had to retreat, and Aung San was able to continue his studies. Both the strike and Aung San's tenaciousness were widely written about in the newspapers in Burma, and all the Bamar organizations and representatives took the side of the students. Aung San had taken his first step toward national fame. He went from being "that madman" to being "the editor." A few years later he was elected to be the chairman of both the student union in Rangoon and the national student organization All Burma Federation of Students' Unions. There even existed a group of students who tended toward fascism and had good contacts with the Japanese Empire. Saw was one of them, as was Ba Maw, and later even activists from the younger generation, for example, Ne Win, who later became Burma's dictator. However, even the more left-wing nationalists, such as Aung San, flirted during a brief period in the 1930s with fascist ideology. Still, the dominating ideology was socialism. In Marxism and in Lenin's criticism of colonialism, the young nationalists found what they understood to be a counterforce to the economic and political system that they hated and from which they wanted to free themselves.

At the beginning of 1937, Aung San was one of those who founded the Red Dragon Book Club, and for some years, until the war, they published articles and made translations of European left-wing literature, including John Strachey's *Theory and Practice of Socialism*, Nietzsche's works, Marx's texts, and several books on the Irish Sinn Fein.

As the nationalists grew more and more radical, internal political tensions mounted. The anticolonial criticism often developed into ideological hairsplitting and debates that were just as much about various individuals' establishing their positions within the different factions of the movement. This partly explained why Aung San gained such a strong position: in contrast to many of the other nationalists, he never lost focus. The aim of the movement was to throw out the British and create an independent Burma. No ideological or internal political conflicts were so important that they should be allowed to hinder the movement from attaining its ultimate goal. This attitude made him into a key figure, independent of whichever faction was for the moment dominating the movement as a whole.

In 1938 Aung San left the university to become a member of Dohbama Asi-ayone (the We Burmese Organization). It had been founded some years previous, and the members called themselves Thakins (gentlemen), a title that was normally reserved for the British. At the same time the social tensions were increasing in Burma. The workers in the oil industry went on strike because of wretched wages and working conditions, and the peasants made their way to Rangoon to protest in the streets. At a student demonstration, one of the students was killed by the police, which triggered a wave of new protests all over the country. In Mandalay seventeen people were killed in a clash between the police and the demonstrators. The situation that time was almost as charged as it would be fifty years later, when Aung San Suu Kyi took up her position at the head of the protests.

Aung San saw the social unrest as an opportunity to create a more permanent resistance movement and to increase the pressure on the British administration. He as well as the other leaders of We Burmese traveled across the country meeting workers' leaders, students, and monks to coordinate the protests. After several months' hard work, We Burmese had become established as the hub of the anticolonial resistance.

The tempo and energy suited Aung San. As general secretary for the organization, he worked around the clock, organizing meetings and writing articles all day long. At night he slept on a blanket on the floor in the organization's office on Yegyaw Street in Rangoon. He still did not bother about his hygiene, and his clothes hung like filthy rags on his thin body. Despite being one of the most talked-about nationalist leaders, he was only twenty-four years old, and several of the older nationalists who came to the office on Yegyaw Street thought he was a servant boy who was there to clean or serve tea.

The British had not been completely insensitive to the political developments. During the 1930s they had given the Burmese greater symbolic influence over their own affairs. The Burmese elected their own parliament now and their own government. For several years in the 1930s, the nationalist Ba Maw was prime minister. However, political power was in practice subjected to severe limitations, and all decisions were submitted to the British governor, the administration in Calcutta, or the government in London.

The protests and the violence in the streets resulted in the resignation of Ba Maw's government, but the only effect was that a new puppet government was appointed.

The nationalist movement had good contacts with India and was for a long time influenced by Gandhi's and Nehru's nonviolent methods. Aung San too perceived the Indian nationalists as role models: well-educated academics, often politically radical, who chose to enter the system in order to reform it from within. But for Aung San, methods were always negotiable. The way to the goal was a question of strategy, neither more nor less. Nearing the end of the 1930s, he started to tire of the sluggishness of the system and he leaned more and more toward the viewpoint that it was time to take up armed resistance. He wanted to acquire weapons and build up a guerrilla army. In the book *Aung San and the Struggle for Burmese Independence* there is a quotation in which Aung San explains the plan he had crudely sketched during the social unrest in the years prior to World War II:

> A countrywide mass resistance movement against British imperialism on a progressive scale . . . series of local and partial strikes of industrial and rural workers leading to the general and rent strike; and finally all forms of militant propaganda such as mass demonstrations and people's marches leading to mass civil disobedience. Also, an economic campaign against British imperialism in the form of a boycott of British goods leading to the mass non-payment of taxes, to be supported by developing guerrilla actions against military and civil and police outposts, lines of communication, etc., leading to the complete paralysis of the British administration in Burma.

At the end of December 1939, Aung San was in Mandalay to speak at a meeting of the nationalist movement. He then very briefly met the British Labour politician Stafford Cribbs. When the latter asked how the nationalists planned to free Burma, Aung San answered with an example. If Stafford Cribbs took a pen from him, he would first ask politely if he could have his pen back. If that did not help, then he would demand to have his pen back, and if that did not work, there would be no other course of action open to him than to take the pen back by force. After having said this, Aung San reached toward the pen in Cribbs's shirt pocket and jerked it out with such force that the shirt was ripped. The Burmese present thought that Aung San was embarrassing, but Cribbs was impressed by Aung San's commitment and charisma, and he told the story of this event when he returned to England.

If Aung San had implemented his idea about a guerrilla revolt, then he would probably have met the same fate as his famous relative in the 1880s. He would have been captured, executed, and would have disappeared into the oblivion of history. However, if there was one characteristic that was typical for Aung San, then it was the ability to accept the situation. He realized that such a vast and loosely formulated plan did not have the qualifications to succeed. A national guerrilla army would never have had the strength to conquer the well-trained and effective British military forces. The nationalists would take to arms, but in order to succeed, they would first be compelled to seek support abroad.

After the protests in 1939, the British administration tightened up the reprisals against the nationalist movement. Several of the leaders were behind bars, accused of treason and agitation. Aung San managed to keep clear of the security police right up until June 1940. On his way from a meeting in the Irrawaddy Delta, he stopped to hold a speech in the village of Daung Gyi. The local police kept an eye on the situation, and just when Aung San was about to speak, one of the policemen held out a hand-written note: under no circumstances was he to mention the condition of the Chin population in western Burma. Aung San read the note, climbed up onto the podium, and declared that he was thinking of devoting his entire speech to the British violations against the Chin population in western Burma.

The police immediately issued a warrant for his arrest, and after that Aung San was compelled to avoid public events.

In this situation, when they were so severely pressed back, somebody suggested traveling to China to seek support from the Chinese communist party, and in August 1940 Aung San and Thakin Hla Myaing left Burma on the *Hai Lee*, a vessel sailing under the Norwegian flag. Their goal was the international enclave Amoy (today named Xiamen) in China. It is slightly unclear how they had imagined contact with the communists would really be established, and the journey was undertaken to the greatest possible degree on a win-or-lose basis. When they arrived in Amoy, they checked into a cheap guesthouse and began their long, hopeless wait. After a few weeks, their money started to run out. Aung San became ill with dysentery and lay in bed all day, every day. Just when the situation was at its most desperate, they were paid a visit by an agent from the Japanese security service.

Japan had become interested in Burma as early as the mid-1930s. They had invited the right-wing nationalist U Saw to Tokyo in 1935, and when U Saw returned home he immediately bought up the newspaper *Sun*, probably with Japanese money, which thereafter carried on propaganda for the Japanese expansion in Asia. The same thing happened with the newspaper *New Burma* after its owner, the pro-fascist politician Thein Maung, had made a similar journey in 1939.

These right-wing nationalists did not have any sympathy for Aung San and his comrades in the socialist movement, but they realized that the Japanese would be able to benefit from his rather hare-brained journey to China. Going behind the back of the rest of the nationalist movement, they made a pact with Col. Keiji Suzuki from the Japanese security service. Suzuki had been sent to Rangoon disguised as a journalist but he was really the chief for Minami Kikan, a secret organization whose only task was to help the Burmese nationalist movement. Japan's goal was to gain control over the so-called Burma Road, a transport corridor going right through northern Burma. The Allies used the road to send weapons and supplies to Chiang Kai-shek and his Chinese nationalist army, Guomindang (GMD). If Japan were to succeed in cutting off the Burma Road, then its chances of winning a final victory over Chiang Kai-shek would increase and thereby also its possibilities of gaining control over the whole of Asia.

The Burmese right-wing nationalists and Suzuki had together formulated a plan, the gist of which was that the Japanese army would take on a group of young nationalists and give them military training. When Aung San and Thakin Hla Myaing had made contact with the Japanese in Amoy, they were then transported to Tokyo to meet Suzuki. It is impossible to determine whether Aung San had any misgivings when faced with cooperating with the Japanese. Several years later in the light of hindsight, he asserted that he had been doubtful right from the start. The stay in Japan was "not as bad as one could expect," as he said, but he also stated that he was horrified over the totally inflexible social hierarchies and the way in which the Japanese army treated women. And he was shocked when Suzuki explained that the only way to get rid of the British was to kill men, women, and children indiscriminately. Aung San knelt before the imperial palace of course, when the 2,600th anniversary of the empire was being celebrated, but only out of politeness, not because he had any ambitions to be the emperor's subject.

In practice it was probably Aung San's pragmatic side that took the upper hand. He saw Japan as a lever: the enemy of an enemy that with its mighty military power and imperialistic self-interest could help drive the British into the sea.

Aung San returned to Burma in February 1941 disguised as a Chinese seaman. With him he had an offer of money, weapons, and military training. Several of the radical nationalists in Rangoon were skeptical. They mistrusted Japan's ambitions, but Aung San convinced them that it was strategically right to trust the Japanese. A group of young Burmese were later chosen to travel to Hainan and receive military training from the Japanese security service.

They traveled there in three groups, and later on there suddenly appeared a fourth group, consisting of nationalists from the fascist faction. Its leader was Thakin Tun Ok, but among its members was also Ne Win, who was to become Burma's dictator. Already at that point it was obvious that the Japanese did not trust Aung San, that they wanted to complement the group of left-wing nationalists with a more loyal, right-wing group. The young men who were given military training on Hainan later came to be called the thirty comrades.

Before Hainan it had still been an open-ended question as to which of the young nationalists would become the leader, but now Aung San came indisputably forward as the driving force. In her book *Aung San of Burma*, Aung San Suu Kyi wrote, "And for all the charges of 'poor human relations' which had been leveled against him, it was he who rallied the men when their bodies and spirits flagged, showed special concern for the youngest ones and counseled self-restraint when feelings ran high against either camp life or the Japanese."

At the end of 1941, Colonel Suzuki and the thirty comrades gathered in Bangkok, where they formally founded the Burma Independence Army (BIA). They were able to move about freely in Thailand—formally a neutral country that for a long time had been squeezed between the warring powers. However, in the end the country's prime minister, Phibun Soggram, held up a finger in the air and felt that the war was blowing in the direction of Japan. He therefore gave a verbal promise that Japan could use Thailand as a way to occupy both Malaysia and Burma. He had also received a vague promise that the Shan state in eastern Burma would be incorporated into Thailand after a Japanese victory in the war.

When Aung San and Suzuki established BIA in Bangkok, the city was always flooded with Japanese agents and officers. BIA served as an embryo for what would later become Burma's regular army. To start with, it consisted of the thirty nationalists who had been trained on Hainan, agents from Minami Kikan, and a few hundred Burmese and Thai who had been recruited voluntarily in Bangkok. Keiji Suzuki was appointed general and commanding officer; Aung San became the chief of staff and BIA's highest-ranking Burmese.

When plans for the Japanese support had been drawn up, Colonel Suzuki was suitably vague as to the role of the Japanese army. One interpretation was that the BIA would constitute the nucleus, get into Burma, and recruit a larger guerrilla army along the road to Rangoon. The Japanese would occupy parts of southern Burma and the Shan states in order to block the Burma Road to China, but they would leave the rest of the country to the Burmese troops. In practice that was not at all how things turned out. It soon became clear that the Japanese were using the Burmese nationalists as a kind of moral excuse for the invasion that they themselves had been planning for a long time. The BIA was marching side by side with the Japanese Fifteenth Army when the attack was initiated at the end of 1941, and the Japanese Air Force had already spent weeks bombing strategic targets inside the country. The British, who had planned poorly for the war and who did not have the resources to respond to the attack, fled north to the province of Assam in India.

Aung San hoped that the nationalists who still remained in Burma would have built up guerrilla cells that would be activated when the BIA initiated its attack. However, no such underground organization existed. The recruitment of new soldiers had to be carried out haphazardly along the way instead, a method that was to have disastrous consequences when undisciplined units indiscriminately turned on the Karen population in southern Burma.

Colonel Suzuki's own organization in Burma worked better.

The Japanese propaganda had boiled down to representing the Japanese troops as liberators, and when the first bombers swept over the countryside in southern Burma, many Burmese did not take cover but instead went out of their houses and into the streets to wave at them.

In the beginning, the new occupiers were also sincere in their ambition to allow the Burmese to govern on their own, and a government led by Tun Ok was installed in Rangoon. However, even at that point in time, Burmese independence was vastly limited. All the vital decisions were in practice made by the Japanese military command. Tun Ok resigned after only a few months and his government was replaced by a long line of short-lived puppet regimes. One of them was led by Ba Maw, who had once been prime minister under the British. He was known for his contempt for democratic principles; as head of the government, he had as his slogan "One blood, one voice, one command."

"The soldiers from Nippon, whom many had welcomed as liberators, turned out to be worse oppressors than the unpopular British," wrote Aung San Suu Kyi in *Aung San of Burma*. "Ugly incidents multiplied daily. *Kempei* (the Japanese military police) became a dreaded word, and people had to learn to live in a world where disappearances, torture, and forced labour conscription were part of everyday existence."

The Japanese army despised the Burmese in the same racist way they despised most Asians. Many officers considered that a people who let themselves be colonized did not deserve to be treated as human beings, and so the Burmese nationalists and dissidents soon filled the prisons that had been emptied immediately after the British had fled. Interrogations were as a rule conducted with the aid of torture. Among other methods used were hanging victims upside down from the roof and pouring boiling water over their sexual organs and into their nostrils.

In every town the Japanese demanded free access to Burmese women. Brothels had always been part of the structure of the towns, but never on the same industrial scale as now. Young women were forced to sell themselves for a couple of rupees, and if there were no prostitutes available, then the soldiers committed out-and-out rape.

Aung San became more and more bitter over the Japanese betrayal. Immediately after the occupation, the BIA had been given orders to march northward in order to carry on the battle against the fleeing British. After some weeks he realized that the only point of this was to keep him away from the political game in the capital. Later, the BIA was disbanded by the Japanese and replaced by a smaller force that was to have responsibility for domestic security. BIA was to become a kind of police force, a far cry from the national army Aung San had seen in his mind's eye that late evening in Bangkok a year earlier.

At a banquet to celebrate the victory in the spring of 1942, Aung San held a speech that clearly marked his stance: "Today, although I attend this banquet, I feel very embarrassed because I know this feast is celebrated to honor the leaders who brought victory to the country. . . . I don't want to be praised as a hero since I haven't done anything remarkable for my country yet."

And during a visit to a military camp in the town of Maymyo, he said, "I went to Japan to save my people who were struggling like bullocks under the British. But now we are treated like dogs. We are far from our hope of reaching the human stage, and even to get back to the bullock stage we need to struggle more."

In 1943 Aung San and some of the thirty other comrades returned to Japan, where they were decorated by the emperor and were given yet another promise that the Japanese Army would withdraw as soon as the Second World War was over. When they returned to Burma, Aung San was appointed minister of defense in a new government, and Ne Win, one of the thirty comrades, was appointed as commander in chief. For a moment it seemed as though independence was within reach.

However, immediately afterward, Colonel Suzuki asked for a private conversation with Aung San. Suzuki had been recalled to Japan, and before he left he revealed the hidden agenda that had steered Japan's politics concerning Burma the entire time. They had no plans to grant the country real independence. Suzuki said that he had pressed several times to increase the influence of the Burmese, but that every time his orders had been counter-manded by the generals in Tokyo.

In that situation Aung San made an about-face that was unusually dramatic even for him: he sought support from the British. If Japan let them down, then the books must be written anew. Now the old colonial power must be used to drive out the new.

The Allies had not given up the hope of retaking Burma. Japan's advance had partly been slowed down by guerrilla troops from the ethnic minorities. In the north, the Kachins had put up effective resistance, and the Japanese soldiers were scared to death when it came to going up into the mountains north of the town of Myitkyina, where disease, tigers, and an almost invisible army of jungle warriors were awaiting them. The Kachins also had a morbid habit of cutting off the ears of their victims and taking them as trophies of war. In the east, the Karens had put up resistance in a similar way, supported by Allied officers who had been lifted air-to-land into the mountainous regions on the border with Thailand. The Karens pride themselves on having killed at least thirty thousand Japanese soldiers during the war.

In order to finance their jungle warfare, the Allies took to accepting the help of the only currency naturally available in the mountainous regions: opium. The mountainous regions of northeastern Burma are perfect for growing opium poppies, and the peasants had for generations sold opium on the local markets. Early in the twentieth century, the Chinese warlords had further stimulated production for export to opium dens in big cities like Beijing, Shanghai, and Hong Kong. Chiang Kai-shek had driven up production even more to finance the ever more hopeless war against Japan, and the Allies took over a great part of the Chinese nationalist army's contacts in the region. It was a practical decision, well described by two ex-officers, Dean Brelis and W. R. Peers, in their book *Behind the Burma Road*:

> Simply stated, paper currency and even silver were often useless, as there was nothing to buy with money. Opium, however, was the form of payment which everybody used. . . . Opium was available to agents who used it for a number of reasons, varying from obtaining information to buying their own escape. Any indignation felt was removed by

the difficulty of the effort ahead. If opium could be used in achieving the victory, the pattern was clear.

The Allies' plan was to retake Burma from the north and open a new road over the mountains to China. The army that was gathered in the Indian province of Assam was one of the most cosmopolitan that had ever been seen. There were soldiers from all parts of the British Empire: Nigerians, Kenyans, Egyptians, Indians, and men from the ethnic minorities in Burma. Americans, Australians, and Frenchmen had been sent to this distant corner of Southeast Asia to participate and to retake one of the most important land areas of the war.

They started their offensive in the autumn of 1943, and in May 1944 they had reached the Kachin people's capital, Myitkyina. If Burma's towns and villages had been badly damaged when Japan invaded, that was nothing compared to the devastation that now struck the country. The Allies advanced town by town, village by village, and everywhere they met with hard resistance from the Japanese forces who had orders to fight to the last man and lay waste to as much of the land the Allies were about to retake. Myitkyina was besieged for five months. More than three thousand Japanese soldiers barricaded themselves inside the town, and when they at last retreated every single building was in ruins. Maj. Gen. Mizukami Genzu, who had received orders never to capitulate, committed harakiri on an island in the Irrawaddy River. When I visited Myitkyina a few years ago, nobody I met could point to a building that had been put up before 1945.

After Myitkyina it was only a question of time before the British would regain control of the whole country, and in Rangoon Aung San carried on talks with Let Ya, Ba Maw, Ne Win, and the other nationalists about when would be the right time to use their weapons against the Japanese. In November 1943 Maj. Hugh Paul Seagrim, who was organizing the resistance among the Karen people in eastern Burma on behalf of the Allies, reported to his superiors that "a certain" Aung San from Burma's nationalist army was planning on turning his forces against the Japanese when the time was right. Yet it was not until March 1945 that Aung San deployed his troops against the Japanese, and by then the war was in principle already won.

In May 1945 Aung San traveled to the Allied headquarters in Meiktila to meet Gen. William Slim. He was dressed in exactly the same clothes as when he had come to Burma with the Japanese forces three years earlier, in a Japanese uniform with a sword fastened at his belt. His appearance awoke a great deal of attention among the Allied troops, but General Slim came to like the strange little man now standing in front of him and claiming to represent the entire Burmese nation. He described him as honest and prudent, a person who would keep his word if he agreed to any action.

The Bamar joined the Allies in their enterprise and drove out the Japanese the same way they had first come, over the mountains of the Karen in eastern Burma.

5

The Shots at the Secretariat

In the summer of 1942 observant inhabitants of Rangoon could see a couple slowly rowing out on the shiny waters of Lake Inya. He was wearing a uniform, and she a longyi and a white blouse, although sometimes she wore the white uniform of a nurse. They used to row out there on Sundays, and on other occasions they took long walks to get to know each other. They talked almost nonstop, about politics, the war, the country's social problems—and their love.

He was already a well-known person in the Burmese capital. Everybody knew who Aung San was. He had led the freedom movement and was celebrated as the architect behind the flight of the British. He was twenty-seven years old and already a national hero.

Her name was Khin Kyi, and she worked as a nurse at Rangoon General Hospital. During a brief period in the spring of 1942 Aung San had been admitted to the hospital with a raging fever, probably malaria contracted during the long march through the jungle. The doctors and nurses were of course aware of their patient's importance, and several of the younger nurses hardly dared to go near where he lay in bed in one of the wards. However, Khin Kyi did not bother at all about the reputation of her patient. "She handled Aung San with firmness, tenderness, and good humor," according to Aung San Suu Kyi's description of her parents' first encounter.

Khin Kyi was three years older than Aung San, but it is obvious that they resembled each other in many ways. Both were politically active. Khin Kyi had already been involved in the Women's Freedom League, even before the war. It was a nationalist organization working for women's rights. Both also seemed to be steered by an inner compass that helped them to find their way even in situations in which circumstances pointed in a totally different direction. Without this characteristic Aung San would never have survived the hard years in the freedom movement. Without it, Khin Kyi would never, as one of the first women in a prominent public position, have embarked on a career in politics after her husband's death.

A person tending more toward conservative values would never have chosen the profession of nurse either. That task was normally reserved for women from the ethnic minorities, such as the Karen, Chin, or Kachin. If a Bamar got involved in health care, it was as a doctor, neither more nor less.

As a child, Khin Kyi had been sent to Kemmendine's Girls' School in Rangoon, and she planned on becoming a doctor. But health care attracted her more, and after a while she got herself a job at Rangoon General Hospital, the same hospital that would see her fading away almost fifty years later after a stroke.

It seems only to have taken a few days for Aung San to decide that Khin Kyi was to be the only woman in his life. In his usual straightforward and practical way he told her about his feelings. He wanted to get married. Now was the time. Khin Kyi was not as sure. However, Aung San insisted, and when the fever had abated and he had returned to his work, they continued to meet.

The relationship came as a surprise to most of Aung San's comrades and colleagues. At the university he had been an oddity and after that always 100 percent focused on the struggle for freedom. Even during the war he had kept his asocial character. He was a respected leader and the voice of the people, but his hygiene had not improved. Maung Maung, who later became Burma's official historian, describes how during the Japanese occupation he once saw Aung San take off his military tunic before a meeting in central Burma. The shirt underneath was filthy and full of holes. He only had two uniforms that he alternated between, and he rejected all forms of personal comfort. His self-denying attitude reinforced his position among the Burmese and made him excessively popular, but no women had appeared in his life. Most people understood Aung San to be "a political animal," uninterested in getting married and starting a family. It seemed to be a luxury that he could not or would not allow himself. On one occasion during the war he had even forbidden his soldiers to sing love songs in the evenings when they had pitched camp, since he was afraid that the singing would make them lose focus on the main target. There is also documentation showing how he had yelled in a fit of fury that all true patriots should subject themselves to castration so that romantic nonsense would not distract them from "the great assignment."

In his book *Perfect Hostage*, Justin Wintle described how many of the people around Aung San reacted with what can only be seen as jealousy when he at last was himself struck by love. They wanted to have Bogyoke Aung San to themselves, and right from the beginning strange rumors spread about Ma Khin Kyi. Some asserted that she came from the Karen people, others that she was a Christian, a Baptist, or even a Seventh Day Adventist. The truth was that her father, Pho Hnyin, had grown up in an ordinary Burmese home where Buddhism was the only conceivable religion. As a young man, however, he had hunted frequently, and many of his hunting comrades, often the best shots, were Christian men from the Karen people. During late evenings on hunting expeditions they used to read selected parts of the Bible for him. They told him about the Christian message of love and forgiveness, and after a time Pho Hnyin converted to Christianity. His conversion was an unusual and controversial step in Burma, with all its conflicts between different religions and ethnic groups and with Bamar nationalism strongly on the march forward.

Khin Kyi's mother reacted very strongly. She came from a religious home, and for a long time she refused to accept her husband's decision. In the end they reached an agreement, the gist of which was that their children would grow up with two religions, so that they would later be able to choose for themselves which they wanted to profess. During the years of her youth in her hometown Myaungmya in the Irrawaddy Delta, Khin Kyi regularly attended both Buddhist convent and Christian church services. In this way it was natural for her to live in a multicultural and multireligious society. The strong tensions between the population groups in Burma as a whole did not exist in her own home.

Aung San and Khin Kyi both understood that their relationship would not be "ordinary," but out on the shining waters of Lake Inya, Khin Kyi said yes to Aung San's proposal of marriage.

And yet it was all nearly canceled since Aung San lost control of himself in an atypical way the day before the wedding, as related in Wintle's *Perfect Hostage*. A group of Japanese officers had taken Aung San out with them on a stag party, happy that the committed and extremely hard-working Burmese had a human side despite everything. Aung San had barely tasted alcohol at all previously, and he did not have a chance when the hardened Japanese escalated the rate of drinking. He got disgustingly drunk, and just after midnight he was dumped on the veranda at the front of the house where Khin Kyi was waiting. She was furious and gave the Japanese a severe scolding for what they had done to her husband-to-be. When they left, she continued to scold Aung San, who responded by being sick on the veranda. At that point Khin Kyi informed him that the wedding was off. That was the end. If he were going to behave in that way, then "the great" Aung San would have to find another woman. After some hours' conversation during which Aung San explained that he had never behaved like that before and had no intention of ever doing so again, she changed her mind and they were married on September 6, 1942.

One can only guess how they both came to influence each other in issues of politics and religion. It is clear that Khin Kyi leaned more toward Christianity, her father's religion, before her meeting with Aung San, but after their marriage she was persuaded to be a faithful Buddhist. On a superficial level, this sounds like a purely strategic decision. In a country so profoundly Buddhist as Burma it would have been difficult for Aung San to make a career with a Christian wife. However, according to her friends and family, it was a seriously and carefully considered decision and her faith grew deeper as she grew older. But she never let go of her tolerant view of other cultures and religions, and as Wintle has asserted, it may have been precisely this attitude toward life that contributed to Aung San's greater understanding for Burma's ethnic minorities after the war and their demands for respect from the Bamar majority.

During the following years Aung San and Khin Kyi had four children one after another in rapid succession. The first-born was Aung San Oo, almost ten months to the day after the wedding. Slightly more than a year later little brother Aung San Lin arrived, and on the June 19, 1945, the couple's first daughter, Aung San Suu Kyi, was born. They had another daughter in 1946, but she died almost immediately after being delivered.

All of Aung San Suu Kyi's names come from older members of the family. Aung San after her father, Suu after her paternal grandmother, and Kyi after her mother. In that way her parents did not follow the traditions in Burma. Burmese do not have family names in the same way Westerners do. A woman who marries does not take her husband's name, any more than children take their parents. If someone is named Win Naing, for example, then both names are his individual first names.

On the other hand, most Burmese are given their names according to which day of the week they were born on. Aung San Suu Kyi was born on a Tuesday, for which names like Cid, Nyi, San, and Zaw are common. This means that the number of names in Burma is rather limited, and that many people have the same names. In order to distinguish between people with the same name, the name of the birthplace is sometimes added as part of a person's name. For example, U Thant, the former secretary general of the United Nations, became known in Burma as Pantanaw U Thant, since he was born in the village of Pantanaw.

Family gathered in Rangoon when Aung San Suu Kyi is one year old. Behind her from the left: Khin Kyi, Aung San Oo, Aung San Lin, and Aung San. *Courtesy of Norstedts.*

Sometimes the similarity in names can be an advantage. Several years ago I met a human rights activist who used to visit illegal Burmese immigrants imprisoned in Bangkok. In order to gain access to the prison, she was always compelled to give the name of the person she was going to visit. The problem was that she never knew with any certainty just who had been imprisoned that particular day of the week. "I always say that I am going to visit Maung Maung," she explained, laughing, "and I am always allowed in."

This morass of names becomes even more impenetrable through the titles often used by the Burmese to precede people's names. An older respected man is always accorded the title "U," meaning approximately "Mister" or "Uncle." U Nu is thus really only called Nu. The feminine equivalent is Daw. When people say Daw Aung San Suu Kyi, it is thus a way of showing her special respect.

Apart from this, many writers and political activists use a nickname or a pseudonym. The habit started during the colonial era as a way of misleading the security police, and it has been common even since the junta seized power. The student leader Min Ko Naing can be named as an example. His real name is Paw Oo Tun, but he changed names after a period of student protests. The name Min Ko Naing means "Slayer of Kings," and it was originally a collective designation for a number of students who had printed political texts in protest against the military rule. When Paw Oo Tun later came forward as the leader of the whole student revolt, it was he who came to be associated with the name (as yet another curious fact it may be mentioned that the author Eric Blair, who worked as a policeman in Burma during his youth, later followed this Burmese tradition by taking the pen name George Orwell).

Aung San Suu Kyi means literally "Strange Collection of Brilliant Victories." She was born on a Tuesday and in Burmese astrology every day of the week also stands for a number of personal characteristics. As a Tuesday's child Suu Kyi was expected to be an honest person with high morals. Her father was born on a Saturday, which means that he would become a troublemaker with a hot temper. The belief in the significance of birthdays is strong in Burma, and it is highly probable that parents' and other adults' expectations actually influence the personality that people develop, in the same way as social demands influence the degree to which we develop so-called typically "masculine" or "feminine" characteristics.

The Second World War in Burma ended only a few weeks before Aung San Suu Kyi was born. After the end of the war it was an open question at first as to which status a future Burma was to be given. From his vantage point in London, Winston Churchill assumed that the English commonwealth would be restored. He had not won a world war just to lose an empire. But Churchill did not succeed in convincing the English voters of his worthiness as a postwar politician. The Labour Party won the parliamentary elections in 1945, and with Clement Attlee as prime minister, the process was initiated to dismantle the most globally comprehensive superpower and its domination in the world.

Aung San and the other leaders of the nationalist movement had learned not to trust British promises, and this distrust was mutual to the highest possible degree. After the war the old colonial civil servants returned to Rangoon, and many of them still had their idea of Aung San and the thirty comrades as half-criminal troublemakers. One of those who distrusted the young generation of nationalists was the governor, Reginald Dorman-Smith. When Japan invaded Burma he had fled to Calcutta, and he was bitter because the Bamar had not taken sides with the Allies right from the start. In his eyes Aung San was a criminal who ought to be brought to justice for war crimes.

Together with the administration in London, Dorman-Smith had produced a "White Paper" on the future status of Burma, since up until then the British were planning to govern the country in the same way as before the war. Aung San suspected that the White Paper was a way of delaying Burma's independence long enough for the British to have time to reestablish the old colonial system. The reconstruction of the country's economy and infrastructure was also to be reassigned to the same Western companies as those that had exploited the country's teak forests and mineral mining before the war.

Aung San did not exclude the possibility of a new necessity for armed struggle, and he prepared the nationalist movement for a guerrilla war. Straight after the recapture of Burma, the British had disbanded the nationalist army and about five thousand men had joined the new Burmese army that had been built the period between colonial rule and independence. Aung San was satisfied with that solution, but for safety's sake he built up a militia, the PVO, as well as the regular army. Formally speaking, the PVO was involved in health care and social work, but in practice it was a private army under the leadership of Aung San.

At this point Aung San was confronted with a choice of action. In world history there is no shortage of leaders who have gotten stuck in the liberation phase and who have not understood the need to lay down their arms in time, thus creating a new system of oppression. If one looks at countries like Zimbabwe, Eritrea, or even Vietnam for that matter, the step from liberation to freedom seems to be the most difficult of all.

However, in precisely that situation Aung San showed that he was more than just a liberator. The struggle for independence had increased his tolerance, not diminished it. He had modified some of his most eccentric personal characteristics and matured as a political leader. He had three realizations. The first was that they could not have a dogmatic attitude toward the British. Even if he rattled his weapons he was basically convinced that negotiations and peaceful methods were now needed in order to build a durable independence. In the autumn of 1945 he left the army for this reason and continued his work as a civilian and politician instead.

The second realization was that the political factions within the nationalist movement must achieve lasting unity, otherwise the country would end up in civil war. Even before the Second World War the communists had opposed seeking help from Japan in order to drive out the British. They were of the opinion—absolutely correctly as would soon become evident—that Japan was a more brutal imperial power than Great Britain, and they wanted therefore to join the British in a common cause, fighting against Japanese expansion in Asia. However, Aung San and some of the other leading nationalists had had to sit still and not rock the boat. After the invasion the communists had become the opposition, and their leaders were being hunted down by the Japanese security service. Two of the leaders fled to India, but the most radical communist leader, Thakin Soe, remained in the country, and he was a perpetual source of worry. If the communists took to arms prematurely, then Aung San would be forced to fight against them. This would lead to civil war instead of a common struggle against Japan. Aung San persuaded Thakin Soe to avoid taking up arms until the time was ripe. The nationalist movement united itself in becoming a member of the Anti-Fascist's People's Freedom League (AFPFL), with Aung San as its first official chairman. The AFPFL was to become the foremost political party in the country right up until the time when Ne Win seized power in 1962.

When the British returned, Aung San worked according to the same principle of unity. The opposition movement had to keep itself together, otherwise the British would exploit its disunity for their own ends.

The third realization was that it was necessary to get the ethnic minorities to join in the process. Aung San realized that this would demand negotiations and great diplomatic skill. The British had consistently favored these groups, and their antagonisms were reinforced by the progress of the Japanese and the Bamar nationalist army, the BIA. The Karens were hit particularly hard. The invading army advanced right through their traditional territories in southern and eastern Burma, and many of the soldiers who had joined up with the BIA as volunteers were former criminals who did not give a damn about what the civilian population thought about the Burmese army. When groups of Karen soldiers later carried out guerrilla attacks against the Japanese, Colonel Suzuki gave orders that they should make an example out of the BIA. Several Karen villages east of Rangoon were attacked and burned to the ground. Men, women, and children were shot to death.

Aung San realized that a Burma of the future would not work without the cooperation of the ethnic minorities, and even as early on as the first months of the Japanese occupation, he made regular visits to their leaders to win their confidence. An understanding developed slowly but surely between Aung San and the ethnic groups.

The rivalry between the nationalist leaders was also an integral part of this difficult equation. Several older right-wing nationalists tried to maneuver themselves into a leading position. Ba Maw, who had already been prime minister on two occasions, was one of the self-appointed candidates, as was U Saw, who had been prime minister under both the British and the Japanese rules. The governor, Dorman-Smith, preferred to speak with these two about the future of Burma, even though it was Aung San whose popular support was the strongest. Both of these politicians had, moreover, their own private militias. Neither of them was as large or influential as Aung

San's PVO, but the mere fact that they were able to launch their own force gave them influence in the shaky political postwar landscape.

At the same time the AFPFL was already on the point of splitting apart. The entire nationalist movement was being torn to pieces by internal conflicts, and early in the spring of 1946 Tun Ok, one of the more right-wing nationalists, attempted to get Aung San out of the way by accusing him of murder. Tun Ok said that he had witnessed how Aung San personally executed a man during the 1942 invasion of Burma.

This provided Dorman-Smith with a golden opportunity to get rid of the young nationalist leader, but he hesitated anyway. The British military leader Hubert Rance asserted that any action against Aung San would lead to civil war. Dorman-Smith summoned Aung San to him, and he confessed immediately. When the BIA had penetrated the jungle regions in the south, he had entered a village near the town of Moulmein. Several days earlier the villagers had arrested their own village chief, an Indian man, because he had been cooperating with the British. Aung San decided to make an example of him, and in a summary trial the man was condemned to death. After that, in front of the assembled villagers, Aung San himself was to carry out the sentence. He struck the man with a sword, but the man survived and Aung San had to order one of his men to kill him with a shot to the head. This bizarre episode casts a long shadow over the memory of Aung San. To Dorman-Smith, Aung San asserted emphatically that the execution had been carried out in a state of war and that he had only done his duty as a soldier and commanding officer.

Dorman-Smith chose to let the case rest but carried on working against both Aung San and PVO. His policy was not appreciated either by the politicians in London or by Lord Mountbatten, the head of the British command in India. Mountbatten was on the contrary impressed by Aung San's calm and integrity, and he understood him to be a unifying force in a Burma that already found itself on the point of total chaos.

Some months later Aung San won a significant victory when London decided to recall Dorman-Smith home. His replacement, Hubert Rance, immediately dissolved the political council that had acted as the country's interim government under British control. He later allowed the AFPFL to occupy the majority of the seats in a new council. It was never said aloud, but it was soon also clear that the era of the White Paper was past. Aung San was appointed as vice chairman in the new council, second only to Rance, and he was also given responsibility for key issues such as defense and foreign affairs. And with that it was also clear that older nationalists like U Saw and U Ba Maw had lost their influence over the process of independence.

Aung San's promotion meant, however, that the AFPFL split into two sections. The communists had hoped for a more radical revolution. They had planned for comprehensive strikes and wanted to exploit the uncertain situation after the war to establish a socialist state with close relations to the Soviet Union. It was unthinkable for them to sit in some kind of transitional government in which the British still had the final word. Thakin Soe had already defected in the spring and fled to the Irrawaddy Delta. He had gathered together a minor guerrilla army (the Red Flag Communists) and was planning an armed revolt against the central government. At that point Than Tun and Thein Pe also broke away from the AFPFL and started their own communist guerrilla group, the White Flag Communists.

Their defection was a heavy breach of unity among the nationalists, but it also meant that Aung San no longer needed to pretend. His political rhetoric grew milder, and he appeared more and more as a pragmatic social democrat rather than as a bombastic communist. Whether it was his personal eminence or real conviction that made him change his image is difficult to say.

In January 1947, a delegation with Aung San at its head traveled to London to meet Prime Minister Attlee and to negotiate the final details in the agreement that was to give Burma its independence. On the way to England Aung San stopped in New Delhi, where he spent a few days at the home of Prime Minister Nehru. True to his habit, Aung San had not taken any notice of the dress code. He was wearing the same shabby uniform as during the invasion four years previous. Nehru laughed when he saw his Burmese colleague and tried to persuade him that a Japanese uniform was not the most suitable outfit for an official visit to 10 Downing Street. Nehru sent for a tailor who sewed a three-piece suit for Aung San; he is wearing it in all the photographs that have been preserved from the visit to London.

In New Delhi, Aung San held a press conference in which he confirmed that the Burmese delegation was planning to make specific demands in

London: total independence, meaning no British domination in any kind of diffusely composed commonwealth where the British would be on top as usual. He also repeated the threat of a new armed revolt. Before their departure the AFPFL had alerted PVO to full readiness if it should be seen that the talks with Attlee were a failure.

However, Aung San and Attlee reached a compromise, and at the end of January an agreement was signed confirming that Burma would become independent within a year. Democratic elections were to be held in April, and the newly elected parliament's first task would be to draw up a new constitution based on democratic and federal principles—federal in the sense that the ethnic minorities would have great influence in their respective regional states and that they would be guaranteed a certain number of seats in parliament and the government. The AFPFL would lead an interim government under British supervision.

The agreement worsened the split within the nationalist movement. U Saw was a member of the delegation but refused to sign the document, and as soon as he had returned to Rangoon he and Ba Maw started their own right-wing party and accused Aung San of having sold himself to the imperialists in return for personal power.

Aung San did not have time to worry about such accusations. They were predictable, and he had always counted on U Saw and Ba Maw starting their own party as soon as independence was a fact. Immediately after his arrival home, he traveled on to the little town of Panglong in the Shan state. Representatives from the ethnic minorities had gathered there to decide whether one state would be established within the borders we nowadays recognize as Burma, or whether they would continue with their demands for total independence. In principle there was nothing to hinder the second alternative. Economically they were of course underdeveloped, but that was the case for most of the Asian states after the war. Administratively, they would have great difficulties to overcome. Several of the regional states had during only a few decades gone from being local tribal communities to regional states in the British Empire. However, that did not make them any different from many other states that had been colonized and now had to build up their own societal structures. Geographically and demographically they were qualified, without a doubt. The Kachin state in north Burma is about as large as Austria. The Shan state has a population today of around four million and is more extensive than most European countries.

Most assertive in their demands for independence were the Karenni people. They had been very close to the colonial power and understood that the British had promised them their own state. On September 11, 1946, one local Karenni leader had appointed a government for the "United Karenni States." Other Karenni leaders had reinforced their arsenals, and if it proved necessary for achieving independence they were now ready for war.

The developments in the Rakhine state in western Burma were just as explosive. There the Buddhist monk U Sein Da had assembled a guerrilla army to restore the old Rakhine Kingdom. At the same time a Muslim guerrilla force had been created to defend the Rohyinga people's rights against U Sein Da's soldiers. The Muslims and the Buddhists had lived side by side for centuries in the region, but that unity was now in the process of cracking.

The Karens were also dubious about becoming members of the new union. The war had deepened their historical distrust of the Bamar. They even sent a delegation of their own to London in the hopes that Attlee would give them an agreement similar to the one Aung San had been given. However, the government in London had decided to stake everything on Aung San, and the Karen delegation did not get to meet any important civil servants or politicians. During some painful days in the British capital, they were shown the various cultural and historical sights.

Several days before the meeting in Panglong, the Karen National Union (KNU) had been formed. The Karens were totally focused on independence and were present in Panglong purely as observers.

Aung San laid all his political prestige on the line and succeeded in persuading the representatives for the Chin, Kachin, and Shan peoples to sign an agreement about becoming members of the new union. The Shan princes were given a special clause giving them the right to secede from the union after ten years if they were not satisfied with the cooperation. The same right was given to the Karenni.

There were still many loose ends, but the success in Panglong demonstrated that Aung San's plan for progress was watertight. In April, Burma's first democratic elections were held and the AFPFL won a walkover. The elections were indeed boycotted by both the "red" and the "white" communists, and likewise by the Karens in KNU, but the election victory nonetheless legit-imized Aung San's leadership. He was on his way to becoming independent Burma's first democratically elected prime minister.

He would have attained that post, if it had not been for those shots at the Secretariat.

The Secretariat is a redbrick building covering almost an entire block in an area near the port of Rangoon. It is surrounded by a high brick wall with barbed wire along the top, and an overgrown garden. Its windows look emptily out in the direction of the shabby center of Rangoon, but although having been abandoned, it is watched day and night by armed guards. In 1947, it was a building completely open to all. Despite Rangoon being the capital for Burma's government-to-be, despite the sensitive negotiations with the ethnic groups, and despite the existence of infinite numbers of weapons in circulation after the war, security around those who were to constitute the new leadership of the country had not been reinforced. Aung San was utterly unprotected.

On the morning of July 19, Aung San did the same as he did most morn-ings during those hectic months in 1947. He awoke at 5 a.m. in the family's house on Tower Lane. It was situated on a verdant hill in a wealthy residen-tial area just north of Lake Kandawgyi. The two-story house was built in a colonial style with a white-plastered tower, and it was completely sur-rounded by a white stone wall.

Aung San ate a breakfast consisting of noodles and drank a cup of tea, and then he hugged his three children before walking out to the waiting official car that would take him to the Secretariat. During the morning he was to spend a couple of hours on administrative tasks before meeting his government cabinet at half past ten. Some of the most promising politicians of the day were members of the government, and Aung San had consciously chosen several representatives from the ethnic minorities, for example the Karen leader Mahn Ba Khaing and Hsam Htun, one of the princes from the Shan people. Normally, the government gathered in the British governor's office, but on this particular day there was nothing on the agenda that war-ranted the attendance of the governor.

It seemed to be a regular working day, but the politician U Saw had other plans. On his command a group of soldiers was on its way to the Secretariat.

U Saw had been planning the attack for months. Thoughts of revenge had taken root as early as when Governor Rance had allowed Aung San and the AFPFL to gain a majority in the interim government. U Saw understood himself to be the rightful leader of the nationalist movement. He was older and had more experience than Aung San. He did not like Aung San's left-wing views, and some months earlier he himself had been the target of an attempted murder. He was certain that Aung San was the person behind it. (Nobody has been able to prove it.)

The vehicle with the armed men drove fast southward through the chaotic network of Rangoon's roads. It passed street markets, pagodas, English cars, and ox wagons from the countryside around the capital. Nobody stopped the vehicle when it drove into the courtyard of the Secretariat, and the armed men were able to make their way up to the second floor, where the interim government had just assembled, without any problem. They fatally shot a guard posted outside the meeting room, and then they jerked open the door and opened fire. Aung San had risen as soon as the first shot was fired; he was immediately hit by thirteen bullets. Six other ministers were also executed. Among them were Mahn Ba Khain and Hsam Htun, along with Aung San's brother U Ba Win. It later turned out that a number of British officers had delivered the weapons used in the attack, but the matter was never properly investigated and U Saw had to bear the entire blame for the murders.

One of the most eminent nationalist leaders in Southeast Asia no longer existed. Aung San had only reached the age of thirty-two. He died at 10:37 a.m. on July 19, 1947, a day that is still ceremoniously held as the Day of the Martyrs in Burma. He had made a remarkable journey from the dusty streets of his childhood in Natmauk to the university and the struggle for independence. Along the way he had not only conquered his own antisocial characteristics, but this oddity of a man had become a national hero.

"He was an intuitive intellectual," said Professor Khynt Maung at the University of Rangoon a long time afterward, in an interview with Angelene Naw, "and at the same time he could be totally undisciplined. I knew him well and I knew many people who worked with him and some of them said he was extremely rude and unpredictable. But of course, he was a genius so people accepted his idiosyncratic manners."

It is impossible to know how Aung San would have tackled the difficulties that Burma was faced with during the 1950s. Civil war broke out only a few months after the formal independence in January 1948. The Karens took up arms, as did the communists. And during the 1950s, the Union of Burma cracked little by little, until the end of democracy in 1962. Perhaps Aung San, with his strong winning instinct and his "independence at any price" mentality might have been just as brutal and violent as the generals who later came to power. Or else he might have been able to stop the breakdown thanks to his diplomatic capacity and the strong confidence he enjoyed among the ethnic minorities. One often hears that view in the Burma of today, where it is said that the murders at the Secretariat meant a death sentence for the whole of the democratic promise that independence and the new constitution brought with them.

U Saw's dream of becoming the country's first prime minister was already dashed the afternoon after the murders. He was arrested, condemned to death for murder and treason, and hanged in May 1948.

Instead it was U Nu who took over as prime minister. He had followed on the heels of Aung San during all the years they were students together, via the Thakin movement and out into the war. But when independence was within reach, he had withdrawn from public life into a monastery. He was a wise leader, considerate and reasoning, and he had been the vice chairman of the AFPFL. However, as a candidate, he was not at all the unifying force that the country needed when it was balancing between stability and chaos. U Nu was not accorded the same confidence by the ethnic minorities and—perhaps most important of all—he did not have the same support from the army. Aung San was understood to be its founder, and with him gone, there was nobody who was able or willing to control the destructive power of the armed forces.

6

The Election Campaign

Critics sometimes accuse Aung San Suu Kyi of being obsessed with her father. What they are implicitly driving at is that she is not a popular leader in her own right; she is totally dependent on Aung San's status as a national hero. This is of course true in the sense that she became famous and rapidly gained a political position because she is his daughter. If she had not had this relationship, then she would not have held that speech at the Shwedagon Pagoda in 1988 and she would not have become a symbol for the democratic movement in the same way.

It is also true that a significant proportion of her own texts and speeches have often revolved around her father. Even before her return to Burma in 1988, she had published *Aung San of Burma*, an outline of his life in which she gives prominence to his good aspects and glosses rather too glibly over his faults and transgressions. She writes only briefly about the accusations against him of murder and nothing at all about his flirtation with totalitarian ideologies in the 1930s. Even Peter Carey, one of her and Michael's friends in Oxford, says that she had "the uncritical and admiring attitude of a daughter to her father."

But obsessed? She has always forcefully rejected that allegation: "I don't think about my father every day. I'm not obsessed by him, as some people seem to think. I prefer to believe that my attitude to him is based on healthy respect and admiration, not obsession," as she said in an interview with Alan Clements.

Of course, the accusation of obsession is really about something else. It is in the interests of the junta to discredit Aung San Suu Kyi, and therefore they are trying to spread the image of her as someone who has nothing worth saying. That she is just being nostalgic, living on and exploiting her father's greatness.

It is particularly strange if one considers that almost everyone in Burma has regarded Aung San as a hero—the military and the democratic movement alike, the country's political elite as well as the ordinary people in the streets. His picture has been put up everywhere, in teahouses, in officers' barracks, and in the offices of the NLD. Streets, markets, and whole blocks have been named after him. In more recent years, however, the junta have been less keen to promote him as an example, well aware that people always think about Aung San Suu Kyi when they see pictures of her father.

Aung San Suu Kyi's possible obsession does not differ much from that of the average Burmese. Basically, it is a battle about historiography. Ever since Ne Win seized power in 1962, the junta's propaganda has drawn a straight line between the national hero Aung San and dictatorship. Aung San's founding of the army and the army's liberation of the country from the colonial powers have been used to justify military rule, as well as implicitly give the generals the right to interpret reality and an eternal right to rule the country.

By invoking her father and pointing to her own connections to the liberation of Burma, Aung San Suu Kyi has torn this argument out of the junta's hands. She has cut loose and shown that the oppression established by the junta is not at all the natural continuation of the state that Aung San sketched in the 1940s. By calling the great popular protests during 1988 "the second struggle for independence," she instead links the opposition and the democratic movement to the struggle for liberation. In that sense, her appearance at Shwedagon was the starting point for a revision of the inheritance from Aung San and the anticolonial struggle.

However, 1988 was also the starting point for a year of intensive election work. Only a few weeks after Saw Maung's and the new junta's seizure of power, Aung San Suu Kyi became one of the founders of a political party, the National League for Democracy. U Tin Oo, the former commander in chief who had ended up in a conflict with the junta in the 1970s, was chosen as the party chairman. Aung San Suu Kyi was the general secretary.

The new junta, the SLORC, had sent out a message that the elections would be held some time during 1990, which meant that the NLD had between one and two years at its disposal in which to carry out an election campaign. After 1962, Ne Win had banned all parties except Burma's socialist party, the BSPP, whose central committee had been more powerful than the country's formal government. When the SLORC took over after the BSPP in 1988, they promised that the one-party state would be abolished and that promise gave rise to enormous activity in civilian society. New parties sprouted like mushrooms out of the ground, and within a couple of months more than two hundred new parties had been registered. Scarcely one hundred of them were later authorized by the junta and actually allowed to participate in the elections.

The junta had given all the new parties the right to use the telephone (which was far from self-evident in Burma in 1988), and they had been given special rations of gasoline so that they could travel around the country. The junta had also started a new party, the National Unity Party (NUP), which replaced Burma's socialist party. Saw Maung saw to it that all the parties that allied themselves with the NUP were able to run their election campaigns with money from the state, while all the SLORC's critics had to manage as best they could. Throughout the entire election campaign the generals refused to meet the representatives of the opposition in debates or in order to make clear which rules were to apply for the election process. "There are more than one hundred political parties. Which one of them are we supposed to meet?" they asked rhetorically. Then Aung San Suu Kyi suggested that the opposition should choose one representative in common, and at a meeting in Rangoon the 104 different parties united in choosing Aung San Suu Kyi to represent the assembled opposition in talks with the junta.

After the meeting, leaders of all the parties except the NLD were called in for interrogation by the security police. A pair of handcuffs had been symbolically placed in front of them on the table, and several of them were pressured to renounce their support for Aung San Suu Kyi. Those who refused were subjected to very tough reprisals. Khin Maung Myint, the party leader for the People's Progressive Party, was thrown into prison where he became very ill several years later. One of his medical orderlies related that the junta gave him an ultimatum right up to the last moment of his life: he would be given medicine and medical care, but only if he rejected Aung San Suu Kyi. Khin Maung Myint had an extremely high temperature, but nonetheless he yelled at his warders: "No uniforms! Don't come here! I'd rather die than sign your papers!" He died after four years in prison.

Despite the junta's efforts, the citizens of Burma knew that Aung San Suu Kyi had support from most of the political parties and groups. She suggested later that in order not to split the votes any further, an even greater degree of coordination was required of the opposition parties, which meant sharing only one candidate in each constituency. No such alliance was ever created, however.

The SLORC had promised political freedom, but it only took a few weeks for that promise to be broken. The military cracked down on the whole of the opposition. The largest student party, the Democratic Party for a New Society (DPNS), that openly supported the NLD, had the whole time to choose new leaders since the junta imprisoned them as soon as they had been nominated. One of them, the young student Moe Thee Zun, went underground when he found out that the security service was searching for him. Some weeks later he turned up on the border with Thailand, where he declared that peaceful methods were no longer of any use. It was time to take up arms in the struggle against the junta. He became one of the leading forces in the student army that warred along with the ethnic minorities against the junta for a number of years along the Thai border.

Aung San Suu Kyi, however, was a tougher nut to crack. She immediately became extremely popular, even among the soldiers in the army, and she launched an election campaign that was several months long. She traveled as though she were obsessed. She held political meetings and met NLD activists all over Burma. Everywhere she went, tens of thousands of people turned up to listen, and in record time the party succeeded in building up a comprehensive network of local offices and party associations. At the end of the year they had registered a dizzying three million members.

Traveling in Burma takes time. The roads are in a terrible state, and a swarm of cyclists, ox carts, and pedestrians make for slow going. The whole traffic situation is made even worse on account of the steering wheel in most cars being on the right, despite the introduction of right-hand traffic in the country way back in the 1970s. For an inexperienced driver, it is in other words lethal to pass since he or she cannot see the oncoming traffic.

For Aung San Suu Kyi and her companions, it was essential to plan the journeys well ahead of time in order to exploit every opportunity of meeting people and recruiting new members. Most of Suu Kyi's meetings were held late in the afternoons or in the evenings. After each meeting she and her companions would spend the night in some guesthouse or another in order to get up as early as four o'clock in the morning and start on their journey to the next village.

"I have never ceased to be moved by the sense of the world lying quiescent and vulnerable, waiting to be awakened by the light of the new day quivering just beyond the horizon," she wrote some years later in a Japanese newspaper.

When I talked to the journalist and author Bertil Lintner, one of the world's leading experts on Burmese politics, he described the election campaign as presenting a much more dangerous challenge to the junta than the protests in 1988. Despite the way that the junta harassed and arrested activists, the democratic movement succeeded in disciplining its opposition. Instead of chaotic and often violent demonstrations through the big cities, people gathered to listen to quiet political speeches, and when the military and the police provoked them, they succeeded in keeping calm anyway. The whole election campaign was transformed into an education in democracy and civil disobedience.

When I made my first trip along the Burma-Thai border in the mid-1990s, I met many political activists: mostly young people who had staked everything on a political change inside Burma but who had lost the struggle and been forced to flee abroad. They spent their days in pulsating Burmese exile communities full of life, in cities like Mae Sot and Chiang Mai. Every single person I met was working for some organization that focused on the situation of political prisoners, women's rights, the Karen people's cultural heritage, or medical care to refugees on both sides of the border. On several occasions I asked which political ideology they represented, and the answer was often just a raised eyebrow. "What do you mean, political ideology? We are democrats." One often meets that point of view among those in political opposition to dictatorships where there is no freedom of the press, where political parties—irrespective of ideology—are strongly opposed, and where a small elite rules arbitrarily.

This broad, basic democratic attitude also characterized the NLD's first party program. It was written by Aung San Suu Kyi and U Tin Oo during the autumn of 1988. It is true that the SLORC had promised general elections and encouraged the people to get politically organized, but in practice matters were quite different. Burma furthermore had no functioning democratic constitution that could regulate the election process. Everything happened according to the conditions set by the junta.

The party program demanded the restoration of Burma as a federal union, with respect for the rights of the ethnic minorities and an explicit distribution of power within a democratic system. The ethnic minorities were even to be given more comprehensive rights than afforded in the Constitution of 1947, which had been shown to be inadequate when it came to keeping the peace and getting all the different groups within the population to cooperate in building the nation.

Aung San Suu Kyi's spirit hovered over the text, not least because it emphasized so clearly that Burma's rulers must respect human rights and allow the citizens to choose their own leaders. The program also established that the "road towards socialism" that Ne Win had tested from 1962 and onward had been a failure. The almost 100 percent nationalization of the country's economy and the cultural isolation had cast the country into poverty. Now was the time for a careful liberalization of the economy and greater openness toward the rest of the world.

The NLD wrote that medical care and schools should be given special priority, which was also a reaction to the junta's policies since the 1960s. While the military devoured more and more of the national budget, the educational system and medical care, for many decades among the best in Asia, had been totally wrecked.

However, one of the most important issues during the election campaign had to do with the path chosen by the opposition. Time and again, Aung San Suu Kyi reiterated the significance of nonviolence as an approach. In the interview with Alan Clements several years later she said, "I do not believe in armed struggle because it will perpetrate the tradition that he who is best at wielding arms, wields power. Even if the democracy movement were to succeed through force of arms, it would leave in the minds of the people the idea that whoever has the greater armed might wins in the end. That will not help democracy."

Yet she still did not completely reject violence as a method. She was compelled to accept that several thousand students had fled into the jungle and founded an army with its base in the rebel stronghold Manerplaw near the border with Thailand. Aung San Suu Kyi realized that they were basically on her side, and chose a diplomatic middle road. She expressed understanding for resorting to violent methods out of sheer desperation but emphasized that the NLD was a nonviolent movement.

Quickly and without any visible effort, Aung San Suu Kyi fell into her role as Burma's leading politician of the opposition. It was as though she had lived her whole life waiting for just this moment in time, when the paths of history crossed, revealing to her what was to be her destiny.

While the election campaign was being carried on with ever greater intensity, it was clear that her mother, Khin Kyi, was not going to survive for much longer. Her condition worsened, and she died at the end of December. She was seventy-six years old, and despite having survived her husband by over forty years, she had never met another man. There is not even a note anywhere about a "male acquaintance" or anything else that might hint at a love relationship. Aung San Suu Kyi has said that her mother had far too great a sense of responsibility to meet anyone new. She was Aung San's widow, and the national consciousness required her to remain just that. Full stop. She had a sense of responsibility that we in the West would normally associate with royal families, if with anyone at all.

The funeral was held on January 2, 1989, and it developed into yet another gigantic protest against the junta. On account of the military violence, people had not dared to venture out and take part in any large demonstrations since September. But the funeral of Aung San's widow was sanctioned by the whole social machinery, and the SLORC could not do a thing when more than a hundred thousand people took to the streets once again. The NLD, fearing new violence, called out several hundred party activists to ensure it was carried out peacefully and in an organized manner as the huge procession slowly advanced along University Avenue.

Aung San Suu Kyi's husband, Michael Aris, and their sons, who had returned to England just after the speech at Shwedagon to start their school term, now traveled once again to Burma to be present at Khin Kyi's funeral. The splitting up of the family had yet been neither painful nor particularly dramatic. As on earlier occasions during their marriage, Michael and Suu Kyi kept in contact by writing long letters to each other, and they spoke on the telephone almost every day. However, Suu Kyi's family's visit to Burma turned out to be brief. Only a few days after the funeral, Michael was recalled to Oxford by his duties, and Suu Kyi increased the pace of the election campaign.

The SLORC continued its brutal, sometimes almost tragicomical propaganda against her. The security chief, Khin Nyunt, explained that Aung San Suu Kyi and U Tin Oo were part of an international right-wing conspiracy that also included several foreign governments. He never declared which ones, but he mentioned that the British BBC and the radio channel Voice of America belonged to those who spread lies about the country. Shortly afterward his criticism did an about-face, and he accused Suu Kyi of being totally in the hands of the Burmese communist party instead. The idea was to link both Aung San Suu Kyi and the NLD to the forty-year-old conflict with the communist guerrillas.

However, the propaganda was most often quite simply about discrediting her as a person. They called her a "Western fashion girl," and since she was married to a foreigner she must, according to the junta's crazy, xenophobic image of the world, per definition be a foreign spy, an "axe in the hands of the neocolonialists."

When Aung San Suu Kyi held election meetings, the security police used to regularly harass and arrest the public. During one campaign trip to the Irrawaddy Delta, her party was followed the whole time by a military truck with a sound system at its back. As soon as they stopped to give a speech, the army started playing military music at top volume to drown her out.

The strategy of strictly monitoring the NLD's meetings boomeranged against the junta in a slightly surprising way. Propaganda portrayed her as a terrorist and agitator, a person who would bring chaos to the country, but out in the field the soldiers met quite another person. When her followers yelled insults at the soldiers and the army (a popular criticism was about the junta leaders not having any education), she encouraged them to stop. Soldiers who had been sent out to disturb meetings often jumped down from their trucks and joined the crowd to listen to her speeches.

One of her bodyguards at that time, Moe Myat Thu, tells the story of something that happened in October 1988 when Aung San Suu Kyi was about to travel to the village of her father's birth, Natmauk. Just before the city boundary she was stopped at a checkpoint, but instead of letting herself be provoked by the soldiers, she began talking to them as though they were old acquaintances. She asked about their children and the living standards of their families, and about how they liked being in the army. For the soldiers this was something quite new. Burma has always been a hierarchical society. Throughout history the distinctions between those up there and those down here have been sharp and impenetrable. People with power have always expected a degree of subordination from those further down the social ladder, irrespective of whether the rulers have been the British colonizers or the Bamar nobility. The junta had sharpened the contrasts by situating a strictly military hierarchy on top of the more traditional class distinction. Officers communicated with their soldiers by means of direct orders, never through social small talk. Aung San Suu Kyi broke all those rules. A few of those I have spoken to in the course of this work have described her as snobbish and haughty. They have seen a side of Suu Kyi that she seems to display when she does not like the person she meets. However, the absolute majority say the complete opposite. Despite her family background, despite her education and her status as a national icon, she treats people as equals.

During the election campaign, she often received questions about why she was married to a foreigner. Moe Myat Thu remembers a meeting in a little village in central Burma, where the question was put by a man at the very back of the audience. "It's not very strange," explained Aung San Suu Kyi with a smile. "I just happened to live in England when I was at the age when you get married. If I had lived in this village I might have been married to you."

The generals in the junta quite simply did not know how to handle a person with such disarming charm.

During those first months of the election campaign there were few direct threats aimed at her person. The junta did not dare. They realized that such a measure might lead to a full-scale revolution. During one trip, however,

Aung San Suu Kyi was only seconds from being shot to death. The occurrence has now become part of the mythmaking around her, not least because it says something important about her personality.

It all happened in Danubyu, a dusty little dump in the Irrawaddy Delta about sixty miles northwest of Rangoon. It was April 5, 1989. During the day Suu Kyi and her people had been out with a boat in the Irrawaddy Delta, carrying out their election campaign. Everywhere they had been met by rejoicing crowds, and neither the police nor the military had intervened to stop their meetings. When evening was approaching, they were on their way back to the town of Danubyu. As they got closer to the harbor area, they saw that it was full of soldiers who were standing with rifles raised and aimed at their boats.

They were not surprised. When they had arrived at Danubyu the same morning, the streets had been full of soldiers. The inhabitants in the town had been ordered to stay at home, otherwise they would risk getting arrested or even shot. Once at the NLD office, they were met by a certain Capt. Myint Oo, who forbade them to hold any political meeting. "For security reasons," he explained. Aung San Suu Kyi had agreed to their demand and met her party comrades inside the office instead.

When they were about to leave Danubyu later on, Capt. Myint Oo tried to stop them again but allowed them to pass after Aung San Suu Kyi had promised that they would be back before six o'clock.

Despite the fact that they were back well before the time agreed on, the atmosphere was now very threatening in the harbor area. Nyo Ohn Myint, who was the chairman of the NLD youth section and also included in Suu Kyi's force of bodyguards, suggested that they should get out of the boats on the beach beside the jetty. Suu Kyi climbed out first onto the clay bank. When the rest of her party had come ashore, they were surrounded by a group of soldiers who pressed them toward the water, pulled at their clothes, and yelled at them to turn around. One of Suu Kyi's bodyguards lost his temper and nearly started a fight with one of the soldiers, but after a couple of minutes the pressure eased and Aung San Suu Kyi suggested that she should walk ahead toward the NLD office.

They walked for three hundred or so feet along the main street, and when they arrived in the vicinity of the town marketplace, they met six soldiers blocking their path. Capt. Myint Oo stood beside them with a pistol in one hand and a megaphone in the other. One of the bodyguards, Win Thein, walked diagonally in front of the rest of the group with an NLD flag.

Maw Min Lwin, who was the chief of the bodyguard force, realized that Suu Kyi was exposing herself to unnecessary danger. Along with Nyo Ohn Myint, he tried to walk in front of Suu Kyi, but she stopped them. "No, you don't need to," she said. "That will only make them nervous. Let me go first."

They continued on their way.

At that time of day, Danubyu was usually teeming with market noise, traffic, and the babble of thousands of human voices. Now not a sound was to be heard.

Ma Thanegi, one of the women in the NLD leadership, was walking a few steps behind the bodyguards. She tried to speak to the captain. "Stop this. You must let us pass," she said. "You must let us walk to our office."

But the captain yelled that they would be shot on the spot if they continued walking in the middle of the road. "Okay," said Suu Kyi, "then we will walk along the side of the road instead." The captain yelled back that they would be shot even if they walked along the side of the road. He started counting from one and ordered his soldiers to open fire when he got to ten. Then Suu Kyi turned around to the rest of her party and asked them to stop. If the captain meant what he said, she did not want to risk a bloodbath. Aung San Suu Kyi herself continued slowly onward.

The soldiers cocked their weapons.

"I was scared to death," says Nyo Ohn Myint, telling me the story of this incident twenty years later. "But just as the captain was about to give the order to fire one of his superiors came running, a major, and stopped the counting."

A violent exchange of words broke out on the pavement. It ended with Capt. Myint Oo tearing off the officer's tabs from his uniform and yelling, "What have I got these for if I can't give an order to fire?" By that time Aung San Suu Kyi had already walked straight through the line of soldiers. As she passed, Suu Kyi saw how they were trembling with nervousness. One of the soldiers was crying. Later on, Aung San Suu Kyi told Alan Clements about this incident: "My thought was, one doesn't turn back in a situation like this. I don't think I'm unique in that. I've often heard people who have

taken part in demonstrations say that when you are charged by the police
you can't make up your mind in advance about what you'll do; it's a decision
which you have to make there and then."

Nyo Ohn Myint remembers how the NLD had an informal meeting later on
in the evening in the Danubyu office. Everyone was shocked by what had
happened. He had been unable to speak for an hour after they had arrived
in safety. One of the local NLD activists also recounted that Capt. Myint Oo
had sat in the local police station after his humiliation earlier on in the day
and swore to kill Aung San Suu Kyi. He had been terribly drunk, waved his
pistol about, and screamed that he had "saved a bullet for the wife of that
Indian!" Among racist Bamar, all foreigners are often called Indians.

Well inside the NLD office, most people thought it was time to go home,
but Suu Kyi refused to cancel the arrangements for the following day. They
were going to visit a monument dedicated to General Bandula, who was
killed at Danubyu in 1825 during a crucial battle against the British in the
first Anglo-Bamar war.

"If I die in Danubyu," she said, "you have to seize the opportunity to
democratize the country." When they arrived at the monument, they were
met by the major who had stopped the shooting the previous day. He told
them that Capt. Myint Oo had been transported away from Danubyu and
assured them that Suu Kyi no longer needed to feel threatened.

The self-sacrificing behavior she had demonstrated at Danubyu was an
important explanation as to why the young activists in the democratic movement joined her after the bloody autumn of 1988. She showed that her own
safety was not more valuable than anyone else's, and she did whatever she
could to protect the activists who gathered around her.

Immediately after their homecoming from Danubyu, Moe Myat Thu, one
of her bodyguards, and five other young people were arrested outside the
gates of 54 University Avenue. The soldiers dragged them out of their car
and took them to an army camp in the vicinity. When Aung San Suu Kyi
heard about this incident, she immediately went out onto University Avenue
and sat down on the pavement. She told the surprised soldiers that she was
thinking of sitting there until her colleagues were released. The soldiers
grew nervous. It was the first day of the annual Burmese water festival, and

they knew that the whole street would soon be flooded with people wanting to celebrate at the NLD headquarters, situated five hundred feet from there. If Aung San Suu Kyi was still sitting out on the street, the whole situation might develop into a demonstration against the junta. After about thirty minutes, the NLD activists were released.

"It isn't a hard choice to make, to follow a leader who acts like that to protect her colleagues," says Moe Myat Thu when I interviewed him in Thailand in the winter of 2010.

Most of all, of course, it shows a strange, sometimes almost death-defying obstinacy. Yet Aung San Suu Kyi will not agree that she is brave. When asked a question about Danubyu, she has replied, "There must be thousands of soldiers who do that kind of thing every day. Because, unfortunately, there are battles going on all the time in this world."

Aung San Suu Kyi often emphasizes that she refuses to allow fear to rule her life, even if there is often good reason to be afraid. "You must not let your fear stop you from doing what is right," she has explained. "You must not deny fear. Fear is normal. But it's dangerous if you let it stop you from doing what you know is right."

In her next breath she usually mentions how as a child she used to handle her fear in the same way she did during the election campaign when perpetually harassed by the junta—by challenging it. During her earliest years, she, like most other children, was afraid of the dark when she was about to go to sleep in the evenings. But instead of pulling the covers up over her head and shutting her eyes, she chose to get up and go down into the pitch-dark cellar. There she sat on the floor and waited until she was used to the darkness, until she controlled it. One of the most famous things she is quoted as saying is "Fear is a habit."

After Danubyu, the junta realized that Aung San Suu Kyi was not going to give an inch even when faced with the threat of death, and the election campaign had shown that both the democratic movement and the ethnic minorities stood behind her. Even a large part of the army looked up to her. Aung San Suu Kyi thus constituted a direct threat against the continuation of the junta's long hold on power. She still believed that they might draw up some kind of formal death sentence against her. If it became public, then it would trigger a revolution. At the same time Capt. Myint Oo's unstable behavior demonstrated that there were elements within the army who wanted to see her dead.

The temperature rose even higher during the spring and summer of 1989. The junta intensified their harassment, and more and more democratic activists were arrested and sentenced to long terms in prison after summary trials.

That did not stop Aung San Suu Kyi from intensifying her criticism of the military rule. Lian Sakhong, who lives in Uppsala nowadays, remembers a meeting immediately before the annual water festival in Rangoon. Lian comes from the Chin people, and at that time he was one of the leaders of the ethnic minorities' alliance, the United Nationalities League for Democracy (UNLD). He was going to give a speech after Aung San Suu Kyi:

> Before the meeting she seemed quite calm. Her face was expression-less, but the look in her eyes was concentrated, filled with energy and focused straight ahead all the time. She was wearing a white blouse with full sleeves, and just as the meeting was about to start, she rolled them up above her elbows. I've never seen anything like it. She looked like a gunman preparing for a shoot-out.

In her speech a few minutes later she went on the attack for the first time against the former dictator Ne Win. In prior speeches, she had avoided pointing him out in any specific way. In Burma one has a duty to respect and revere those who are older, even if they are guilty of a brutal genocide, and nobody else in the democratic movement had dared to criticize the former dictator. It is true that he had given up his power in the summer of 1988, but both the people of Burma and the international community assumed that he still ruled from the wings. Aung San Suu Kyi accused him now of having corrupted her father's legacy, having dragged the country down into poverty, and not having had the ability to make peace with the ethnic minorities.

This last issue—relations with the ethnic minorities—was controversial even for the democratic movement and the NLD. With July 19, 1989, in view, Aung San Suu Kyi sent out information that she was thinking of arranging an alternative demonstration in memory of her father on the forty-second

Meeting at NLD's head office (spring 1989). From the left: Salai Ngai Sak, Lian Sakhong, Ram Ling Hmung (standing), Daw Aung San Suu Kyi, and U Tin Oo. *Courtesy of Lian Sakhong.*

anniversary of his murder. Ever since 1962, they have transformed this memorial day into a celebration of the country's military power. However, instead of taking part in the celebrations of the regime, Aung San Suu Kyi was now planning a peaceful march of her own along the streets of Rangoon. On July 19 a meeting was held between the NLD and the ethnic groups' UNLD. Lian Sakhong, one of the participants at the meeting, relates that Aung San Suu Kyi and the representatives from the UNLD planned to make it into a shared demonstration. However, U Tin Oo and the other generals in the executive for the NLD reacted very strongly and threatened to join the regime's demonstration if the suggestion was accepted. The pensioned generals in the executive of the NLD distrusted the ethnic groups, and several of them wanted to keep the national control of the federal states in one way or another. Aung San Suu Kyi, on the contrary, was of the opinion that a federal constitution was necessary in order to create peace in the country, and she strove for even closer cooperation with the UNLD. She also suggested that the NLD refrain from running for office in the federal states so that the ethnic parties would not suffer competition from her own party.

The conflict within the NLD never became acute during the election campaign. When the SLORC heard about the plans for an alternative July 19 demonstration, they called in several battalions from the regiments stationed around the capital and let them patrol the streets at the same time the state-controlled mass media trumpeted out that the junta was going to keep law and order at any price.

With this threat of a new bloodbath hanging over it, the demonstration was canceled, but the junta had now been given an excuse to tighten the thumbscrews. Early in the morning of July 20, 1989, eleven covered trucks drove up along University Avenue. The vehicles were parked so that they blocked all transport past Aung San Suu Kyi's house. Soldiers poured out of the backs of the trucks and stopped the forty NLD activists and family members who were inside the house from leaving.

Several hours passed without anything happening. The soldiers wanted either to spread anxiety and uncertainty among those inside the house, or else they were waiting for orders from above. Aung San Suu Kyi realized that the time had come and spent the day packing. "I thought if they were going to take me to prison then at least I should have a bag packed with essentials," said Suu Kyi a few years later, in an interview with Barbara Victor, "such as toothbrush and a change of clothes. After I did that, we all had a nice time just waiting."

Suu Kyi was able to spend the day conversing with her party comrades and being together with her sons, Alexander and Kim. They had come to Rangoon some weeks earlier with their father, but Michael had returned to attend his own father's funeral in Scotland. Sixteen-year-old Alexander was old enough to understand that the soldiers constituted a threat, but Kim mostly thought that it was exciting. "I remember the soldiers coming to the house," he said in an interview in 2004 in the magazine *The Weekly*. "There was a huge amount of activity and lots of guns and shouting. Of course, I wasn't really aware of what it was all about, but, for a young boy, it was incredibly exciting. Mother tried to be reassuring, at least when I was around, and I can't remember ever being frightened."

One of Suu Kyi's assistants played Monopoly with the children to pass the time. At about four o'clock in the afternoon the wait seemed to be over. Half a dozen soldiers entered the house and searched through the office spaces on the ground floor. They turned desk drawers upside down and poured out the contents on the floor. They tore items out of the wardrobes and the kitchen cupboards. After them, an older officer made his entrance. He exhorted U Tin Oo and U Kyi Maung to leave the house. The others there were arrested and thrown into prison. Some of them were released after two or three days, and others received long prison sentences.

The officer who had forced his way into the house read a document with allegations against Aung San Suu Kyi. She was a "dangerous" and "subversive" person, he said, since she was planning to carry out an alternative ceremony to commemorate her father's death, and therefore she would now be committed to house arrest. The house was emptied. Only her sons and two maids were permitted to remain.

Aung San Suu Kyi was now a prisoner in the shabby white stone house on the shores of Lake Inya, the very house in which she had spent so many years of her childhood.

7

Childhood

Burma in the 1950s was a country full of sharp contrasts. On the one hand, there was a civil war and unrest. Aung San was dead and society was going through an ever more blatant militarization. On the other hand, there was a strong belief in the future, with an economy that was on its way to being built up after the war and a freedom in society that Burma had never before experienced.

The Danish doctor and author Aage Krarup Nielsen writes about the bright side of Burmese life in his book *De gyllene pagodernas land* ("The Land of the Golden Pagodas"), published in 1959. His narrative is about Burma's immense natural resources, wide-stretched teak forests, and fertile paddy fields. He also describes how the system of education was well developed and the literacy rate was the highest in Southeast Asia. Krarup Nielsen met businessmen and politicians who all described Burma as a successful example for other Asian countries. The concept had not yet been invented at that time, but everybody took for granted that Burma would become one of the "Asian tigers."

Burma was, however, confronted with enormous problems. To start with, large areas of the country were bombed to bits after the Second World War. The Japanese attack and the Allies' counterattack had razed whole towns and villages to the ground, leaving them in ruins. The harbor in Rangoon had been wrecked, and more than five hundred trains and railway carriages had been blown up by the Japanese before they retreated. And just as reconstruction was about to begin, the communists went underground and started an armed struggle against the central government. At that point three months had passed since independence, and shortly after that the Karenni people's guerrilla army and the Karens with their armed wing, the Karen National Liberation Army (KNLA), declared war on the central government. The first phase of the civil war was extremely bloody, hindering all further development in the countryside. During this period, U Nu's government was only in control of the region around the capital. After a few years the Karen guerrillas had been driven back, but even so they were in control of the greater part of the Karen state and in practice they established an independent nation in the mountains between Burma and Thailand.

Most of the other ethnic groups were at first loyal to the government in Rangoon, but they took care to arm themselves. No group fully trusted the Bamars' assurances of independence within the framework of a federal union, and it was easy to obtain weapons. Both the Japanese and the Allies had left behind large arsenals, and most groups had of course been drawn into the world war in one way or another.

Amid this chaos, Burma also became a pawn in the Cold War. When Mao Zedong's communists took power in Beijing in 1949, the nationalist leader Chiang Kai-shek fled to Taiwan. His Guomindang established a military dictatorship on the island and swore to retake mainland China one day. The Western world supported GMD for a long time, and right up until the 1970s Taiwan was allowed to represent China at the United Nations.

That part of the story is relatively well known. Less well known is that two of Chiang Kai-shek's army units planned to do what Mao had once done, that is to say remain in a distant part of the country, keep a hold on that region, and then start the counteroffensive from there. They decided that Jonghong in the southern Yunnan province would be their "base," but before they had realized their plans, Mao's People's Army had already gained control of the town. Instead, about 1,700 soldiers from Chiang Kai-shek's Eighth and Ninth Armies marched over the border into Burma. So as not to be discovered and pressed back by Burmese government troops they traveled right through the inaccessible jungle of the Shan state. One of the officers, Zhang

Weicheng, had fought together with the Allied forces during the war and knew the area. In the end they settled in the town Mong Hsat in a green, fertile valley in the eastern Shan state. There were plenty of supplies and the local people seemed to be friendly. During the coming years, GMD established its own state in northeastern Burma.

The Central Intelligence Agency (CIA) immediately made contact with them and initiated an operation to retake China from the communists. The White House supported the basic elements of the strategy that the CIA developed. President Harry S. Truman saw how the communist guerrillas were winning terrain in the whole of Southeast Asia and drew the wrong conclusion that all these movements were linked together via Moscow and Beijing. But even if the leading politicians in the United States supported the basic elements in this analysis, it was still extremely controversial to support the guerrillas directly in an independent country like Burma. The extent and character of the operation were therefore kept secret by the civil servants responsible within the CIA, even from the White House and Congress. During a number of years, enormous number of weapons and supplies were shipped out to the mountains in the Shan state. An aviation company called Civil Air Transports (CAT) was established to take care of the deliveries. Several other companies based in Thailand looked after contacts with the rest of the world.

Burma's army was sent to the Shan state but did not succeed in driving out GMD. U Nu chose to take up this issue in the recently established United Nations General Assembly, which agreed on a resolution in April 1953 demanding that GMD lay down its arms and hand over the region to the government of Burma. However, GMD and the CIA flouted this resolution. New soldiers were recruited from the ethnic groups in the border region, and by the end of 1953, GMD was able to muster as many as twelve thousand soldiers.

The Chinese troops in the Shan mountains neither could nor would rely completely on support from the United States. They needed their own resources and turned therefore to the only asset that was able to bring in any income to speak of in the mountains: opium. Under the alleged supervision of the CIA, opium production in the Shan mountains exploded. CAT aircraft started in Thailand, and on its way north it carried arms and ammunition.

On the return journey the aircraft conveyed ton after ton of opium, which was later refined into heroin and shipped out to the world markets via Bangkok.

In the beginning of the 1950s, GMD twice attempted to retake China. Its troops marched over the border with a couple of thousand well-armed soldiers and military instructors from the United States, but the popular support that GMD had counted on never turned up and the attacks were easily repulsed. After a brief period in the 1950s it was clear that GMD was going to "get dug in" in Burma.

The central government in Rangoon increased its military ventures in the region. The commander in chief of the army, Ne Win, sent thousands of soldiers to the mountain areas, and the historically independent Shan people felt pressured from two directions, since both armies were perceived to be "foreign."

At the same time, China increased its support to Burma's communist party, partly to combat GMD, and Beijing provided new fuel for the civil war. U Nu was fully aware of the threats from both the United States and China. The vast neighboring country in the north has always had an ambition to expand southward, to open up trade routes, and to gain direct access to the Indian Ocean. On that point Mao was no different from Beijing's previous rulers.

Aung San Suu Kyi did not see much of this with her own eyes. She grew up in the early 1950s in Rangoon, a city that was characterized more by optimism and belief in the future than were the problem-filled border regions. Burma was on its way to establishing itself as an independent nation. It joined the newly created United Nations and a series of international delegations whose members visited the country to study the political development and investigate investment opportunities. Several of these foreign guests also found their way to Aung San's house on Tower Lane. During the war, Aung San had built an impressive network of contacts in India, Japan, Great Britain, and the neighboring countries. Khin Kyi's home remained an important meeting place for the political and military elite in Burma. When Khin Kyi became a widow, she first had plans to take up her old career as a nurse. However, U Nu and the others who ran the country were of the opinion that this assignment was all too limited for the widow of the country's national hero. Instead she was appointed as the head of a committee working to develop the welfare of women and children. She took over Aung San's seat in parliament and even led a Burmese delegation to the World Health Organization (WHO), which had started a large project in Burma to reduce malarial diseases. Khin Kyi thus played an important role in the political postwar landscape.

On the morning of January 16, 1953, the family was once again struck by tragedy. Aung San Suu Kyi was playing with her brother Aung San Lin outside the house. The two children, seven and eight years old, were very close to each other. They slept in the same room, went to the same school, and often romped around in the garden together. On that morning they were running around for a while outdoors; Aung San Suu Kyi got tired and went indoors to rest while her brother ran down to a pond that lay near the driveway up to the house. There he dropped a toy weapon in the water, and when Aung San Lin went to pick it up, one of his sandals got stuck in the clay. He rushed into the house, gave the toy to Aung San Suu Kyi, and called over his shoulder that he was going to fetch his sandal. A little while later he was found dead, floating facedown in the pond.

People in Burma have learned to live with death as part of everyday life. Poverty has always harvested many victims, and the country has been at war almost continually, with violent death and sudden disappearances of political dissidents. As one effect of this, Burma has had one of the highest levels of child mortality in Asia during the entire postwar period, right up until the present day. The problems have gotten worse in recent years, when the junta have escalated the war against the guerrilla armies and invested all their resources in military armament with only a marginal portion on medical care.

Many are of the opinion that Buddhism equips people with better readiness than other religions when it comes to handling grief and tragedies. One basic idea in the Buddhist faith is that of life's transience. Happiness always changes into grief, and no grief lasts forever. As a human being, one must learn to live with these changes but also with the insight that life does not end with death. It takes on new forms. The soul lives on.

However, all this is theoretical reasoning. In practice it is hard to imagine anything other than the deepest grief when a child dies.

"I was very close to him . . . ," Aung San Suu Kyi recalled, talking to

Clements, "probably closer to him than to anybody else. We shared the same room and played together all the time. His death was a tremendous loss for me. At that time I felt an enormous grief. I suppose you could call it a 'trauma,' but it was not something I couldn't cope with. Of course, I was very upset by the fact that I would never see him again."

On the surface, Khin Kyi took her son's death in the same stoical way as she had received the message about the murder of Aung San. At the time of the accident she had just been promoted to head of the planning commission in the social department. When one of her colleagues entered her office and told her the terrible news, she did not go home at once but stayed and finished her tasks for that day. It sounds absolutely bizarre, and some of the biographies of Aung San Suu Kyi's life imply that this is a later reconstruction fabricated by the junta with the intention of casting a shadow over the daughter as well. However, the information comes straight from Aung San Suu Kyi, so there is really no reason to doubt its truth. She used her mother's reaction as an example of her parents' feeling for social and societal responsibility. An almost inhumanly rational attitude in that case: her son's life could not be saved, and so there was no reason to hurry home from the job she had been employed to take care of.

Even if this story is true, Khin Kyi must reasonably have landed in a state of shock and the deepest grief, and after her son's death she no longer wanted to live in the house on Tower Lane. In the spring of 1953 the family packed their belongings and moved to the white stone house at 54 University Avenue, on the shores of the beautiful Lake Inya, a few miles north of Tower Lane. The area had previously been inhabited by British colonial civil servants and top businessmen, but after independence several of the villas around the lake had been taken over by the rulers of the new Burma. The commander in chief of the army, Ne Win, lived, for example, in a spacious villa on the opposite side of the lake. When Aung San Suu Kyi was confined to house arrest forty years later by Ne Win's underlings, they could have waved to each other across the mirrorlike waters.

Aung San Suu Kyi had a materially privileged childhood in a country where most people lived in poverty and misery. Yet her upbringing was not characterized by any luxury. Khin Kyi had the same ascetic attitude as Aung San had had. She was careful not to spoil her children.

"The toys of my early childhood seemed luxurious in post–World War II Burma, but they were quite modest," wrote Aung San Suu Kyi in a newspaper chronicle in Thailand in the 1990s. "I had a series of round-eyed, hairless dolls made of thin, pink plastic, which buckled and cracked easily, and with moveable limbs attached by means of brittle elastic string that could ill withstand the attention of restless little hands."

When things got broken, they were to be patched up and mended. There was no question of buying new ones. Suu Kyi really thought that the dolls were ugly and unpractical, but she regarded them with respect since she had heard some adults saying that Japan's industrialization had started with the manufacture of precisely that kind of toy. In her childhood fantasies, the dolls were transformed into keys that could open the door to a better world.

Her favorite toy was a kaleidoscope, a tube with bits of glass and beads that kept on creating new patterns when one turned it round and round. When the kaleidoscope got broken, her oldest brother, Aung San Oo, built his own homemade version with mirrors and colored glass. But in Suu Kyi's eyes the copy was never able to compete with the original.

Nowadays, most of the traces of the British colonial era in Burma have been erased. Apart from the architecture, the dusty and shabby houses in central Rangoon, which look as though someone has chucked a couple of blocks from London into the middle of Southeast Asia, everything has been more or less swept away. English is taught in some schools, it is true, but for many years after Ne Win's takeover of power even that was forbidden. He reintroduced English as a school subject when it turned out that one of his daughters was not admitted to a college in the United States on account of her inadequate grasp of the language.

That was not at all the case during the early 1950s. Many British people had chosen to remain in the country after independence. English companies still carried on trade and commerce in the country, and the prime minister, U Nu, was keen on attracting more foreign investors. The Indian population was still intact. During the colonial era, there had sometimes been more Indians than Bamar living in the capital.

To put it briefly: when Burma was still standing at the crossroads, Rangoon was a multicultural city, and Aung San Suu Kyi's youth was stamped by that.

For her mother, nationalism did not seem to have been about "driving out" the English or about setting the Bamar up against any of the ethnic minorities. Nationalism was about the right to rule over one's own destiny and to nurture, and be allowed to nurture, one's own culture. That other cultures coexisted in the country was not a threat, and it was not possible or even desirable to drive them out.

Khin Kyi's broad international network meant that many of the conversations in their home were carried on in English and she wanted her children to become bilingual quickly. On that point she had the same outlook as Aung San. Even as a boy he had demanded to be able to learn English at school, since it would not be possible to educate himself and influence the development of society if he did not master the language of the colonial power.

When Aung San Suu Kyi reached school age she was first placed in a private school, Saint Frances Convent, where education was carried out bilingually. A few years later she was moved to the prestigious Methodist English High School (MEHS), a school for the absolute cream of society, with high school fees, strategically situated in central Rangoon. MEHS was one of several schools in Rangoon that were administrated by Christian communities. Saint Paul's was only for boys, Saint Mary's and Saint John's were girls' schools. MEHS accepted pupils of both sexes. Many British children attended the school, and even Gen. Ne Win's six children went there. Bamar was a compulsory subject, but many lessons were held in English.

"Everybody knew who Aung San Suu Kyi was. As the daughter of Aung San, she was never able to remain anonymous. But she was not treated differently in any way," says Jenny Tun-Aung, who attended the same class as Suu Kyi. "On the other hand it was already obvious that she was stubborn and that she always held her ground. Just as at other schools, the boys used to be nuisance to us girls, but every time they went for Suu Kyi she shouted at them and chased them all the way into the boys' lavatories."

Her cousin Sein Win paints a similar picture. In the 1990s he became prime minister in the exile government that was formed when the junta refused to hand over power to the popularly elected politicians. Sein Win was born a year before Aung San Suu Kyi, and his father, U Ba Win, had been murdered together with Aung San in the Secretariat in 1947.

"Our common experiences made the bonds between our families unusually strong," he explained when I talked to him in the spring of 2010. "We were neighbors and we children often played together. Aung San Suu Kyi was an ordinary girl who liked playing with her friends, but she had an extraordinary sense of fair play. If anyone tried to cheat at baseball or any other game we were playing, she always put a stop to it at once."

The Swede Clas Örjan Spång, today working as a teacher in Stockholm, was in the same class as Aung San Suu Kyi in 1958. He stayed for a year in Rangoon, where his father worked at the Swedish company LM Ericsson. He remembers his classmate very well, not the least for her name. Everyone else in their class was given an English name by their teacher, Mrs. Brindley, but she insisted on calling the daughter of the famous national hero by her father's name. After a couple of days Suu Kyi corrected her teacher. "My name is not Aung San," she said. "But you are related to him, aren't you?" asked Mrs. Brindley. After this Suu Kyi was called by her real name.

"That's why I remember her so well," said Clas Örjan when, many years later, I met him for lunch in a small apartment on the outskirts of Stockholm. "If she had been given an English name it's possible I never would have picked up her real name or her background."

There were around forty students in their class, and both Suu Kyi and Clas Örjan sat in the front, close to the teacher and far away from "the noise in the back of the room" where a group of young boys always talked and threw things at one another.

"Actually it was Aung San Suu Kyi who persuaded me to study French," said Clas Örjan.

Many people say these kinds of things about Aung San Suu Kyi's school years, along with the observations that she found schoolwork easy and that she particularly enjoyed languages. As soon as she had learned to read, she left the world of dolls behind her and threw herself into the world of books. Sein Win relates that she always had a book with her, and when his own family came on a visit, they often found her sitting sunk into an armchair, deep in a book.

When she was nine years old she was given a tip by one of her cousins that she should read a book about Sherlock Holmes, and after that she was sold on detective novels. "How could Bugs Bunny adventures compare with those of a man who could, from a careful examination of a battered old hat, gauge the physical and mental attributes, financial situation, and the matrimonial difficulties of its erstwhile owner?" she wrote in one of her texts about literature. In her everyday sympathetic manner she commented that "some of the most relaxing weekends I have ever enjoyed were those I spent quietly with a sense of all work to date completed, and absorbing a mystery."

She soon read her way through all the detective classics, like those by George Simenon and Agatha Christie, but also threw herself into the more hard-boiled stories of Raymond Chandler and Dashiell Hammett. Later on in life she was very fond of P. D. James's stories about the quiet police inspector Adam Dalgliesh. Dalgliesh in particular seems to have struck a chord with Suu Kyi. "The dash of French artist's blood in his veins makes him more fascinating than supposedly exotic investigators like Hercule Poirot," she wrote in a commentary that sounds more like a political stance for mixed marriage than a critical literary point of view.

She read everything and everywhere. She used to take a book with her when she went shopping with her mother. Reading during car trips was

Class photo from Methodist High School (1959–1960). Aung San Suu Kyi is fifth from the left in the middle row. *Courtesy of Jenny Tun-Aung, who is standing last to the right on the same row.*

unthinkable in the chaotic traffic of Rangoon. She would begin to feel sick. But as soon as the car had stopped, her eyes turned once again to the pages of her book. "The moment the car stopped anywhere, I would open my book and start reading, even if it was at a traffic light. Then I would have to shut it and couldn't wait for the next stop."

When she was about ten she dreamed of being a soldier and an officer, preferably a general like her father. "Up to then, of course, the army was an institution that served the people and not one that took from them," she said in an interview conducted by Alan Clements. However, the dream of a soldier's life soon faded, possibly for the simple reason that women were not permitted to enter the army. Influenced by all the books she devoured, she now wanted to become an author instead. She wanted to write stories that fascinated and gripped the reader, such as those she enjoyed reading.

Later in life she was to realize part of that dream. During the 1980s she published several documents and books: one book about her home country and one about Bhutan (both written for children and published in Australia), an essay about her father, and several articles on political issues. But as yet she has not become an author of fiction.

It's obvious that Aung San Suu Kyi's main influence in her early life, her role model and guide during the years of childhood, growing up without a father, was her mother, Khin Kyi.

It is sometimes said about Khin Kyi that she did not get married to a man but to a destiny. The opposite is often said about Aung San, that he got married to a woman who had morals and backbone sufficient to hold up his ideals even after his death.

His ideals, not her own.

Apart from the fact that this reflects a patriarchal worldview, it is of course both false and true. False in the sense that Khin Kyi had very strong political ideas and pronounced concepts of right and wrong of her own, and they guided her during her very successful professional career. It is also true that she never remarried after Aung San. His significance for Burma's collective unconscious was far too important for her to "besmirch" it with a new love affair.

During the whole of the 1950s she toiled away to keep everything going in their daily life. Her working days were long and there was not much time to spend with the children. In that sense she was no different from her deceased husband. They had the same ability to focus on the task at hand and to be absorbed by their work. At the same time she saw to it that the children were given a strict and rather conservative upbringing. Khin Kyi was not the least careful about her children's appearance. When they had guests at home the children always had to wear their best clothes, well ironed and without flecks of dirt. This is what Suu Kyi related for Alan Clements:

> My mother was a very strong person and I suppose I too am strong, in my own way. But I have a much more informal relationship with my children. My mother's relationship with me was quite formal. She never ran around and played with me when I was young. With my sons, I was always running around with them, playing together. Also, I would have long discussions with them. Sometimes I would argue with them—tremendously passionate arguments, because my sons can be quite argumentative, and I am argumentative too. I never did this sort of thing with my mother.

Khin Kyi's views basically reflected a traditional Burmese outlook on upbringing. Children were expected to manage on their own to a great extent. U Thant, the secretary general of the United Nations and a member of the Burmese liberation movement in the 1940s, has described how his own childhood felt like an endless stream of days when the adults were quite simply not there. The children on the block roamed around as they liked, returning home only to eat, and there was always rice ready in the kitchen.

Children are also expected to show respect for their elders. They learn early on to bow in front of adults, in the same way that one learns early on to bow in front of the Buddhist altar before going to bed in the evening.

That Khin Kyi was often busy with work did not mean that the children were alone during the day. The concept of family in Burma in the 1950s was not as broad as in India, for example, nor was it as narrow as the modern nuclear family in Western countries. A household usually consisted of children, parents, and one or several grandparents, perhaps also an aunt or uncle.

One or more housekeepers lived in the house on University Avenue and also for long periods of time an aunt, as did Khin Kyi's father, Pho Hnyin, the man who had converted to Christianity during his forest jaunts with the hunters of the Karen people.

When reading about Aung San Suu Kyi's mother, one is struck by the fact that she, despite the great geographical and cultural distance, resembles famous Swedish politician and diplomat, later Nobel Peace Prize laureate, Alva Myrdal. Both were born at the beginning of the 1900s and were active during a time when women were starting to help themselves to a more public life. They had the same fields of political interest and both participated in forming the social politics of their respective countries, with a particular focus on women and children. Both had an ability to concentrate fully on their work while at the same time, paradoxically enough, accepting a traditional female role. They allowed their husbands to be the star and adapted a great deal of their lives to fit in with the man of the family, dead or alive.

To take the similarity between Alva Myrdal and Khin Kyi one step further, it is actually likely that these two successful women met each other when they were both working as ambassadors in India. When Khin Kyi was appointed as Burma's first female ambassador in 1960, Alva Myrdal had already spent four years in New Delhi. They were both acquaintances of India's prime minister, Nehru, and moved in the diplomatic circles of the Indian capital.

Aung San Suu Kyi was fifteen when they moved to India. Khin Kyi wanted to have her daughter close to her, so there was no question of her staying behind in Rangoon. For her big brother Aung San Oo the situation was different. He was seventeen years old and had already been sent to boarding school in England.

Aung San Suu Kyi and her mother left a country on the brink of total chaos. The government had not succeeded in handling the communist guerrillas, several smaller ethnic groups had taken up arms, and GMD was still a perpetual source of unrest in the distant mountains of the Shan state. In an interview with the Dane Aage Krarup Nielsen, Prime Minister U Nu admitted that there were dark clouds in the otherwise bright skies. The reconstruction of the country had been interrupted on account of the eternal battles. Before the world war the rice exports had been three million tons per year and now they had still not reached more than two million tons. The farmers did not dare to cultivate their lands for fear of plundering and theft. "We can't fortify every village or protect every stretch of road!" proclaimed U Nu. "But we shall get at them! We know that their battle morale is low and we also know that the guerrilla battles that have flamed up recently are a sign of weakness, the final desperate struggle with their backs against the wall."

Despite the fact that the civil war had been going on for ten years since it first broke out, there was still great tolerance in the world at large for the government army's tough measures against the rebels. The Bamar sometimes compared their history to that of the United States. In the United States it took one hundred years and a civil war before the federal state could be seriously established. Burma had quite simply a historical baptism by fire to go through.

This view would turn out to be basically wrong. As in all societies characterized by war, the military successively reinforced its power, and the 1950s were marked by continual clashes between the civil government and the commander in chief of the army, Ne Win. With the civil war as a bloody background, the army devoured an ever greater proportion of the national budget, and the generals began step by step to dominate the greater part of the business sector. This started in 1951 when the army-owned Defence Services Institute opened a grocery shop in Rangoon. The idea was that army personnel should be able to buy goods that were otherwise hard to come by in Burma with its war economy; the concept was somewhat like the shops for the higher-level state employees in the former Eastern Bloc. Many officers and soldiers soon realized that they could buy more goods than they needed and sell them on the black market. Before long eighteen similar shops had opened. After that the army opened a bookshop that at first was just to sell goods to soldiers but which soon started selling paper, books, and pens to civilians too. The next step was a newspaper, *Myawaddy*, that was owned by the army and that was given the task of "balancing" the press that was otherwise fairly critical of the government. The newspaper became successful and was able to offer higher salaries to journalists, four-color printing to advertisers, and simple entertainment to the readers. At the end of the 1950s, the army owned building companies, shipping companies, chains of shops, and one of the country's leading import companies.

Parallel with the economic expansion, Ne Win built up an army that was loyal to him, as well as an effective security police force and a network of informers. He made use of what he learned both from the British security police and from the feared Japanese military police during the war period. He had shown great interest in the Japanese army's intelligence activities and methods of torture as far back as 1941 during the thirty comrades' military training camp on Hainan, and as commander in chief of the army with his power continually increasing, he had the opportunity of exploiting the knowledge acquired during that time.

Toward the end of the 1950s it was quite clear that the situation in the country was in the process of becoming too much for U Nu to cope with. The war did not come to an end, and in the autumn of 1958 the democratically elected prime minister gave up and handed over power to a military government under the leadership of Ne Win.

The takeover of power was quite undramatic, and the population of central Burma supported the measure, generally speaking. They still had confidence in the army and many were of the opinion that military rule for a short time was the only way to come to terms with the country's problems. For the ethnic minorities the changes were more dramatic. Ne Win changed the balance of power between Rangoon and the border regions. For the first time in history the regions belonging to the ethnic groups were to obey the same laws as the central regions of Burma. Local political leaders in the Karen, Shan, Chin, and Kachin states lost their power and had no right to make decisions about the budgets of the regional states in the same way as they had earlier.

Military rule was supposed to be a temporary solution for six months, but not until February 1960 were democratic elections held. The AFPFL won by the same simple means as before and U Nu was able to be reinstated as prime minister.

At this point U Nu made two crucial mistakes. Before the elections he had promised that Buddhism would be the national religion in Burma. After the elections he partly backed down on this, but by then the damage was already done. The ethnic minorities that had joined the union according to the Panglong agreement did not trust the central government and had no plans of remaining in a federal state that denied them freedom of religion. After that, U Nu came to an agreement with China about a border conflict that had been going on for several years. The agreement meant that a number of Kachin villages ended up on the Chinese side of the border. Both the Kachins via the Kachin Independence Army and groups of Shan rebels declared war against the central government in Rangoon.

In order to save the situation, U Nu called a meeting of representatives of the ethnic groups who wanted to see a peaceful solution to the country's political problems. They were assembled at a seminar in Rangoon at the beginning of March in order to draw up a new federal constitution that was to safeguard the independence of the border regions even more explicitly than before. However, that measure created a deep fissure in his own party, which consisted mainly of Bamar, and it caused the military with Ne Win at their head to turn openly against him. Before the seminar was over Ne Win had seized power in a coup d'état.

8

Suu from Burma

Aung San Suu Kyi grew up in a completely different political climate from that of her parents, and also under more privileged circumstances. They seemed to have been aware even as teenagers of which path they were going to choose in life: that they would contribute to the struggle for independence. For Aung San Suu Kyi, there was not the same obvious mission in life nor the same external need to make a decision early on.

"He was a better person than I am, and I'm not just saying this because I want to appear modest. My father was one of these people who were born with a sense of responsibility, far greater and more developed than mine. From the very moment he started going to school, he was a hard worker, very conscientious. I wasn't like that. I would study hard only when I liked the teacher or the subject. I had to develop my sense of responsibility and work with it."

This self-portrait is not, however, in total agreement with the person whom her friends and acquaintances describe from the 1950s and 1960s. Malavika Karlekar, who attended the same school and shared a class with Suu Kyi during the years in India, says that Suu Kyi was a person with very strong self-discipline right from the beginning. This was even visible in her posture when she was sitting down, not to mention how she carried herself and spoke. She also showed great self-discipline in her studies. Karlekar described the class as being populated by insecure teenagers at first. However, during her time in India, Suu Kyi developed from being a shy girl into a self-confident woman, from having been an almost self-effacing schoolchild into a person with strong and unshakeable convictions, according to Karlekar.

People often say this. Even the young Aung San Suu Kyi is described as a person with self-control, integrity, and strong moral convictions. This was probably an effect of her mother's upbringing but also of the strict rules that applied in the schools she was sent to. And in that way her first school in India, the Convent of Jesus and Mary School, was no exception. The school was Catholic and for girls only. Teaching was carried out mainly by nuns, and discipline was rigorous. The school had been founded in 1919 by a religious order, and it was situated behind the Sacred Heart Cathedral in central New Delhi. A number of well-known Indians had attended the school, among them one of Sonia Gandhi's daughters. Suu Kyi started there in 1960.

It was in India that Aung San Suu Kyi first became closely acquainted with Ma Than É, an older woman who for many years was to play an important part in her life as mentor and role model. Ma Than É was born in 1908 in Burma. Before the Second World War she had been a famous singer in Rangoon, and when Aung San and Khin Kyi started to get to know each other in the summer of 1942, they often listened to her recordings.

Ma Than É fled from the country due to the Japanese occupation. She lived for a time in India but later moved to San Francisco, where she worked for the United States Office of War Information, which later came to be known as the Voice of America. After the war she ended up in London where she met Aung San, who was there to negotiate Burma's independence with Clement Attlee. In one of her texts she has given a graphic description of those cold January days in 1947. Aung San and others in the delegation had meetings with the British government officials during the day, and in the evenings they made an effort to meet as many Burmese living in London as possible. They gathered at the Dorchester Hotel around a "feebly glowing electric fire," eating Burmese food and singing traditional songs together. Some of the delegates intervened with songs they had learned during their cooperation with the Japanese during the war. They discussed the 1930s and the anticolonial struggle, and one of the men told of the Japanese training camp on Hainan. The war itself was not mentioned. It was a sensitive question since most of the exiled Burmese in London, including Ma Than É, had supported the British during the Japanese occupation.

When reading her story, one almost gets the impression that Aung San fell in love with her. They seemed at any rate to have developed warm feelings for each other, and just before the journey back to Rangoon, Aung San asked whether she would not accompany them back to Burma. She declined, and immediately afterward she was given a post at the United Nations. During the 1950s, after Aung San had been murdered, she often visited his widow and the remains of the family in Rangoon. Suu Kyi was then still a child and called her Aunt Dora, after the name that Ma Than É had been given when she attended a mission school in the 1910s.

When Khin Kyi and her daughter moved to New Delhi, Ma Than É was working at the United Nations information office in the city and they began to see each other more regularly. "This was a wonderful opportunity to explore and understand the country of Mahatma Gandhi and Jawaharlal Nehru. Her father had been here and met and consulted Nehru, with whom he came to a close understanding," Ma Than É wrote in an essay published in *Freedom from Fear* about her friendship with Suu Kyi.

Khin Kyi saw to it that her daughter was always fully occupied during the years in India. Apart from school, Aung San Suu Kyi attended courses in Japanese flower-arranging, learned how to play the piano, and took riding lessons. Even so Aung San Suu Kyi still seemed interested most of all in sinking into an armchair and reading. She often received books from her father's friend U Ohn, who worked as a journalist in London and was at one time also ambassador to Moscow. On every visit to New Delhi he brought new books for Suu Kyi, in Burmese and English.

Khin Kyi was also particular about maintaining and transmitting the traditions of her homeland to her daughter. One of the things she took upon herself as new ambassador was to organize the renovation of a Buddhist center on the outskirts of New Delhi. After that, Aung San Suu Kyi often visited this place together with her mother, to meditate and to attend Buddhist festivals.

On a few such occasions her brother Aung San Oo also came to visit them from his boarding school in London. He and Suu Kyi acted as hosts at the receptions in the ambassador's residence. But even then it was noticeable that the siblings did not get along with each other. Aung San Suu Kyi wanted to live up to her mother's, and perhaps also her father's, expectations. She behaved correctly, spoke correctly, and gradually acquired the right education for being able to carry on the work her parents had started. Aung San Oo was not as interested in his social heritage. He had already begun to adapt to a more Western lifestyle and did not plan on returning to Burma.

After eighteen months at the Convent of Jesus and Mary School, Aung San Suu Kyi progressed to Lady Shri Ram College (LSR). Sir Shri Ram, an Indian industrialist, had founded the school in memory of his wife in 1956. He wanted to create an institution for higher education for women and also to give the school an international character. According to the LSR website in 2010, the school aims at "nurturing and creating women who are equipped to be world citizens. Women who take pride in their culture and heritage but also have a cosmopolitan understanding of the world today and a sensibility that celebrates diversity."

If this description weren't so pompous, it would have been quite suitable as a personal description of Aung San Suu Kyi.

In her day the school was situated in Daryaganj in central New Delhi. The main building had been built of gray-white stone in the colonial style, with tall colonnades and green shrubberies beside the school gates. Suu Kyi studied political science; Malavika Karlekar is of the opinion that it was at LSR that Suu Kyi received her first insight into Mahatma Gandhi's theories of nonviolence and civil disobedience—the recipes for political opposition she so consistently applied when she stepped forward as the leader of the democratic movement in Burma. According to Karlekar, Suu Kyi did not express any distinct political ideas during her time at LSR, but it was obvious that she thought about and reflected on politics the whole time. "As her father's daughter she of course acquired opinions in due course. She did not talk about them but it was clear anyway that they existed."

There was, however, no political activity. "The only thing that I remember is that we started a campaign to keep the school gates open for longer in the evenings," says Karlekar, who later became a respected sociologist and the director of the Centre for Women's Development Studies. "We won that battle, but I can't remember that we did anything else political."

Khin Kyi had been appointed as ambassador while U Nu was still prime minister, and despite the fact that she was deeply critical of developments in her home country, she chose to remain at her post even after the military coup in 1962.

Burma's transition to a military dictatorship was not in any way unique to the region. In South Korea, Gen. Park Chung Hee had just established the dictatorship that was to last for twenty-six years. Neighboring Thailand was governed by Field Marshal Sarit Thanarat, and in Pakistan a similar military dictatorship was controlled by Ayub Khan.

What made Ne Win unique was his extreme choice of path after the coup. To start with, he ordered the imprisonment of the democratically elected politicians. U Nu was locked up at a military base (he was the first to be released four years later). Soon after the coup, Ne Win made a journey to China. He returned after only a few days and declared that he was deeply impressed by what Mao and the Chinese communist party had achieved since the revolution in 1949. In April 1962 he presented two peculiar documents. One of them drew up the guidelines for "the Burmese way to socialism," and the other had the title "A System to Correct Humanity and Its Environment." Taken together, these programs were neither particularly Burmese nor socialist, but were mostly an expression of Ne Win's own prejudices and totalitarian ambitions for power. All companies were nationalized, from the largest manufacturing industries to the smallest teahouses. The popularly elected parliament was abolished, and Ne Win stated that the country would never again return to a system that was influenced by Western ideals. Instead, he started Burma's Socialist Program Party (BSPP). It was governed by a revolutionary council, with subordinate regional and local councils. All the posts at all levels were occupied by officers, and after some years it was impossible to distinguish in any meaningful way between the BSPP and Tatmadaw, the army. The party became a parallel structure in the machinery of the state, and the members in its highest executive were considerably more powerful than the ministers in the formal government.

To start with, many Burmese understood Ne Win's takeover of power as a new transitional solution while waiting for the next democratic election.

That was how it had been during the years of military government in the 1950s. But on that occasion civil servicemen and politicians had been allowed to retain their assignments. Now the whole social machinery was militarized, and that made first and foremost the students at Rangoon University protest. They did not intend to keep quiet while their country was being transformed into a military state, and they decided to carry out a peaceful demonstration on the university premises. On July 7, 1962, several thousand students gathered on the university campus, in what was to become their "democratic fortress." Their protest was almost like a popular festival, with singing and dancing and long speeches inside the student union building. Ne Win responded with the bloody practice that has since been repeated every time large demonstrations have broken out in Burma. The military opened fire against the defenseless students and killed dozens, perhaps hundreds.

In order to show that he meant business, Ne Win also gave the order to blow up the student union at Rangoon University. Ne Win thus erased one of the foremost symbols of the struggle Aung San had carried out against the British colonial power.

The junta's puritanical aspect soon also became obvious. It forbade all Western dances, horse racing, and beauty competitions, and the few nightclubs in Rangoon were closed. Foreigners were not to be encouraged to travel to Burma, and it was only possible to get a visa for a twenty-four-hour visit to the country.

Most serious of all was perhaps the junta's program to "Burmanize" the border areas. The ethnic minorities were forbidden to publish newspapers and books in their own languages, teaching in the schools was changed to Burmese, and the minorities' political structures were crushed. Several of the princes in the Shan state were kidnapped and murdered. A couple of years after the military coup, most of the ethnic minorities had armed themselves, and with that Burma sank with increasing rapidity into total chaos. Even today, although the junta has come to an agreement with most of the guerrilla armies about a cease-fire, there are over twenty armed groups in the Shan state alone.

The junta also threw out all the Western organizations that were active in Burma, not least that of the Christian missionaries who were working

among the ethnic minorities. The last of them, the Swedish American
Herman Tegenfeldt, who had worked among the Kachin villagers, left the
country in 1966. But many of the Indians and British who had lived in
Burma for generations had chosen to flee even before the military coup.
"We saw which way the wind was blowing. We managed all right, but those
who stayed until 1962 didn't have the same luck," says Peter Carey, who
was eight years old in 1956, when his parents moved from Rangoon. "Before
they were put on a plane out of the country they were plundered of all their
belongings. The soldiers ripped off their wedding rings and jewelry and
stole their cash."

It was perhaps that period of which a close friend of Aung San Suu Kyi's
was thinking several years later, when she urged her on the anniversary of
Aung San's assassination not to grieve for her father's early death. "In a way
it was a blessing for him not growing old," she said. "He didn't have to experience the destructive years."

Khin Kyi endured being an ambassador for five years after the military
coup, but then it became morally impossible for her to represent a government she neither believed in nor respected. In 1967 she moved back to
the house on University Avenue in Rangoon. She resigned from her public
commissions, and during the last twenty years of her life she spent her
days looking after the garden, reading, and immersing herself in religious
matters. Ne Win understood the signal. He and Aung San had never been
able to agree on anything, and there is evidence that Aung San even warned
his party comrades in the AFPFL not to give Ne Win too much power over
the armed forces. When Khin Kyi cut off all contact with the regime, he
took revenge by imposing a forty-thousand-kyat back tax on her. Normally
speaking, diplomats were released from tax during the time they were
working abroad, but the junta chose to make an "exception" for Khin Kyi,
who had to borrow money right and left from family members and friends
in order to pay it back.

When her mother retired, Aung San Suu Kyi had already been living in
England for two years. She had moved there in 1964 to study at St Hugh's
College in Oxford. At that time there were ten male students to every female
student at the very traditional university, and St Hugh's was one of five col-

leges reserved especially for women. "I noticed her straightaway," says Ann Pasternak Slater when I reached her over the phone in England. Pasternak enrolled at the college on the same day as Suu Kyi. "I saw her on the opposite side of the room when I was at some reception or other for new students and I thought, 'God, what a lovely person! I must get to know her!'"

When speaking to people about Aung San Suu Kyi's time in Burma after 1988, they always return to the fact that she demanded a great deal of those around her, since she demanded a great deal of herself. "Privately as well as politically she is driven by the conviction that people with privileges also have special responsibility, and that one must live up to that responsibility," said a Burmese activist who worked with her in the 1990s. Those who met her in Oxford confirm this. When she was in her twenties, it is true that she did not moralize over her friends, but she was of the opinion that many of them took their studies too lightly and wasted their years at university.

"Suu's tight, trim longyi and upright carriage, her firm moral convictions and inherited social grace contrasted sharply with the tatty dress and care-less manners, vague liberalism and uncertain sexual morality [of others]," wrote Pasternak Slater in her essay "Suu Burmese." The title comes from the nickname she gave Suu Kyi. When they both got to know each other, she already had several English friends called Sue, so the new Burmese acquaintance simply had to be called Suu Burmese.

The rules at St Hugh's were as strict as they had been at Suu Kyi's previous schools, with the crucial difference that the female students at Oxford did all they could to break them. The students were compelled to be back at home before ten in the evening, so many of them often sat on their beds and talked and drank hot chocolate until late at night. Most of them also made little excursions out to see friends or boyfriends, and they stole back over the stone wall to the dormitory in the early morning hours.

This was something Aung San Suu Kyi did not do. She took great care of her traditional upbringing while also being far too curious not to try what a number of her Western friends used to talk so much about. After two years she decided, for example, that she wanted to see what it was like to climb back into St Hugh's late at night. She asked an Indian male acquaintance whom she trusted completely to take her with him to a restaurant, so that he could later help her over the wall when it was time to go home. "No infringement of university regulations could have been perpetrated with greater propriety," wrote Pasternak Slater.

On another occasion Suu Kyi decided that it was time to find out what the fuss about alcohol was really all about. For social and religious reasons she had refrained from drinking beer, wine, or spirits. But she did not like the thought of saying no to something without knowing what she was talking about. So one evening at the end of her first year she bought a miniature bottle of sherry or possibly dessert wine, and along with two Indian friends she retired to the shabby ladies' restroom. "There, among the sinks and the cubicles, in a setting deliberately chosen to mirror the distastefulness of the experience, she tried and rejected alcohol forever," Pasternak Slater remembered.

With sex it was completely different. When it came to that she was already convinced: she would never have sex with anyone other than the person she married. "Everyone was on the hunt for boyfriends," according to Pasternak Slater, "[and] many wanted affairs, sex being still a half-forbidden, half-won desideratum. . . . To most of our English contemporaries, Suu's startled disapproval seemed a comic aberration." When one girl asked whether Suu really did not want to go to bed with anybody, she replied, "No! I'll never go to bed with anyone except my husband. Now? I just go to bed hugging my pillow."

This did not mean that Suu Kyi was without feelings. She spent much time with the Indian students, and at the beginning of her studies she fell in love with one of them. But her interest was not returned and their contact never developed into a relationship. "One did catch a glimpse of her persistency in that case," says Pasternak Slater. "It was clear from the start that he wasn't interested in the same way as she was, but she refused to give up. She held on to it for much longer than anyone else would have done."

When she applied to St Hugh's she had chosen to study philosophy, politics, and economics, which was a common combination of subjects among the Indian students at the university. But Suu Kyi really longed for something else, and after her first year she applied to change her course and study to be a forest warden instead. She considered that a practical subject would make it easier for her to return to Burma and do something for her country. But Oxford did not appreciate students' changing their minds about their academic direction, and they rejected her application. When she had passed her examination, she made a new attempt and applied to an English course, but she was not accepted there either.

Many of Suu Kyi's student comrades were politically involved. It was an era when radical internationalism was about to establish itself in Europe and the United States. The world had opened up, the colonial systems were about to be dismantled, and TV had brought the world into people's living rooms. The students who could afford it and who had the time traveled abroad to learn more in places where "reality" seemed to come a little closer than in the chilly lecture halls of Oxford University. One was not in tune with the times if he or she had not picked fruit on some Israeli kibbutz or walked among the poor in India. And one was not truly radical if he or she had not gotten involved in the nuclear disarmament movement or protested against the apartheid system in South Africa.

Through her background and family contacts, Suu Kyi was of course more well traveled and familiar with the ways of society than most of her contemporaries, but she kept away from all openly political activities. "As a student I was caught up in the concern about apartheid, contributing my tiny bit of support by refusing to buy products from South Africa," Suu Kyi has written in an article published in the Thai newspaper *The Nation*. As the leader of the democratic movement she has often used South Africa as an example of how economy and politics are bound up with each other and of how sanctions can in certain situations be a functional recipe for creating political change.

One explanation for the fact that she was not more explicitly political was her mother's position, during the time she was an ambassador as well as later after she had returned to Burma. Khin Kyi could have been landed with great problems if it had emerged that her daughter was active in human rights politics along with a crowd of young British radicals. "I don't believe that she went and listened to debates or was involved in any kind of activism," says Pasternak Slater. "On the other hand she was perpetually aware of what was going on in the world and we often talked about her background in Burma, the culture and traditions there. And she often expressed her irritation over her older brother. She did not consider that he upheld the family traditions."

During summer vacations, Aung San Suu Kyi traveled most often to see her mother in India, but one summer she visited Ma Than É in Algeria. At that time Ma Than É had just left her post in New Delhi in order to build up the United Nations information offices in the Algerian capital, Algiers. The trip gave Suu Kyi the opportunity to experience some of that "adventurousness" that her middle-class friends at Oxford had told her about in connection with their summer travels.

Algeria had just dragged itself out from under the claws of French colonial power and was slowly recovering from the eight-year-long civil war, a situation not entirely unlike that of Burma after the Second World War. The cities were shabby and demolished, and there were only a few hotels that were able to receive guests. Suu Kyi arrived there a few weeks after Algeria's counterpart to Aung San, Ahmed Ben Bella, had been overthrown by his former colleague, the more moderate Houari Boumediene.

Suu Kyi was invited to plenty of social events and parties, but she chose mostly to go out onto the streets in order to meet ordinary Algerians. After a few days she made contact with a man who ran an organization to help the widows of men who had been killed in the war of liberation. He explained that he was busy organizing a project to build homes for these women and he needed volunteers who could help him. For several weeks Suu Kyi worked and lived on the building site. Among her workmates were Russians, British, Lebanese, Dutch, Germans, and Algerians, all of whom were given free lodging and food but no wages. Her Algerian friends took her with them to a wedding in the Kabylian mountains. She saw the Sahara desert and made a short trip to Morocco and the Strait of Gibraltar. Then she returned to Oxford.

On one occasion, just before her finals, Suu Kyi was invited to visit Ne Win. The Burmese dictator had confiscated the passports of millions of Burmese and done everything he could to close the borders; yet he himself made trips to Europe every year, sometimes to Austria where he stayed at a spa and visited doctors, and sometimes to Wimbledon where he rented a spacious villa for himself and his party consisting of women and officers. When Suu Kyi was invited to visit him, her mother had just left her position as ambassador and resigned from all her public undertakings. Suu Kyi had therefore no problem in distancing herself from the regime in her home country, in her own way. She declined the invitation and excused herself on account of having no time: she was studying for her finals.

During the term, Suu Kyi usually lived at St Hugh's, but on the weekends she did the little more than one-hour journey to London by train and stayed at the home of Sir Paul Gore-Booth and his wife, Patricia, in Chelsea. The Gore-Booth couple had come to know Suu Kyi's family when Paul was the British ambassador in Burma from 1953 until 1956. After Rangoon he had been transferred to a post as high commissioner at the British Embassy in India, and there the friendship between the families deepened. When it was time for Suu Kyi to apply to Oxford, Khin Kyi wanted to find somebody who could help her daughter find her way in her new environment and the choice fell naturally on the Gore-Booths, who at that time had returned to London. During the next few years Suu Kyi became almost like a child to the family. "Like an extra daughter," Patricia Gore-Booth has said. Suu Kyi sat at the table when Paul's colleagues were there to dine and she gained insight into the English diplomatic corps' way of reasoning. She often took part in the discussions since the visitors were interested in the situation in Burma and in her mother's work in India.

The Gore-Booths' twin sons were a few years older and among their friends was yet another pair of twins, Anthony and Michael Aris. The Aris brothers had in several ways the same variegated international background as Suu Kyi. They were born on March 27, 1946, in Havanna, Cuba, where their father was working for the British Council, with the task of spreading English culture and the English language in the world. Their mother was the daughter of a French-Canadian diplomat. The family moved from Cuba to Peru and finally landed in England.

In the mid-1960s, both Michael and Anthony were studying to become orientalists at the University of Durham in northern England. There they came to know Christopher Gore-Booth, and since the Gore-Booth family's house in Chelsea seems to have acted as a gathering place for the circle of friends and acquaintances of the whole family, it sometimes happened that the Aris brothers accompanied him up to London. Anthony was the one who first noticed Suu Kyi. "You must see this astonishing Burmese woman from St Hugh's," he said to his brother.

Michael fell head-over-heels as soon as he met her, but Suu Kyi's approach was considerably more wait-and-see. She had not the remotest intention of having a relationship with, let alone marrying, a man who was a Westerner.

Many of her friends and relations at home would have strong objections to such a marriage. It is also possible she already realized that it might turn out to be a problem if she were at any time to play a public role in her home country. But still, she fell in love and started quietly spending time with the lanky, rather Bohemian, yet conservatively brought-up and proper student from Durham.

After her finals Suu Kyi stayed for a longer period of time at the Gore-Booths' home in London. She was given a room in the attic in the large stone house, with her own entrance and her own kitchen. She was able to choose how much time she wanted to spend in the company of the English family. In order to earn a little extra money, she worked as a private tutor to children of the upper class in Chelsea. She also worked for a time as an assistant to the Southeast Asia expert Hugh Tinker at the School of Oriental and African Studies in London. Tinker had published the book *Burma: The Struggle for Independence 1944–48*, and it was a great advantage to have an assistant who was personally a part of the history he had chosen to research.

While Suu Kyi was taking her first steps in her professional life after her studies, Michael Aris had already left the country. During his undergraduate education in Durham he had specialized in Tibet, Bhutan, and Nepal, and in the course of his work he had come into contact with the researcher and author Marco Pallis, who was the last Westerner to leave Lhasa after the Chinese occupation of Tibet. Pallis had introduced Aris to the court in Bhutan, who had given Aris an offer that no student with his specialization could afford to say no to: he became adviser to the royal family in Bhutan. As a twenty-year-old he thus had a unique opportunity to learn more about the Himalayas and the local history and religion while actually living there. He would have preferred to study Tibet, but in 1967 the vast mountain state was totally closed to foreigners. China had taken a stranglehold and was in the process of destroying the country's unique traditions. Bhutan was therefore the best possible starting point for Aris. He quickly learned to speak the local language, Dzongkha, and even became reasonably skilled in Tibetan. There, among the green mountains of the Himalayas at the end of the 1960s, he discovered his mission in life and his identity as a researcher. He was going to become an expert on the culture and religion of the Himalayan mountain states.

At the same time Suu Kyi decided to move to the United States. She wanted to continue her studies in order to earn a master's degree. Once again she was able to take advantage of the family's extensive international network. In 1969 she was accepted to New York University with Frank Trager as her adviser. Trager was a professor of international relations who had been working for several years on an American aid project in Burma. His book *Burma: From Kingdom to Republic* had just been published, and he was looking forward to helping Suu Kyi with her studies.

For Aris and Suu Kyi it was clearly not any easier to maintain their relationship when they were now not able to meet at all. But on another plane it suited her perfectly. She wanted to put time and distance between herself and Michael in order to test her own feelings and at the same time assure herself that he was serious. If what they felt for each other was still there after that time, then she was aiming to follow her feelings and not bother about the conventions.

In New York she stayed with Ma Than É, who had moved there after her sojourn in Algeria. They shared a small apartment with two rooms and a kitchen a few blocks from the United Nations' skyscraper on the corner of Forty-ninth Street and First Avenue. They read, talked, and cooked Burmese food together whenever they got hold of the right spices, which was not that often.

As with all other people who arrive in New York for the first time, Suu Kyi was overwhelmed by the size of the city and the lights, the skyscrapers, the throngs of people, and the sheer number of different cultures and individual expressions. But she did not at all like the bus journeys between the apartment and the university near Washington Square. This was a long time before Mayor Rudolph Giuliani's "zero tolerance" against crime, and Suu Kyi often felt nervous when she had to walk alone in the early mornings and late evenings between her home, the bus, and the university. Therefore she did not hesitate when she was offered the opportunity to work at the United Nations, only a six minutes' walk from her apartment. "After applications, recommendations, interviews, and the usual delays and difficulties, Suu was in," wrote Ma Than É in her essay in *Freedom from Fear.*

The secretary general of the United Nations was at that time U Thant, politically the most successful Burmese of all and in several ways a symbol for what Burma might have been without the civil war, the military coup, and the xenophobic isolation from the rest of the world. U Thant grew up in a small village in the Irrawaddy Delta. His father worked in education and was one of the founders of the *Sun*, a newspaper that in the 1920s and 1930s supported the idea that Burma should be given a greater degree of independence but should remain within the British Empire. But his father died when U Thant was only fourteen years old, and the family landed in great economic difficulty. Despite this, U Thant succeeded in gaining an education as a teacher, and when he was only twenty-five years old he became the headmaster of one of the schools in his hometown. Alongside this job he wrote a great number of articles and essays, in which he argued for increased independence, just like his father. During his time at university he had come to know Aung San, U Nu, and others in the young nationalist movement. U Nu had worked as a teacher at the school in Pantanaw, and when he became prime minister in 1948, he asked U Thant to come to Rangoon. For a number of years in the 1950s U Thant was the speechwriter, personal secretary, and political factotum to the prime minister.

In 1957 U Thant was appointed Burma's representative in the United Nations, and he immediately made himself known as an effective and pragmatic politician. His mild, gentle, and in several ways typically "Burmese" manner appealed to most parties in the otherwise very split United Nations. Not to all, however. He acquired enemies, for example, when his negotiations led to Algeria's independence at the beginning of the 1960s. "It was the job I liked the best," he later told the author June Bingham, "but it took me a long time to regain confidence from the French."

Despite that, when United Nations secretary general Dag Hammarskjöld was killed in an airplane crash in September 1961, U Thant was selected to be his successor. He had strong support among the African and Asian countries, and the superpowers understood him to be no great threat to their dominance in the Security Council. The Burmese was, quite simply, eminently suitable for the role that President Roosevelt had suggested that the world organization's secretary general should play: he should be a moderator, not a player in his own right.

But unlike most secretaries general, who had often been recruited on account of their administrative gifts, U Thant was not satisfied with that role alone. He pursued the policy that the United Nations must be impartial but not morally neutral. In cases where the United Nations Charter and the organization's fundamental principles are subject to gross violation, one must react, he felt. He was, for example, deeply critical of the United States' war in Vietnam and offered several times to mediate in the conflict, but President Lyndon B. Johnson declined each time. Perhaps U Thant foreshadowed the debate on human rights and humanitarian intervention that characterized the United Nations several decades later, when the Wall had fallen and a more open international climate seemed to be within reach.

When Ne Win seized power in 1962, U Thant had already been appointed as secretary general, and Burma's new dictator could not attack him, however much he wanted to. Ne Win detested U Thant, partly because he had been such a close ally of U Nu, and partly because he remained Burma's most brightly shining star on the firmament of international politics. That role was one Ne Win would gladly have awarded to himself.

There is nothing to indicate that U Thant was directly involved in the decision to give Aung San Suu Kyi an appointment at the United Nations, but it is not unthinkable that he had something to do with the matter. The bonds between the Burmese living in New York were close, and Aung San Suu Kyi often spent time in the company of the secretary general's family.

But it was also clear that there were two factions among the Burmese in New York: the ones who were critical of the regime and the ones who supported it. The latter had as their base Burma's embassy and the United Nations delegation appointed by Ne Win. U Thant often invited both groups to Sunday lunch at his home in Riverdale in the Bronx, a house with a large garden and a beautiful view out over the Hudson River. "Other Burmese friends would be there, a convivial company, and Burmese food much to our taste would be served. On special occasions, such as the birthday of one of his grandchildren, the grounds of the house would be decked out to receive the Burmese, and also the heads of many of the permanent delegations to the UN," remembered Ma Than É.

Aung San Suu Kyi was given a post on the Advisory Committee on Administrative and Budgetary Questions, and the work assignments were just about as entertaining as they sound. The committee had the task of scrutinizing the budget and costs of several of the United Nations' most important executive institutions, like the World Health Organization, and the aid programs within the UN Development Programme (UNDP). The committee was independent of both the secretary general and the general assembly. Soul-destroying or not, it gave Aung San Suu Kyi unique insight into the work of the world organization.

In the evenings she involved herself in volunteer work, something that the younger members of the United Nations personnel were at that time more or less expected to do. Suu Kyi did her "social service" at the Bellevue Hospital at the top of First Avenue. The hospital had been founded way back in 1736, and it is today the oldest publicly owned hospital in the United States. Over 80 percent of the patients come from socially vulnerable conditions and do not have comprehensive health insurance. The situation was about the same in the 1960s. Suu Kyi spent many weekday evenings and often one of the days on the weekend at the hospital. She read for the little ones in the children's wards and sat on night duty by the beds of the elderly. The hospital also takes in many patients with psychological problems, and Suu Kyi acted as a support in the waiting rooms before they got to see a doctor.

Ne Win had now been in power in Burma for over eight years. The economy had collapsed and the civil war had been aggravated by an unwillingness of the regime to negotiate with the ethnic minorities, or even to recognize their right to their own culture. The conflict with Guomintang had been resolved at the beginning of the 1960s, thanks to the Chinese and Burmese forces making a combined attack on its strongholds in the northeastern Shan state. The soldiers had been driven over the border to Laos, where many of them joined the United States' escalating war in Indochina. Other parts of the GMD forces ended up in northern Thailand, where it is still possible to distinguish a number of villages that in principle are populated entirely by aged GMD soldiers and their descendants.

But peace there was not. GMD was only a part of the problem, and in the political power vacuum that arose after the flight to Laos and Thailand, other local warlords and ethnically loyal guerrilla groups saw an opportunity of increasing their influence. In order to meet the guerrilla uprising, Ne Win chose to put his trust in the local militia, the so-called Ka Kwe Yes (KKY). The system amounted to allowing the warlords in the Shan mountains full freedom to sell opium and heroin, and in many cases the Burmese Army helped them with transport and protection. In return, the warlords promised to fight against the guerrilla groups that were at war with Rangoon.

The Burma expert Bertil Lintner is of the opinion that there were three reasons why Ne Win chose that solution. First, there was no money in the public treasury to finance a comprehensive, long-term war against the ethnic guerrilla groups. The trade with opium was decisive for supplying the soldiers with weapons, ammunition, uniforms, and necessities. Second, it undermined the Shan rebels' own possibilities of gaining income from the opium fields if the KKY militia took the trade monopoly into its own hands. Third, it was already clear that Ne Win's economic politics were a failure. There was a great shortage of all kinds of goods on the markets inside Burma, and the international drug trade became a way of acquiring capital and everyday commodities for the country.

KKY transported the opium to the market city of Tachilek, which is situated on the border between Thailand and Laos, and there they were paid in pure gold—hence the region's "golden triangle" moniker. Despite the ever more chaotic situation, Ne Win was convinced that his Burmese "socialism" was the only conceivable road. At the same time, relations with Khin Kyi and her family grew frostier and frostier, which even Suu Kyi was made to experience during the time she was living in New York. Ma Than É tells of an episode at the home of U Soe Tin, Burma's ambassador to the United Nations. He was a liberal person who served the junta in a diplomatically correct manner, but he was also keen on keeping in contact with those of the Burmese diaspora who were critical of the regime. One autumn when the General Assembly had its annual meeting they were invited to his home for a formal lunch. The ambassador's residence was also situated in Riverdale, but the house was not as striking as U Thant's. When Suu Kyi entered the spacious rectangular-shaped living room she saw that the sofas had been arranged so that they stood against the walls, with small tables in front of them. U Soe Tin's wife moved quietly around from table to table serving fruit juice and snacks before she retired to the kitchen to prepare the lunch. Suu Kyi was invited to sit down on one of the sofas where two of the delegates at the General Assembly were already sitting. Ma Than É sensed from the atmosphere in the room that all was not as it should be. After a few introductory courtesies, the leader of the delegation started interrogating Suu Kyi. How did she come to be working for the United Nations, despite the fact that nobody in her home country had given her such an assignment? What passport did she use when traveling to the United States? Was she not aware that her diplomatic passport had expired since her mother was no longer working as an ambassador in India? She was committing an illegal act when using that passport and she must immediately hand it in. During this whole maneuver, the others in the room looked unceasingly and with anxious expressions at Suu Kyi, and they mumbled in agreement as soon as a new accusation was aimed at her. It was clear that somebody in Rangoon, in all probability Ne Win personally, had given them the task of degrading Suu Kyi, but she showed no signs of taking the criticism to heart. She explained calmly and collectedly that she had of course applied for a new passport in London, she had handed in her papers several months previously, but the application had for some reason gotten stuck in the bureaucratic process. She was unable to understand why the whole business had been so delayed, she said, and anyway, all the "uncles" in the room certainly understood that one could not travel to another country without any passport at all, did they not?

At that point, Burma's ambassador in London came to her relief. He confirmed that the application had been handed in and sent to Rangoon for approval, but that it had gotten stuck in the system there. Everyone in the room knew that the bureaucracy in Burma under Ne Win had become extremely corrupt and ineffective, and some of those who had muttered supportively when Suu Kyi had been attacked now started instead to fidget uncomfortably. Through her quiet, simple explanation, the barely twenty-five-year-old Aung San Suu Kyi had not only gotten out of the question about her passport, but she had also turned the whole discussion into a criticism of developments in Burma.

9

Family Life in a Knapsack

The contrast could not have been sharper between the cosmopolitan life Aung San Suu Kyi had lived when she was growing up and the daily life she would later have to get used to during the years in house arrest. But still she seems to have taken the whole thing calmly when she was isolated in the house on University Avenue in July 1989. Most of those around her had been arrested during recent months. She had learned to live with the risk.

"My only worry was that my sons got back safely to England, especially if Michael was not allowed to come and get them," she said later.

However, the junta had no plans of stopping Michael. They hoped that he would take both the children and Suu Kyi with him back to Oxford. If Aung San Suu Kyi left the country, they could prevent her from returning. A one-way ticket out from Burma, and they would be rid of that problem.

Michael's journey at the end of July was given almost greater international attention than the arrest of Aung San Suu Kyi a few days earlier. He has written about it in *Freedom from Fear*. Suu Kyi was still a relatively unknown politician belonging to the opposition in a country that nobody in the West had bothered about for decades. Michael was no celebrity either, but he was a Western academic who disappeared without a trace for twenty-one days in one of the world's toughest dictatorships. The scenario fitted hand-in-glove with Western media logic.

When Michael landed at the shabby, badly maintained Mingaladon Airport in Rangoon, the whole runway was occupied by soldiers, military vehicles, and officers, all waiting for the tall Englishman to descend from the plane. He was immediately taken to the VIP lounge inside the main building, where an officer told him that he was to be allowed to visit his wife and sons, but only if he accepted certain specific conditions. He was not permitted to leave the house on University Avenue and he was not permitted under any circumstances to speak to the press or anybody from the British Embassy during his stay in Burma. He agreed to these demands. His only aim with this visit was to see his family again and to take their sons with him back to Oxford. Contrary to what the generals thought, he did not believe for one minute that Suu Kyi would accompany them back home. "She had decided this was her task, and I had no ambition whatsoever to talk her into something else," he said later, as quoted in the *New York Times*.

After the brief interrogation at the airport, he was put into a military vehicle and driven away. No outsider knew anything about his whereabouts. It was as though he had gone up in smoke. The international press wrote about the English academic who had been kidnapped by a junta refusing to answer questions about where he was being "held prisoner."

The military drove him straight to the house on the shores of Lake Inya, and as soon as he had crossed the threshold, he was confronted by the news that Aung San Suu Kyi was on a hunger strike. She had stopped eating three days ago in protest against the torture her friends and party comrades were being subjected to in the prisons. She refused all special treatment and demanded once again that she be thrown into the Insein prison along with the others.

The family lived through twelve days of uncertainty. Kim and Alexander played, read, and watched from the sidelines as their mother's condition slowly worsened. Guards were posted everywhere around the house and on the street outside, but they all behaved correctly and in a disciplined manner toward the family. The soldiers had great respect for Aung San's child and grandchildren, despite everything. Some of them looked after the boys and taught them judo and karate in the garden. The boys did not openly show any emotions, as one of Aung San Suu Kyi's assistants said later: "It's the British stiff-upper-lip training, and the training of their mother, who's been trained by her mother" (quote from Barbara Victors, *The Lady*).

According to Michael Aris, Suu Kyi lost twelve pounds in weight during her twelve-day hunger strike, which is a lot for a person who was already so tiny.

When she was in the process of fading away the junta promised that she would partly get what she wanted: her comrades would be spared torture in the prisons and be given a fair trial in court. Aung San Suu Kyi hesitated. She really wanted to continue her hunger strike until they also agreed to her final demand and threw her into prison. Michael did not doubt that she would continue for as long as necessary, but he succeeded in persuading her to accept the conditions and to accept help from a doctor, who immediately gave her an intravenous drip.

On August 12, 1989, when Michael Aris had been unlocatable for twenty-one days, he was given permission to speak to the British ambassador. He told him about Suu Kyi's health status, and what her demands to the junta involved. The ambassador spoke to the press, which reported that the hunt for Michael Aris was over and that he was now at his wife's side, under heavy military surveillance.

In practice, of course, things did not turn out as the generals had promised. Many of the activists who had been arrested during the election campaign were subjected to brutal torture and had to sit in prison for years without a fair trial. Min Ko Naing, who had led the student revolt the previous year, was imprisoned in March 1989 and not released until 2004. Several of his friends were given similar punishments, and they later revealed that they had been subjected to systematic torture and execrable prison conditions. However, Aung San Suu Kyi had made a point. She would not tolerate just anything and would do whatever she could to oppose the junta, even from her position under house arrest. She also communicated the fact that she under no circumstances was going to do what they wished and leave the country. If they wanted to get rid of her, they would have to drag her in chains to Mingaladon Airport. She had taken upon herself the role of leader of the democratic movement. She was ready to wait until the junta tired, and during the coming years the generals would only permit exceptional visits by Michael and the boys. The family was split up.

They had married on January 1, 1972, in a Burmese wedding ceremony in the drawing room at Paul and Patricia Gore-Booth's home in Chelsea. There is a fantastic wedding photograph, slightly yellowed and worn by time. Michael is wearing a dark suit with a white shirt and tie, and he has a flower in his buttonhole. His hair is as wild as was only possible during 1970s. Suu Kyi, more than a head shorter than her husband, is wearing a white dress with bare shoulders. Her hair is worn up in a fashion-forward style with flowers, and she is wearing a white pearl necklace.

She had chosen to leave New York late in the autumn of 1971. Not because she had tired of the city, her work, or her social life there. She was happy at the United Nations and thought that her volunteer work at Bellevue was useful. The years in the United States had, in reality, taught her more than the years at university. However, in the end she decided that she wanted to spend her life with Michael Aris. During a holiday in the spring of 1971 she had visited him in Bhutan. There they got to know each other seriously. They made long trips into the mountains and Michael introduced her to the country he had lived and worked in for years. They talked about the future. She returned to New York, and during the subsequent eight months she wrote 187 letters to Michael. She wrote about the advantages and disadvantages of a marriage and explained that her loyalty to her native country would always be great and that this might influence their marriage. But ultimately she said yes.

Michael Aris's family attended the wedding in London, as did several of the friends they shared. Aris's siblings joked that all of Suu Kyi's bridesmaids were men. "A number of her old admirers from her time at Oxford were there," said one of them, speaking about the wedding almost forty years later. "They looked up to her and had become close friends to both of them. Michael was lucky that he was the one to be chosen."

Khin Kyi was not at the wedding. She did not approve of her daughter getting married to an Englishman. It was only a year later, when Michael and Suu Kyi visited her in Rangoon, that she recognized her daughter's choice of husband. Suu Kyi's brother Aung San Oo was not at the wedding either. At that time the siblings had not had a close relationship for many years, not even when they were both living in the United States.

In recent years it has become obvious how great the conflict is between Aung San Suu Kyi and her brother. During her second period of house arrest at the beginning of the 2000s, he suddenly demanded to be given ownership of half the house on University Avenue. It was generally assumed that he acted by commission of the junta and that he was thinking of selling his part to the authorities, who would then be able to keep watch on Aung San Suu Kyi more easily. The matter went to court. The court's decision was that her brother, as an American citizen, did not have any right to own property in Burma. The junta has fiddled about with the laws, which in a way means that the matter is still of current interest. When Aung San Suu Kyi wanted to repair the house after Hurricane Nargis, Aung San Oo did all he could to stop the project, and it was only at the end of April 2010 that the plans for renovations were approved by a court in Rangoon.

A close relative of theirs implies that it was her marriage to Michael Aris that definitively put an end to the siblings' contact with each other.

The presence of an official representative from Burma was out of the question at the wedding ceremony. "The Burmese people would not like the daughter of Aung San marrying a foreigner," said London ambassador U Chit Myaung in 1995 when he was interviewed by *Vogue* magazine. "I knew that if I attended the wedding, I would be fired that day."

Michael and Suu Kyi later moved to Bhutan. Now they were going to live together for the first time. Michael was going to continue as tutor to the royal family and at the same time prepare himself for an academic career with the Himalayas and its cultures as his specialization. Suu Kyi had been given a post as adviser to the country's foreign minister. Bhutan wanted to join the United Nations, and the little mountain state that had always been isolated from the world was in acute need of learning more about the United

The wedding of Aung San Suu Kyi and Michael Aris (January 1, 1972).
Courtesy of Norstedts.

Nations' system. Suu Kyi's experiences from New York were suited perfectly for the post.

It can scarcely have been regarded as politically correct to work for the regime in Bhutan. It was and is one of the world's smallest and poorest countries. The highest mountains are over twenty thousand feet high and between them people live by means of farming and trade. The capital, Thimphu, situated at almost a mile and a half above sea level, stretches along the western valley of the Wang Chu river. For many years the king of Bhutan personally constituted the government and saw it as his most important task to drive all "foreigners" out of the country, which in practice meant expelling all Indians and Nepalese. They had in many cases been living in the country for several generations. As recently as the 1990s, the Swedish king received massive criticism from human rights organizations because he and Queen Silvia went on a holiday trip to that country. Meanwhile, Bhutan has been quietly going through a process of modernization and democratization, which in fact began during the years when Michael Aris and Aung San Suu Kyi were working there. Michael was among other things tutor to the crown prince, Jigme Singye Wangchuck, who was crowned king in 1974. During his reign, the country slowly started to change and open itself up to the world around it, even if it's still far from being a democracy. It is probable that Michael Aris played a part in that process of change.

They remained in Bhutan for little over a year and then returned to England. Michael had been accepted as a postgraduate at the University of London. Furthermore, Suu Kyi was pregnant with their first child, Alexander Myint San Aung Aris. He was born in London in April 1973.

They only lived there for a few months. Shortly after Alexander's birth, Michael received an offer from the University of California to lead a research expedition to Nepal. He accepted, and Suu Kyi, who did not want to be left alone with their newborn son, decided to accompany him on the trip. They were already well acquainted with the mountains and the culture in the Himalayas, so it would be wrong to say that they set off for an unknown country. However, how many other young parents of their generation would have had sufficient courage or sense of adventure to take a newborn baby with them on a journey lasting several months to the Himalayas?

When they returned to England at the end of 1973, they moved for a short time to Michael's parents' house in Scotland. After that Oxford University offered Michael an appointment at St John's College. There he could continue working on his thesis on Bhutan's historical roots. At the end of the 1970s the thesis was published in a more accessible form under the title *Bhutan: The Early History of a Himalayan Kingdom.*

During the late 1970s, they lived a traditional family life. Aris worked on his academic career and Suu Kyi stayed at home to take care of the children. Their second son, Kim Thein Lin, was born in 1977. After that, Suu Kyi had her hands full with diaper-changing, cooking, and other household chores, and there was not much time for anything else. She gave up her own professional ambitions, and even though she often visited her mother in Rangoon, she had no real plans for getting involved in the politics of her native country.

Simultaneously, the problems were accumulating in Burma. The war in the Shan state and other border regions escalated almost without a break. In 1968 every single valley and every single mountainside had been occupied by some local warlord, drug cartel, or ethnic guerrilla group. The politically motivated groups that were fighting to secure their respective people's independence from the central regime in Rangoon included the Shan State Army; the Lahu National United Party; farther north, the Kachin Independence Army; and farther south, the Karen National Liberation Army.

However, during the 1970s it was not mainly these groups that reinforced their power over the border regions. It was instead the drug cartels and the leaders of Ne Win's local militia, the KKY, often the same people. The most well-known warlords, like Khun Sa and Lo Hsing-Han, built up modern armies and made enormous fortunes for themselves from the trade in drugs. They became internationally known and hunted during the 1970s, when the United States, Australia, and Europe were flooded with white heroin from the Shan mountains.

The situation was further complicated in 1968 when the communist rebels in the Communist Party of Burma (CPB), invaded the northern Shan state from China. Open, grim battles took place between the CPB and the militia that the military junta had linked to themselves before the CPB could consolidate its power in the area along the border to China and establish what was in practice a state within a state. Paradoxically enough, the communists then governed almost the same region as had previously been controlled by GMD with the support of the CIA. And in the same way as GMD, the communist guerrillas were more and more drawn into the drug trade as time passed.

In central Burma, dissatisfaction with the military government also increased. Unemployment was at an all-time high, and there was a shortage of almost all everyday goods. In May 1974, a strike broke out among the workers in the oil industry. The protests spread to Rangoon, and railway workers and employees at a weaving mill joined forces with the strikers. Ne Win did as he had done in 1962 and beat down the protesters with violence. As usual, the real fatality figures were kept secret, but about a hundred people were probably killed when soldiers opened fire on the crowds. Then it was the students' turn. In November 1974, U Thant died of lung cancer. He had served as the secretary general until 1971 and after that lived with his family in New York. After his death, he should have been buried in his home country, but despite his having been Burma's best-known politician for ten years, Ne Win refused to give him a state funeral. The relationship between the two men had never been good, and it became even frostier when the last democratically elected prime minister, U Nu, had appeared in 1969 at the United Nations and aimed hard criticism at the regime. U Thant had not had anything to do with this affair, but Ne Win understood it to mean that the secretary general had finally turned his back on him.

The plan was therefore to bury U Thant in an obscure cemetery, and when his coffin arrived by air from the United States, it was met only by the acting minister of education, U Aung Tun, who was later dismissed because he had disobeyed Ne Win's orders. The coffin was temporarily stored in a building at Rangoon's disused racecourse, but in the morning when the coffin was to be taken to the cemetery, it was hijacked by a group of students from the university. They bore it to the university area, and the former secretary general of the United Nations received a burial place he would probably have appreciated. His coffin was lowered at the place where the former student union had been—the same building Ne Win had had blown up in 1962. The students took their chances and spent several days demonstrating against the military junta. This time, too, the military went on the attack, recapturing the coffin and transporting it to a new burial place at Shwedagon Square. However, now the genie had yet again been let out of the bottle. Enormous crowds of people went out onto the streets, and the military responded by opening fire and killing hundreds of people.

An important explanation for the fact that the protests did not make a greater impact was that they had been unorganized and spontaneous. A unifying force was lacking, something that could channel the popular anger and transform it into a constructive political movement. Ne Win survived the crisis. He had purchased several more years in power for himself.

During this time, Aung San Suu Kyi was living a peaceful life in Oxford. The family lived in an apartment they had been allowed to rent by St John's College: an open, light two-bedroom with a high ceiling and large windows looking out onto the garden. On the walls hung colorful mats from Bhutan and paintings from Tibet. The bedrooms were small. One of them, barely bigger than a cupboard, acted as both a nursery for the children and a guest-room when they had visitors from Burma or Bhutan, Michael's research colleagues or some family member from Scotland. Suu Kyi was in that sense very Burmese. The traveler in her home country is immediately met with enormous hospitality, and if it had not been for the laws of the junta that forbid "strangers" to spend the night in one's home, it would have been easy to spend a month in the country without having to resort to a hotel.

One of the visitors was Thant Myint U, a grandchild of U Thant. In his book *River of Lost Footsteps* he describes an everyday summer afternoon in the garden in Oxford. The children were playing on the lawn. They drank tea together while Michael Aris smoked his pipe. Aung San Suu Kyi encouraged her young compatriot to study in England. His brief account paints a picture of a relatively normal academic family, with the house full of books and thoughts occupied with research and writing.

Ann Pasternak Slater had lost contact with Suu Kyi during the years in New York, but now they were both in Oxford and also had small children of the same age. They rekindled their friendship. Pasternak Slater often marvelled over how Suu Kyi was able to stand all those visitors living there for weeks at a time in the cramped guestroom. Not for a second did she hint that it was an inconvenience. The friends often met when Suu Kyi came cycling from a hasty shopping trip in the center. The bicycle was always fully loaded with plastic bags full of milk, bread, and cheap fruit from the market. "When I called in the afternoons with my own baby daughter, I would find her busy in the kitchen preparing economical Japanese fish dishes, or at her sewing machine," she wrote in her essay "Suu Burmese." Visitors to their home remember how she often did all her household chores with Kim hanging in a square of cloth on her back and Alexander playing at her feet.

Their neighbor Nalini Jain recounted in an interview in the 1990s that Suu Kyi was a mother who enforced strict discipline in the home, a discipline that applied to herself as well as the others in the family. The children were expected to eat whatever was served and not to complain about the food. Michael has said something similar, that Alexander and Kim were so drilled to eat whatever was put on the table that they would, without hesitation, have gobbled up a snake if that was what Suu Kyi was serving that day.

Thanks to the university, the family was able to live well in the house in central Oxford, but basically these were frugal years for them. They only had Michael's meager researcher's salary to live on and at the same time two growing children to provide for. The couple never owned a car or a TV set.

Simultaneously, Suu Kyi was searching for something meaningful to do outside the home. "Suu maintained a house that was elegant and calm," wrote Pasternak Slater, "but battened down at the back, hidden away among the kitchen's stacked pots and pans, was anxiety, cramp, and strain." Peter Carey, who got to know them at the end of the 1970s, has the same picture of Suu Kyi. "She was very meticulous and disciplined, and extremely friendly by nature," he said in my interview with him. "She loved the life of a wife and mother, but it was also as though she was searching for an objective. Something in which to invest her talents and gifts. She had lost her father very early on, perhaps even lost her country, and she had as yet not found a new mission in life."

At the beginning of the 1980s, the most intensive years with small children were over, and Suu Kyi gradually started to consider her possibilities of resuming a professional career. Even when Kim was a newborn, she had worked for several hours a week at the university's Bodleian Library building in its Burmese section. She had also organized courses in Burmese for the staff there. A couple of years later she and Michael together became the editors of the anthology *Tibetan Studies in Honour of Hugh Richardson*. After that she began writing herself, and in this way she took a few first steps toward her old dream of becoming an author. In rapid succession she published the children's books *Let's Visit Bhutan*, *Let's Visit Burma*, and *Let's Visit Nepal*, three countries that she knew well but that were completely unknown to most Europeans. The books are simple, easily understood introductions that neither touch on the political systems of these countries nor take up the violations of democracy and human rights. The subjects are history, culture, and religion.

During those years around the shift from the 1970s to the 1980s, Suu Kyi also decided to get to know her father better. Aung San had never ceased to fascinate her and to affect her choices in life. "When she was a young mother, living in Oxford, England, she'd occasionally meet former British colonials who had served in Burma at the end of the war. 'Did they know General Aung San? What was he like? What did he look like?' One of them said, 'He did look a little like Yul Brynner,' which she liked quite a lot," Peter Carey has said.

In 1984 Suu Kyi published the book *Aung San of Burma* in a series on Asian leaders at the University of Queensland Press. It was a short biography of her father. In contrast to her books for children and young people, her text on Aung San is of a political character. Even then, four years prior to her entry into the democratic movement, one notices that she has an ambition to wrench the interpretation of Aung San and thus of Burma's postcolonial history out of the hands of the military junta. Although she does write about her father's revolutionary aspect and his experiences of cooperation with Japan, she is above all concerned with emphasizing his pragmatism and the fact that he left the army to shoulder the role of a civil political leader in a democratic system.

The book gave Suu Kyi a taste for more, and when it had been published she wanted once again to have a go at an academic career. Michael had moved his research to the School of Oriental and African Studies in London and now Suu Kyi also applied to attend this college.

Their various academic projects caused the family to split up yet again. Michael was given an exchange appointment as a researcher in the old colonial town of Simla in India, and Suu Kyi was offered the opportunity of working for eighteen months at the University of Kyoto. The idea was to learn more about the contacts between Burma and Japan during the Second

World War, and she also planned to interview Japanese war veterans who had known her father.

Aung San Suu Kyi had always found languages easy and did her utmost to learn Japanese before her journey out. Author Justin Wintle describes how she transformed the family's bathroom at 15 Park Town in Oxford into a language laboratory, with Japanese words and sentences taped up all over the bathroom walls, so that she could go in there and review at any time of day. However, it was a time-consuming and boringly repetitive task, much harder than the other languages she had learned.

When she later ended up under house arrest in Rangoon, she once again took up her language studies, and with the help of books that Michael had sent her, she improved both her French and her Japanese.

Kim accompanied his mother to Japan and Michael took Alexander with him to Simla. Kim was only seven years old and neither he nor Suu Kyi felt particularly at home in Kyoto. For some unknown reason, Kim had been placed in a school where Japanese was the only language spoken, and he had difficulty in keeping up with the lessons and in finding new friends. There was a school for English-speakers nearby, so the decision appears strange, but the idea seems to have been that he should learn Japanese the hard way.

The Burmese Michael Aung-Thwin was also at the University in Kyoto, one of the few people whom Suu Kyi had met over the years who did not speak well of her. They had their studies right next door to each other and spent time there almost daily during the course of a year. Aung-Thwin has said in several interviews that he perceived her as a wandering hub of conflict who was in addition obsessed by her father. "We argued about Burma almost every day and had honest disagreements," he said in the Web-based newspaper *New Mandala* in 2009. "So, when I said she was divisive, that's because she was. It's no secret. Everyone knew it, we, as well as her Japanese hosts. . . . And she was, indeed, always harping about her father. I would too if my father were as famous as hers. She even tried to convince my daughter how famous her father was by showing her a Burmese coin with his face on it. My daughter was hardly seven and couldn't give a damn."

The political conflicts between them were about their different attitudes toward the military junta and which paths forward were feasible for Burma.

Aung-Thwin considered that there was a certain justification for Ne Win's dictatorship and that Burma's political system must be coupled with the specific culture and history of the country. Democracy means decentralization, he wrote in an essay a few years after having worked with her, and in Burma, as in many other countries, decentralization means anarchy. Aung-Thwin concluded that many people would prefer military rule if the alternative was chaos.

He wrote this essay about Burma, but also partly as an argument against the foreign policy of the United States, which often meant forcing its own political and economic system onto other countries without adapting it to local conditions. In Burma the ethnic conflicts and the hierarchical traditions demand the formation of the system in a different way than that of the Western world. It would have been easy to sympathize with that position, if it were not for the problem that he used this criticism to give moral support to the military junta.

Aung-Thwin's wife, Maria, was also skeptical toward Suu Kyi: "It was as if she didn't have a husband. She never once said anything about missing him . . . and actually it seemed that the farther she was from him, the better it was for her, or at least more convenient for what she wanted to do with her life."

This quotation has been diligently used in the junta's propaganda against Aung San Suu Kyi, and it often creeps into articles and short biographies about her. It implies that she came to Burma some years later for reasons other than that of looking after her mother, and it makes her appear as a cold, calculating person who puts her own political ambitions before her family.

Kim and Suu Kyi stayed in Kyoto for one year, after which they traveled to join Michael and Alexander in Simla. They remained there for almost a year and after that returned to England, where Suu Kyi was to begin in earnest the task of writing her thesis. According to the rules of the university about the length of postgraduate appointments, she would not be able to earn her doctorate before October 1989, but she planned on working fast and to have her thesis completed in the autumn of 1988. Ma Than É, who also lived with them for three months in Kyoto, has described that time as a period of very hard work and great decisiveness.

There was something restless about Suu Kyi during that period. The feeling that she was searching for a mission, something to which to apply her energy and gifts, grew stronger. Early in the autumn of 1987, Khin Kyi arrived in Oxford to undergo a complicated eye operation. She stayed with Suu Kyi and her family for a couple of months. Suu Kyi was simultaneously applying for a post as assistant professor at the University of Michigan. Peter Carey helped her with her application, and when she was about to post it, she sent him a letter of thanks at the same time. She wrote,

> I'm having a wonderful time experimenting with my new Amstrad 9512—I can't quite take writing seriously at the moment because it's just like a game with the word processor! But I must try to be serious— I have just done my application to Michigan and I am sending you a copy together with my copies of my CV and thesis outline. Thank you very much for agreeing to be a referee, Peter. I don't know if they will consider my application seriously enough to ask you for a reference but it is very good to have the encouragement of people like you and John [her supervisor at the university]. All those years spent as a full-time mother were most enjoyable and rewarding but the gap in professional and academic activities (although I did manage to study Tibetan and Japanese during that time) makes me feel somewhat at a disadvantage compared to those who were never out of the field.

She does not seem to have had any greater hopes of being awarded the post, but her application shows that she took her academic career seriously. She was thinking of establishing herself as a researcher in Burmese history and literature. It may well have been so, if it had not been for that telephone call on the evening of March 31, 1988.

10

House Arrest

When she was confined to house arrest for the first time in 1989, Aung San Suu Kyi knew nothing about the future. One cannot prevent oneself from wondering about what she would have thought if she had known that when she would be released in November 2010 she would have spent fifteen of the past twenty-one years under house arrest.

How can anyone cope with such a sacrifice? How does one manage to avoid getting broken down physically and psychologically?

For Aung San Suu Kyi the answer has always been integrity and discipline. She has described the strict daily routine she set up right from the first autumn. She got up every morning at half past five and meditated in the faint dawn light. She read. After that she listened for a while to the radio, the BBC, the Burmese transmissions from the Voice of America, and after a time also from the Democratic Voice of Burma, which was transmitted from Oslo. When Michael Aris came for a visit he was somewhat amused by the fact that she was more up-to-date on world news than he was.

After that she spent some time exercising, eventually on a simple Nordic Track she had succeeded in getting into the house. She had breakfast, listened again to the radio, and then read books and played the piano.

"I tried to keep the same routines during my latest house arrest," she told me when I interviewed her in February 2011. "But I wasn't as strict as I had been before. This time I had two companions in the house, and it would have been dreadful for them to follow my schedule."

This time she also found herself preferring to read poetry rather than prose.

"Maybe it's something to do with age," she said in an interview with *Financial Times*. "I have discovered some rather beautiful bits by Tennyson. I used to think he was an old fuddy-duddy, but it's not quite like that. Some of the poems from *The Princess* are quite beautiful."

Most things during house arrests were the same, though, for example the fact that she was denied access to the telephone. At the beginning of the first arrest back in 1989, a soldier had marched into the house, cut the telephone line, and carried off the telephone, so she was unable to talk to her friends or family. However, Michael Aris had obtained the right to send her parcels and was able to supply her with a steady stream of books. She read political books in the mornings and fiction in the afternoons. After a number of years, she acquired a copy of Nelson Mandela's recently published autobiography, *Long Walk to Freedom*. Mandela's story about life under apartheid and his prison years on Robben Island inspired her and helped her keep up her courage. She was able to link together her knowledge about the resistance to apartheid in Great Britain in the 1960s with her own highly concrete experiences of imprisonment and oppression.

During the initial period of her isolation, she often worked in the garden, particularly in the mornings before the sun became too sweltering. She took care of the lawns, the garden beds down by the lake, and the lilies growing along the walls of the house. However, after a while she no longer had the strength. The grounds surrounding the house are extensive. They accommodate a small woody area and two buildings apart from the main house, and the climate in Burma assists nature in its conquest within a few months. Soon a joke began to circulate in Rangoon: the junta is trying to silence Suu Kyi by allowing the jungle to grow so thick around her house that no human being could possibly either enter or leave. A kind of Sleeping Beauty legend, though without a prince coming to break the enchantment.

Michael and her sons had returned to Oxford at the end of August, just before term began. Several days later they received a message that the boys'

Burmese passports had been retracted. In contrast to Suu Kyi, both Kim and Alexander had had dual citizenship, which made it possible for them to travel to Burma without special visas. Now they would be denied the right to return to their mother in Rangoon. The junta counted coldly on the fact that if Aung San Suu Kyi did not want to accompany her family to Oxford, and if they were not allowed to visit her, her longing for the boys would in the end become so strong that she, too, would choose to leave.

However, the travel ban only concerned Kim and Alexander to start with. Michael was permitted to return to Rangoon late in the autumn. "The days I spent alone with her that last time, completely isolated from the world, are among my happiest memories of our many years of marriage," he wrote in *Freedom from Fear*. They carried on long conversations with each other and celebrated Christmas together. "It was wonderfully peaceful. Suu had established a strict regime of exercise, study, and piano which I managed to disrupt."

In the meanwhile, the junta rejected Suu Kyi's candidacy to the election in 1990. They had made an addendum to the constitution that forbade a person who was married to a foreigner to run as a candidate in a general election. The NLD thus had to enter the election without its most important leader, and the junta assumed that this would take the sting out of the democratic movement. But once again they made a gross mistake about the strength of the popular dissatisfaction.

The election was to be held on May 27, 1990. Before the election day, the SLORC displayed a striking openness. For months they had done all they could to crush the opposition. They had stopped people from attending political meetings, threatened and imprisoned activists, and carried out hard-as-nails propaganda in the state-owned mass media. The university and the higher secondary schools had been closed so that the students would not be able to assemble and organize oppositional meetings. Yet the NLD and almost ninety other parties, several of them from the ethnic minorities, were still permitted to act freely for a few days before the election. International media and observers were allowed into the country, and to judge by reports, there was not much to indicate that the SLORC was considering manipulation of the election results. Hopes had increased in January the same year, when Gen. Saw Maung had said that Tatmadaw and the junta were not thinking of nominating the next government—that would be the task of the people via their newly elected parliament. Despite the obvious suppression of freedom to hold meetings and the violations during the election campaign, his statement had given the voters the impression that their votes could make a difference. As many as 73 percent went out and voted on election day, an unusually high rate of electoral participation in a country that had not carried out an election since 1960. And despite the fact that Aung San Suu Kyi's candidacy constituted a block, the NLD won an overwhelming victory. The party received 80 percent of the seats in parliament. The parties of the ethnic minorities, all allies of the NLD, took home 14 percent. The junta's party, the National Unity Party (NUP), received almost 20 percent of the votes, but since they applied the British election system with majority elections in one-person constituencies, this only gave them a few seats in parliament.

The people had made a monumental statement against the military junta. Aung San Suu Kyi had not only succeeded with her election campaign during the months she was free to act politically, she had also received broad support for her nonviolent perspective. On the day of the election only a few outbreaks of violence were reported from the thousands of polling stations around the country. A closer analysis of the results showed that the NLD had won in regions where the military and their families were in great majority. Only a small number of them had given her their support publicly, but protected by electoral anonymity they had voted for the NLD anyway. Even the soldiers and their officers wanted a new regime in Burma.

During the days following May 27, people celebrated all over Burma, and everyone was counting on the release of Aung San Suu Kyi. The paradox was that the junta had created just the kind of personal cult around her, by imprisoning her, that they had wished to avoid. They had made her into a martyr and a symbol for the opposition. Zin Linn was one of those who took part in the organization of the election campaign in one of the constituencies in Rangoon.

"My candidate himself had a military background," he recounted when I met him twenty years later at a café in Bangkok. "That made people skeptical, but they chose to vote for him anyway since he was Aung San Suu Kyi's candidate. One voter told me that he would even vote for a dog if it was backed up by Aung San Suu Kyi."

After the election, two months of confusion followed. The generals seemed almost paralyzed by their total misjudgement of the situation, and out in the streets the first delirium of victory had been replaced by uncertainty. Why was nothing happening? Would the junta acknowledge the election results or were the generals searching for an excuse to declare the whole process null and void?

During this period the NLD had its chance to have assembled parliament on its own. The NLD could have proclaimed a government that other countries would have been able to recognize, in that way increasing the pressure on the junta. But even the NLD did not want to rock the boat. Aung San Suu Kyi was isolated in her home, and others in the party leadership chose to wait and see. Most of them were themselves former generals and officers, and they probably planned on the SLORC getting in touch with them to initiate talks about the way forward. However, that was not what happened. On July 27 the head of the security service, Khin Nyunt, gave a speech in which he declared that the election had not been about voting for a new parliament at all. The election had instead been about choosing a new assembly to formulate a new constitution. The election results were in the process of being declared null and void.

The day after, the NLD gathered in Gandhi Hall in central Rangoon, but its members did not choose to proclaim a new government on that occasion either. Instead they gave the junta another two months in which to recognize the election results, and they demanded an open and unconditional dialogue in order to put a stop to the crisis that the country found itself in. This final wording bears the stamp of Aung San Suu Kyi. Her critics inside and outside the military junta often accuse her of being uncompromising and stubborn to the point of stupidity. However, during the entire election campaign she underlined that she was not demanding any kind of revolution in Burma. It takes time to change a political system, she has said, and it is going to require cooperation from everyone in our society. Even the military.

During this time, Michael, Alexander, and Kim were at home in Oxford. Michael had had certain hopes of traveling there in the summer but had been denied an entry visa. Now they were hoping that Suu Kyi would be freed and that the family could be reunited. But in a letter to Michael dated July 17, 1990, Suu Kyi did not mention any date for her release. Instead she asked Michael to send her the almost impenetrable Indian epics *Ramayana* and *Mahabharata*. The rest of the letter was about her longing for the children and practical family matters. Between the lines, Michael understood that she was calculating on a long time under house arrest.

When it began to dawn on the people that the election was going to be declared null and void, their anger intensified once again. On August 8, 1990, on the anniversary of the massacres two years earlier, a large protest action was held in Mandalay, and this time it was the monks from the monastery who took the lead. The action on August 8 had not been advertised in advance. The monks just might have been out on their morning walk to collect donations for the monastery. However, the number of monks and the symbolic significance of the date meant that nobody could avoid being aware of what it was really all about. Tens of thousands of civilians joined them. The students flanked the monks to protect them from attack. The soldiers were called in, and when one of the students unrolled a peacock flag, they got nervous and opened fire. Nine monks were shot to death and an additional fourteen were badly beaten. Several of the injured disappeared without a trace after the military had cleaned up the streets.

The incident was covered up by the state-owned mass media, which asserted that only one monk had been killed and that the violence had been sparked by the students who had attacked the armed guards.

The violence and the attempt to conceal what had really happened triggered a new wave of protests, and all over the country monks assembled to show solidarity with the killed and wounded. When they passed officers and their families during their morning walks, they turned their begging bowls upside down and refused to accept alms from them. Not to be allowed to donate money to the monasteries gives bad karma and is among the worst that can happen to a Buddhist. When the boycott had been going on for some time, the officers became so nervous that they brought in by plane monks from Thailand who had to accept their alms.

This challenge by the monks was one of the greatest threats the junta had encountered, and the generals realized that they would have to act quickly. Gen. Saw Maung gave the command that all the monastery orders that had taken part in the protests were to be dissolved, an utterly exceptional decision given the fact that the worldly powers in Burma had never had any mandate for direct rule over the monasteries. He proclaimed that those who opposed this decision no longer had the right to be monks. The local commanders were given the authority to tear the orange clothing off the backs of those monks who refused to cooperate. In October the army carried out raids against the monasteries. Thousands of monks were harassed and thrown into prison. Later the traditional religious leadership was dissolved, and the junta appointed on their own initiative a new, more easily controlled and centralized group of monks to lead the sanghan.

The democratic movement's hope of rapid political change had already diminished dramatically in September. At that point a smallish group of parliamentarians from the NLD had assembled in Mandalay to form a shadow government, which the party should already have done in the summer. The SLORC discovered that the meeting was going to be held, and they started a mass hunt-down of all the elected parliamentarians. The entire remaining leadership of the NLD had been taken prisoner, among others U Kyi Maung, the retired general who was acting as chairman during the absence of Aung San Suu Kyi. All remaining hope was crushed when the junta demonstrated that they had no hesitation whatsoever in striking at the monk orders or putting themselves above the religious traditions. The signal could not have been clearer: the junta was intending to remain in power, whatever the price.

The junta had no intention of letting Aung San Suu Kyi go. On the contrary, they readjusted the laws once again so that it would be possible to keep her out of the public eye in the foreseeable future. It had previously been possible for the police to keep somebody under house arrest for one year without a trial. Now the time was prolonged to five years.

Aung San Suu Kyi took this, too, in her usual calm manner, so well known nowadays. In order to tease the guards who visited her now and then, she filled the walls of her house with pasted-up quotations by Gandhi, Nehru, and her own father, Aung San. She had a large portrait of him in her reception room on the ground floor. Sometimes when she was unable to sleep at night, she went downstairs and looked at the picture. She was able—perhaps for the first time—to feel that they were close, that he was present. She looked into his eyes and said to herself, "Okay, now it's you and me against them."

She read books about vipassana meditation and practiced purposefully in order to improve herself. When she had been released some years later and was asked about what she would do if she were to be arrested once again, she replied with a laugh that she would in that case see to it that she reached even higher levels in her meditation.

Meditation is central for understanding how she and the other political prisoners coped with their time in isolation. "For a Buddhist it is not necessarily a negative thing to shut out the world. Even as children we learn to withdraw into ourselves, to shut out the world and purify our senses," said the student leader Min Ko Naing in an interview in 2005. At that point he had spent sixteen years in an isolation cell and had meditated every day.

Every time Suu Kyi is asked about the years under house arrest, she emphasizes that she has been treated very mildly when compared to many other political prisoners. In a television interview with the Swedish journalist Malou von Sievers, she said that she has not felt like a prisoner since she has not been held in a prison, and that many of her party comrades had had a much harder time. They had been tortured and not known what had happened to their families. Her own family was safe in another country, and she has said in several interviews that she has felt a security in knowing that they were not directly threatened.

On another occasion she recounted that the Buddhist principles of self-control and inner peace were crucial for her to cope with the period during which she was under house arrest. She "accepted" the circumstances under which she lived and tried only to influence those parts of her life that were still hers to control. "I simply stopped worrying about my family," she said in 1996. "I couldn't do anything about the situation so I learned to control my thoughts."

Restraint. Self-control. Suu Kyi often speaks about these as goals for one's personal development. One cannot influence everything around him or her. The only things that one can control with any certainty are his or her own thoughts and actions. Inside yourself you can always in some sense be free; even under strict imprisonment there is room for action. It is ultimately a matter of preserving one's integrity. As is often the case with Suu Kyi, she seasons this philosophical reasoning with humor and a peal of laughter. "I believe that some people who have been in prison also did not feel like prisoners," she told Alan Clements, and then she quoted her party comrade U Kyi Maung as having said, "If my wife knew how free I felt in Insein prison she'd be furious."

Even though Aung San Suu Kyi kept up her courage and was "free in thought," those six years, as well as the later periods of house arrest, must have been both mentally and physically stressful. One problem was money. She was not allowed to receive money from the outside, and at the same time she refused to accept free food from the guards who were stationed by the dozen outside her house. The junta was not going to be given any kind of hold on her. However, after a short time she had no money left and she had to be satisfied with eating two small portions of rice a day. In the end she came to an agreement with the junta. They would deliver food to her and she would pay with furniture and fittings from the house. Slowly but surely the building was emptied of the furniture her mother had collected throughout the years. The officers who were responsible for the guard could not bear the thought that Aung San's daughter should be totally destitute, so they secretly stored all the furniture in a warehouse a little distance away from 54 University Avenue. When she was freed in 1995, they wanted to give her back her belongings, but Aung San Suu Kyi refused to receive them and demanded that she be allowed to buy them back. No favors.

Even after the furniture-for-food system had been established, she was compelled to live frugally. Her breakfast usually consisted of tea and a piece of fruit. Never bread, that was too expensive. Once every weekend she allowed herself the luxury of eating a hard-boiled egg. The effect of this diet was that she rapidly lost a lot of weight, from 110 to around 90 pounds, and during that period she must have been on the brink of malnutrition.

The economic problems were partly solved when Michael Aris published the book *Freedom from Fear*, with texts by Aung San Suu Kyi and people who had come to know her over the years. The income from the book was deposited in an account in Rangoon and was thereafter at the disposal of Suu Kyi.

In the meantime the junta continued to slander her, consistently and without any sign of shame for their blatant racism and narrow-mindedness. On one occasion a cartoon was published in one of the state-owned newspapers. It showed a lone boy beside a group of children. The boy was ugly and crippled, and his caption made it clear that he was of mixed race, a direct allusion to Kim and Alexander. The group of children were athletic and full of well-being, and under this group of children the caption stated that they were "real citizens."

The junta also exploited the fact that Michael was able to send parcels to her, and one day pictures were published showing the alleged contents of one of the parcels. They were a tube of lipstick and a couple of American fashion magazines. In the text Aung San Suu Kyi is described as a "Western fashion girl." Clearly something very reprehensible in the eyes of the junta.

During her first period under house arrest, changes also occurred at the top level of the junta. During 1991 Gen. Saw Maung, who had led the SLORC's seizure of power in 1988, displayed several signs of being mentally ill. Rumors went around that he was an alcoholic and had heart trouble. During a visit to a golf course he pulled out his pistol and threatened others there while yelling at them that he was the reincarnation of King Kyanzittha, a Bamar king in the eleventh century. He was forced to resign from his appointment as the leader of the SLORC in April 1992.

He was succeeded by Gen. Than Shwe. Than Shwe was born in 1933 in the vicinity of Mandalay, and during Ne Win's years in office he rose in rank until he was appointed brigadier general and acting minister of defense in 1985. After the SLORC's power takeover in 1988, he became the second-in-command of the junta.

Now he formed a leadership troika with Gen. Maung Aye and Khin Nyunt. The latter was formally third-in-command, but as the chief of the powerful military security service and with the support of Ne Win from the sidelines, he was understood by many to be Burma's strong man. Khin Nyunt has Chinese roots, and after his military career he had been called to Rangoon in 1984 to investigate a bloody terrorist action against a group of politicians from South Korea who were visiting Burma. Khin Nyunt quickly took control of the military security service, which became a state within the state under his leadership. Khin Nyunt was considered to be Ne Win's favorite among the younger officers.

It soon turned out that the SLORC had a plan. The junta hoped that the economic development after liberalization would assuage people's anger. It was only a matter of keeping Aung San Suu Kyi imprisoned until they had constructed a political framework that would enable them to stay in power and finally ignore the election results from 1990.

The first step in the plan was to set up a national convention with the task of drawing up a new constitution. More than a thousand delegates were handpicked by the junta. Only a very few of them were politicians who had been elected to parliament in 1990. The convention assembled for the first time in 1993, and initially the NLD chose to cooperate in the process, despite Aung San Suu Kyi still being held under house arrest.

After that, Khin Nyunt succeeded in achieving a truce with most of the ethnic groups, who were tired of decades of war. None of them handed in their weapons, but they had realized that they would never be able to conquer the regime in Rangoon by military means.

Khin Nyunt's biggest victory was the agreement he concluded with the remaining members of the old communist party, the CPB, in the northeastern Shan state. The CPB had controlled the region since 1968, but China had withdrawn its support at the end of the 1980s, and the dissatisfaction among the soldiers had increased dramatically. The old leadership of the CPB refused, however, to give up and said no when Beijing offered them a place to retreat to in China. The troops mutinied in the spring of 1989, driving their leaders into a humiliating exile. What was left was a number of loosely connected armies. The biggest of them, with its base among the Wa people, took for itself the name United Wa State Army (UWSA).

Khin Nyunt called in the notorious drug smuggler Lo Hsing-Han to mediate between the junta and the new groups. The result was a truce with the regime that was reminiscent of the agreement Ne Win had concluded with the KKY units in the 1960s. UWSA received the green light to produce heroin and methamphetamine in return for a promise of support in the war against other guerrilla groups.

Some of the major resistance armies, such as the Karen National Liberation Army and the Shan State Army, still refused to cooperate, and the truce with the UWSA meant that the junta was able to send in greater military resources against the groups that were still at war. Step by step, often with extremely brutal methods, the SLORC gained control over regions that had previously been controlled by the ethnic groups.

Parallel to this, Khin Nyunt was also carrying on talks with Aung San Suu Kyi. Some of her earlier collaborators assert that she actually experienced these talks as being meaningful. At one meeting with Khin Nyunt, she put forth a suggestion the gist of which was to open the NLD offices that had been closed and to allow the democratic opposition to elect its own delegates to the convention. It is possible that Khin Nyunt actually considered this, but that he was stopped by other powers within the junta.

On July 10, 1995, Aung San Suu Kyi was released from house arrest. In the few photographs of her that exist from those first days, she looks almost impudently full of energy. None of those who met her could see that she had just spent six years under house arrest. It was as though six years of isolation had just been a brief interlude, an unwelcome but manageable interruption to the work she had now made into the mission of her life.

11

The World Wakes Up

Michael Aris was an academic and teacher, and he was happy with that life. However, during the first period of house arrest he also became Aung San Suu Kyi's mouthpiece in an international context. It was a public role that he neither liked nor felt especially suited to. Yet he persevered with bravura. He argued her and the Burmese democratic movement's case before the United Nations, innumerable human rights organizations, and foreign governments that wanted closer insight into the conditions at University Avenue.

"Michael was an impressive person," says Peter Carey. "He had no ambition whatsoever to promote himself. He was really happiest out of the limelight, but now he had taken upon himself the task of supporting her, and this he did very skillfully. He emphasized her situation but was careful not to put his own words in her mouth. It was almost the role of a martyr, and unfortunately it ended up that way too."

Michael Aris was driven by the will to protect his wife. "I was not a politician, nor am I Burmese," said Michael. "I was literally just her husband and as her husband I did and said everything I could to get her released."

According to friends of his at Oxford, he was convinced that the best method was publicity. By focusing the international spotlight on Burma, Aung San Suu Kyi was provided with a kind of life insurance. The generals would never be able to cause her any injury without being held responsible for it.

His hard work contributed to the fact that in the autumn of 1991, Aung San Suu Kyi was awarded the Nobel Peace Prize, a distinction that suddenly placed her in the same category as Desmond Tutu, Lech Wałęsa, and Mother Teresa. The SLORC realized instantly that this was an extremely significant distinction and protested loudly, but they were not able to prevent Alexander and Kim from receiving the prize at the ceremony in Oslo. Alexander, who was nineteen at the time, made a speech of thanks on his mother's behalf.

I know that if she were free today my mother would, in thanking you, also ask you to pray that the oppressors and the oppressed should throw down their weapons and join together to build a nation founded on humanity in the spirit of peace.

Although my mother is often described as a political dissident who strives by peaceful means for democratic change, we should remember that her quest is basically spiritual. As she has said, "The quintessential revolution is that of the spirit," and she has written of the "essential spiritual aims" of the struggle. The realization of this depends solely on human responsibility. At the root of that responsibility lies, and I quote, "the concept of perfection, the urge to achieve it, the intelligence to find a path toward it, and the will to follow that path if not to the end, at least the distance needed to rise above individual limitation.

"To live the full life," she says, "one must have the courage to bear the responsibility of the needs of others . . . one must want to bear this responsibility."

For Michael Aris, it was a moment filled with disparate feelings. Pride over Alexander's speech, which reached a whole world, was mixed with the longing for his wife. "It's a dark time," said Michael at the press conference after the ceremony. His voice trembled and his eyes welled with tears. "But I'm sure there will be a change. I am optimistic about the future. Burma will open up. It's just a question of when."

The junta chose to exploit Michael's public role in their own propaganda. That Aung San Suu Kyi was married to a "foreigner," and furthermore one from the former colonial power, had been one of their main points of attack right from the beginning. Now, in addition to this, he was acting as her defender, a piece of evidence as good as any that neocolonial conspiracy was being plotted against Burma. And they did all they could to drag their marriage in the mud. The author Barbara Victor met some of the generals during a trip to Burma in the mid-1990s.

"Why did she decide to leave her children and her husband?" asked a professor and supporter of the junta at the Rangoon Institute of Technology. "I talked to her when she was first married to Mr. Aris and had only one baby and came back during Ne Win's time to lay a wreath at her father's grave. She told me then that she had no intention of ever moving back to Rangoon. Obviously, by the time she was placed under house confinement, there was already trouble in her marriage or she never would have suddenly decided to abandon her husband and two children."

One of the ministers in the government followed the same bizarre line of reasoning: "Frankly, it is a perverse way of running one's emotional life when the alternative to divorce is house arrest. Why should our country be involved in the domestic troubles of one couple?"

The world at large did not allow itself to be convinced. On the contrary, international prizes and distinctions rained down on the prisoner at University Avenue. She was awarded the Norwegian Thorolf Rafto prize for human rights, the European Parliament's Sakharov Prize, UNESCO's Simón Bolívar prize, the Victor Jara distinction, the Jawaharlal Nehru prize, W. Averell Harriman's democracy prize, and some years later the Freedom of the City of Dublin award as well as the Swedish Olof Palme Prize. And these are only a few of the many distinctions.

One explanation for the enormous attention was of course Suu Kyi's personal character. She dared to stand up against one of the world's most brutal dictatorships. It was a classic David and Goliath situation.

Perhaps the Western world's strong reactions were also dependent on its bad conscience. Many countries had more or less consciously shown tolerance during Ne Win's military rule. Bertil Lintner writes in his book *Burma in Revolt* about how leading academics and politicians in the West turned a blind eye to the violations of the Burmese regime, how the British era and the brief period of democracy in the 1950s were regarded as a parenthesis in history, and how it was only natural after the colonial era that the country reverted to its traditional forms of rule. The ethnic minorities were perceived as fanatical separatists—rather like the general picture of the southern states during the American Civil War. Modernization demanded quite simply that these small "tribal societies" conform to the formation of a greater state. That these groups of people had legitimate reasons for demanding more independence from Rangoon did not seem to be of any importance. This understanding was not least common among the left-wing groups of the 1960s and 1970s, which lay the whole of the blame for the civil war on the former British colonial power.

The Burmese had repeated over and over again to foreign visitors to Rangoon that the regime was hated by the people, but very few had listened to them. And on the few occasions he was put under pressure concerning this matter, Ne Win always asserted that the civil war and the unstable situation in the border regions made it impossible to revert to democracy. The time would soon be ripe, he avowed. The process of democratization would shortly begin.

Of course it did not.

Lintner gives a most amusing description of how foreign diplomats stationed in Rangoon were kept quite unaware of the real political development in the country. The regime did not contribute any information of its own, and the diplomats were quite content to hang around in hotel bars and play a few rounds on the golf courses of the capital while waiting to be transferred to a more interesting country.

Many countries also cooperated with the junta in order to combat the drugs in the golden triangle. Guomintang's time in the mountains had brought with it an enormous increase in the drug trade, and after Ne Win's agreement with local warlords Burma had become one of the world's foremost exporters of heroin. Ne Win had received hard international criticism for his KKY strategy at the beginning of the 1970s, and had then formally cut off all contact with warlords like Khun Sa and Lo Hsing-Han. But this change was only cosmetic. In practice, several of the largest drug cartels had the support of the junta, and many of the officers in Tatmadaw made great private profit by supporting the drug trade through protection and safe conduct for the opium transports over the border to Thailand.

Despite this, Ne Win succeeded in convincing the international community of his honest intentions. The United Nations organ for combating drugs, UN Drug Control Programme (UNDCP), cooperated with the Burmese authorities, as did the Drug Enforcement Agency in the United States. In the mid-1980s, Washington supplied Burma with Bell 205 helicopters and the herbicide Agent 2,4-D. This substance is closely related to Agent Orange, which was used to defoliate large areas of jungle during the Vietnam War, and its use was forbidden in the United States since, according to several health investigations, it increased the risk for cancer. After that, helicopters and airplanes swept in low over the regions belonging to the ethnic minorities, spraying their fields with poisonous chemicals. Their harvests died, as did the population, sometimes. Those who drank water that had been sprayed or ate food that had been stored near the fields became ill with appalling stomach pains.

And this had no effect at all on the production of opium. First, the junta used the American equipment in the war against the ethnic groups. The opium traders who were in collusion with the junta avoided getting their crops destroyed, and those who challenged Ne Win got their farmlands mercilessly sprayed with Agent 2,4-D. It was the same for the guerrilla groups, for example among the Kachins and Karens, who were fighting for their right to independence without financing their activities via opium.

Second, many farmers were compelled to increase their production of opium as an effect of the spraying. The farmers in the Shan state at this time grew three main crops: coffee, tea, and opium. But it was only the opium that could be economically profitable in a single season. Those who kept their coffee and tea plantations risked getting their entire annual income destroyed if a government helicopter suddenly turned up on the horizon. Those who changed over to opium reduced the risks and increased their chances of quick profits.

However, the United States was far from being the only country to give support to Burma at that time. At the end of 1982, Ne Win wanted to purchase the Carl Gustaf recoilless antitank rifle from Bofors, for example. The political section at the Swedish Ministry of Foreign Affairs had advised against the sale on account of the civil war, but when the matter landed on Prime Minister Olof Palme's desk, he dismissed their objections. In Björn Elmbrant's biography of Palme, his comment is quoted: "Oh, that." Palme had said, "That guerrilla war has been going on since the Second World War. They are drug dealers more than guerrillas. The situation is stable. Just get on with it."

Norway also gave the junta its support. Via the United Nations, Norway financed a project to find replacement crops for the farmers in the Shan state, but the project was limited to the areas that "might become" sites for opium production. The areas where the drug trade was already the dominant enterprise were left alone.

Against this background, the demonstrations and massacres in 1988 acted as an eye-opener for the international community. When the junta employed the same methods inside Rangoon as they had earlier used against the ethnic minorities, the world at large was no longer able to shut its eyes to it.

However, the zeitgeist in the 1990s played a part in the sharp reactions against the violations and the support for the democratic movement. Autumn of 1989 saw the collapse of the Iron Curtain, only months after Aung San Suu Kyi had become a public figure. The Cold War was at an end, and the West seemed to have won. The economist Francis Fukuyama spoke of the end of history. The world would now open up. People and rulers would realize that the Western world's model with its mixture of political democracy and market economy was the only feasible one. Fukuyama was met by stony and justified criticism for being shortsighted and unhistorical, but most people held the view anyway that the fall of the Eastern Bloc had opened up a window of opportunity. Dictators and autocrats would no longer be able to conceal themselves behind the great powers. Human rights and humanitarian issues, not crass realpolitik, would be the center of attention for the international community.

Burma became a test for the possibilities of the international community. It was as though the military junta had only understood the first half of Francis Fukuyama's thesis. After the SLORC's seizure of power in September 1988, they got rid of the ideology of the socialist state and redirected the economic policy, and just as in the 1960s, they found their model in China. The generals wanted to privatize sections of the economy and admit foreign companies, but they were not planning for democracy. Crass market economy would be combined with continued political control.

In the autumn of 1990, Sweden took the initiative with a resolution in the United Nations General Assembly that criticized Burma for its violations against its own civil population. This was the first in a series of initiatives on the part of the United Nations General Assembly, but while it was an indication of several countries' anxiety, it also demonstrated that the world community was deeply split. China, India, and several other Asian countries opposed the proposal. Sweden had to withdraw the resolution and came back later with a watered-down proposal that could be accepted unanimously by the assembly. The United Nations Commission on Human Rights also appointed an independent expert to examine the development in Burma, and in 1995 Álvaro de Soto was appointed as the special envoy from the secretary general of the United Nations. A long line of rapporteurs and envoys has followed after him, but each has failed in breaking the stalemate in Burma.

The United States chose to go further on its own. Immediately following the massacres in 1988, it introduced a weapons embargo against Burma and ended several of the antidrug programs that had been administrated by the regime in Rangoon. Later on during the 1990s it introduced even more directed sanctions, among others a prohibition against new investments in Burma and travel bans on members of the junta.

The involvement of the European Union has in principle mirrored the American involvement, with an arms embargo and gradually sharpened sanctions during the 1990s and the 2000s. The sanctions of the European Union have never been as comprehensive as those of the United States, mainly because the member states of the European Union have not been able to agree on a common objective. The Nordic countries along with Holland and Great Britain have been the "hawks," while France has often blocked the issue. The French oil company Total has extensive interests in Burma, which have constituted a hindrance for the European community when it comes to introducing sanctions against the gas and oil trade.

In the mid-1990s, a broad grassroots movement emerged whose aim was to stop companies from investing in and trading with Burma. By means of consumer boycotts, mainly via activists in the United States, they succeeded in getting companies like Pepsi Cola, Levi's, Ericsson, and Motorola to pull out of Burma. At the end of the 1990s, four American states and twenty-three cities had decided not to carry out any public deals with companies that had enterprises in the country. The campaign became global in due course. Hundreds, perhaps thousands, of organizations in the civil community became involved with human rights in Burma. These organizations often cooperated with activists from inside Burma, who had fled from oppression and were now in the process of establishing a resistance movement in exile.

One central agent at work was the exile government that had been formed by six parliamentarians under the leadership of Sein Win. They had succeeded in fleeing to the regions bordering Thailand in 1990, and there they were received with open arms by the Karen guerrillas and other armed groups that had established a base in the little village of Manerplaw.

Sein Win, a cousin of Aung San Suu Kyi, had not had any prominent role within the NLD, but he was now one of those who had succeeded in escaping. On December 18 in Manerplaw, the National Coalition Government of the Union of Burma (NCGUB) was founded with Sein Win as the prime minister. The NCGUB remained in the border regions for some years but nowadays has its main offices in Washington.

China chose a completely different road than the European Union and the United States. One might actually read the development in China and Burma as a pendulum movement. First, the economic policy, in which Burma tried to imitate China. Then the massacre at Tiananmen Square (the Square of Heavenly Peace), which was carried out barely a year after the generals in Rangoon had done the same against their people. Burma was the only country in the world that publicly defended the Chinese communist party's action.

Then came Aung San Suu Kyi's house arrest, implemented only a few weeks after tanks had rolled into the streets of Beijing. After that, China quickly became the ally of Burma, and Burma's main supplier of aid, consumer goods, and—not least—arms. The first arms delivery was shipped in at the same time as the protests of the monks were crushed in the autumn of 1990. After them followed fighter aircraft, patrol vessels, tanks, radar equipment, and hand firearms sufficient for seventy-four new battalions. As thanks for this assistance, Chinese companies were permitted more or less without impediment to exploit the natural resources of Burma.

The borders that have since characterized the way the world community deals with the Burma issue were drawn at this point. China and Russia assert that the United Nations should not interfere with the domestic affairs of member states, and they have consistently exploited their veto power in the United Nations Security Council to block all serious proposals concerning Burma.

The military junta has in turn exploited the situation to play the countries of the world against one another. If China has wavered in its support, then the junta turns to India or Russia. If either of these has increased its pressure on Burma, it draws up new agreements with neighboring countries in Southeast Asia.

During all these years the junta also used Aung San Suu Kyi as a regulator. When the pressure from other countries became too great, restrictions around her was eased, and some envoys from the United Nations or the European Union or the United States were permitted to meet with her. Then the trap was closed again as soon as the attention of the world at large turned in another direction. During the fall of 2011, after her release a couple of month earlier, this seemed to change, with politicians from all around the world coming to visit her. It's impossible to say whether this is a more permanent openess in the regime's policy.

12

"My Suu"

At first the NLD had certain hopes that the release in 1995 was the start of a real process of reconciliation. Aung San Suu Kyi hoped that the junta, the NLD, and the ethnic minorities would get down to solving the country's problems together. "There is more in common between the authorities and us of the democratic forces in Burma than existed between the black and white peoples of South Africa. Why shouldn't Burma be able to start a process similar to that in South Africa?" asked Suu Kyi rhetorically at a press conference immediately after her release.

The talks she had had with Khin Nyunt during 1994 were one explanation for these hopes. In February of that year, U.S. representative Bill Richardson had traveled to Burma. He met both Suu Kyi and representatives for the junta, and after that a number of preparatory talks were held.

Another explanation for Suu Kyi's belief that talks would be meaningful was her awareness of the enormous problems confronting Burma. The economy was still stagnating. The junta's economic "liberalization" had not worked out. The international campaigns were one explanation, but just as important was the fact that the generals did not understand what was necessary to attracting foreign companies. Burma was far too corrupt. Companies that were considering investing in the country withdrew as soon as they understood that they were expected to pay a certain percentage of their investments as bribes to the civil servants and officers in charge. When the state-owned companies were to be privatized, they were given away to the generals and members of their families, who resaddled and became company executives without any previous knowledge at all about how one was supposed to act in a market economy. Many companies from other countries were scared away by this obvious incompetence and also by the fact that several of the new actors in the Burmese economy were former drug barons from the Shan mountains who were exploiting liberalization to launder money from the trade in heroin and methamphetamine.

It soon became apparent that the junta had no serious intentions of taking steps toward democracy with the release of Suu Kyi. A first indication came when the state-owned newspapers did not even mention that she had been released. When the United Nations envoy Álvaro de Soto demanded that the junta should hold talks with Aung San Suu Kyi, the generals replied that she was an ordinary citizen and that it was impossible for a government to carry on a dialogue with all its citizens. Some months later, Burma's ambassador in Bangkok said that the regime did not have any plans to discuss reforms with Suu Kyi. He referred to the national convention: "We don't need a dialogue with anyone."

In November 1995, the NLD withdrew from the national convention in protest against the continued harassment, which made the junta further escalate their propaganda. Aung San Suu Kyi and the NLD were accused of being traitors who threatened the stability and security of the country. The state-owned newspapers, like the English-language *New Light of Myanmar* and *Myanmar Times*, published—and are still publishing—a piece every day with the headline "People's Desire"; its themes were encapsulated in four points:

1. Oppose those relying on external elements, acting as stooges, holding negative views.
2. Oppose those trying to jeopardize the stability of the state and progress of the nation.
3. Oppose foreign nations interfering in internal affairs of the state.
4. Crush all internal and external destructive elements as the common enemy.

Of course most of this was directed at Suu Kyi personally. During her years under house arrest, the propaganda had made her out to be a puppet in the hands of her husband, who in his turn was alleged to be allied with foreign security services and powers that wanted to cast Burma into a state of chaos and anarchy.

Yet Suu Kyi managed to remain optimistic. On her birthday in the summer of 1996, Peter Carey traveled to Burma. It was his first visit to the country since his family had moved away from there in the 1950s, and what struck him most was that Suu Kyi seemed so full of confidence. She also seemed almost completely untouched by the period of house arrest:

> She really believed that things were on their way to changing in Burma, however hard her life had been in house arrest. Michael thought the same when I spoke to him at home in Oxford. He believed that a change was imminent. We talked and spent time together for a few days and she was the same Suu whom I had met in Oxford many years earlier, with a jasmine blossom in her hair, just as full of energy as ever. In Burma she is called "the iron butterfly." She is frail and simultaneously intractably strong and stubborn. I believe that she is very like her father in that respect.

On one level she had, however, already surpassed her father: during her time under house arrest she had become a political superstar of a caliber that was unthinkable in the 1940s, and after her release, her fame came as a shock. "She stood in the center for the whole world but did not even have an assistant to call her own," recounted Debbie Stothard when I met her in Bangkok. "Most of those who were active were still in prison and the NLD had no resources for employing people."

Debbie Stothard comes from Malaysia, and in the mid-1990s she started the organization ALTSEAN. Burma was then on its way to becoming a member of the Southeast Asian cooperative organization ASEAN, and Debbie founded ALTSEAN as a lobby organization with the aim of getting countries like Thailand, Malaysia, and Singapore to increase the political pressure on Burma. When Aung San Suu Kyi heard about this organization, she invited Debbie to her house on University Avenue. The meeting ended with Debbie becoming a kind of press secretary for Aung San Suu Kyi. All inquiries about interviews, meetings, and statements passed through ALTSEAN's office in Bangkok, and Debbie often traveled to Burma to work directly with Suu Kyi.

"Everybody wanted to know how she coped with the time under house arrest, what her view was of the military junta, and what plans she had for the future," says Debbie. "Everyone wanted to capture a small part of her time and attention for themselves."

It sounds somewhat like the situation after her release in 2010. Diplomats and journalists from all over the world were lining up in the same way as I had done before my interview. And everyone was hoping to get a piece of her attention.

Suu Kyi was especially irritated by the need to answer the same questions over and over again. Few people "come alive on the screen" in the same way as Aung San Suu Kyi does, but she could not understand the logic that steers the Western mass media. "I've answered those questions once already! Why can't the journalists be satisfied with that?" she exclaimed in frustration to Debbie Stothard.

"She began every day by finding out whether any NLD activists had been imprisoned during the night," said Debbie. "She worked for several hours every day on helping the families of those in prison, and it happened often that we received information about the death of one of her friends in prison. So at one moment it was a case of life or death, and at the next she had to sit and answer the same questions that she had received the previous day, but from a new journalist from some new media company or other. She often became angry and irritated because the pressure was so great, and when Suu Kyi gets angry it is no fun getting in her way," Debbie continued, laughing. "That's a side of her that many people forget. She has a terrible temperament. It passes just as quickly and at the next moment she is just as sparkling and full of positive energy as usual. But I can imagine that people who don't know her might get upset at her anger."

Debbie Stothard media-trained Suu Kyi. She explained that repetition is essential for the mass media. Just because one journalist has reported something does not mean that all the others will write the same thing. Debbie taught her to look straight at the journalist in interviews and to talk straight into the camera when she recorded appeals or speeches to international conferences on videotape. Then she helped to smuggle the tapes out of the country.

One such videotape was smuggled out and sent to the great international gender equality conference in Beijing in 1995. Aung San Suu Kyi had been invited to give the inaugural speech. In her taped speech she explained why it was impossible for her to participate in the conference in person: she would be shut out of Burma. After that she argued for women's right to political power and she criticized her own country's patriarchal traditions. She pointed out that only 14 of the 485 politicians who had been elected to parliament in 1990 were women, and they all came from her own party, the NLD.

In the beginning it was a classic speech for equality, but later she changed her tack and devoted a considerable part of the speech to linking together the Buddhist tradition with the striving for democracy. She said that there is a philosophical similarity between the Buddhist tradition of mutual forgiveness (pavarana) and the parliament in the democratic political systems. The pavarana tradition aims at gathering together the monks in the monasteries to talk about the unjust deeds committed between people, and then to encourage all involved parties to forgive: "This ceremony, during which monks ask mutual forgiveness for any offense given during the retreat, can be said to be a council of truth and reconciliation. It might also be considered a forerunner of that most democratic of institutions, the parliament, a meeting of peoples gathered together to talk over their shared problems," Aung San Suu Kyi writes in her essay "In Quest of Democracy," published in *Freedom from Fear*.

This may sound like a far-fetched, almost rather naive connection, but among the monks in Burma there is really a strong sounding board for such an interpretation. As we have seen earlier, the monk system—the sanghan—has always had an independent role in relation to the Burmese state apparatus. During times of deep oppression and strong state repression from autocratic kings or colonial powers, the monasteries have been a refuge where people have been able to carry on an open and unconditional political dialogue. It was no mere chance that after the election in 1990, a group of monks offered the NLD the possibility of assembling the new parliament in a monastery in

Mandalay, just as it was no mere chance that the monks have always played an important role in the popular protests against the military junta.

In "In Quest of Democracy" Aung San Suu Kyi develops the thought even further. She describes how members of the protest movement that emerged in the middle of 1980 were searching for examples for their own thoughts about power and popular influence, and how they found that support both in the Western ideological tradition and in their own history. She takes an example from the stories about Buddha and his ten recommendations for how a king should act. One of the king's "duties" is not to govern against the will of the people. In Buddhist mythology there are plenty of examples of kings and rulers who have abused the trust placed in them, through brutality or corruption, and who have therefore been dethroned by their subjects. "It is a cogent argument for democracy," writes Aung San Suu Kyi, "that governments regulated by principles of accountability, respect for public opinion and the supremacy of just laws are more likely than an all-powerful ruler or ruling class, uninhibited by the need to honor the will of the people, to observe the traditional duties of Buddhist kingship."

Another paragraph in the text is devoted to the issue of human dignity. Buddhism is basically about the innate dignity of human beings. All human beings bear a potential to attain nirvana, to see the truth, and through their actions to help others to do the same. However, to attain a true image of life one must also question life, and that questioning is completely at odds with the logic of dictatorships. Dictatorships demand a belief without doubt, writes Aung San Suu Kyi: "An unquestioning faith more in keeping with orthodox tenets of the biblical religions which have held sway in the West than with the more liberal Buddhist attitude."

The author Bertil Lintner wrote in his book about Aung San Suu Kyi that her political thinking after her house arrest has been more tinged by mysticism and Buddhist thought. During her time abroad her texts were often about Burma's unfinished modernization, about practical political issues and analyses of colonialism and the military dictatorship. In that sense she is paradoxically more like her father before her return to Burma. As early as his first political speech as a student, he embraced how the monk system and politics were kept separate, and even if the nationalist movement were influenced by Buddhism, he held on tightly to that principle even later in life. After her house arrest, with six years' time for religious studies, Suu Kyi tries on the contrary to actively weave together politics and religion. She refrains consciously from regarding Buddhism or any other religion as exclusive, but she often uses ancient Buddhist terms and moral recommendations to mirror her own political philosophy: *metta*, *karuna*, *parami*, *sati*, *vipassana*, *nibanna*, and so on.

All this may be interpreted as a mystification of or, to use a more derogatory term, a mixed-up way of approaching Burma's political and economic problems. Lintner writes that it is to some extent reminiscent of the Bhutanese king Jigme Singye Wangchuck's striving to replace gross national product with "gross national happiness" as a measure of the progress of a nation. Aung San Suu Kyi had gotten to know King Wangchuck during her time in Bhutan in the 1970s, so the connection is natural.

However, her new focus on religion and spirituality might just as well be interpreted as an attempt to talk about democracy and freedom in a way that connects with the more traditional Burmese way of thinking about societal matters. Michael Aung-Thwin, who worked together with Suu Kyi in Kyoto in the 1980s, has accused both her and the democratic movement of forcing the development of a "democratic jihad": democracy at any price and according to a Western model. His criticism is reminiscent of the arguments the junta usually employs. Ever since the coup in 1962, the generals in Burma, as in many other dictatorships in the third world, have asserted that democracy is a Western import, foreign to the cultural and religious traditions of their own country. In Asia many rulers talk about "Asian values," which is often just a way of excusing a continued totalitarian government.

Aung San Suu Kyi continues to show that striving for popular influence in the political decision-making body is not only common to all humanity but is also rooted in a tradition that is valid even in Burma. She has not written any more comprehensive political texts, and her long period of house arrest has prevented her from drawing up a more coherent, concrete description of her political program. However, by mirroring democracy and Buddhism in each other she actually makes an important contribution to the discussion of the legitimacy of democracy.

The years of isolation had not diminished Aung San Suu Kyi's popularity among the Burmese either. On the contrary, the isolation had increased the mythmaking around her, and when she was released the interest in listening to her was greater than ever. During the first days after her release in the summer of 1995, thousands of people gathered outside her house. In the end, the pressure became so great that she and her helpers placed a table on the inside of the gate on University Avenue. She climbed up on the table with a broad smile on her lips. She was dressed in a green blouse and a grayish-blue longyi. Several NLD activists stood beside her and looked out over the crowds while she gave a short speech.

The following day even more people collected outside the gate. The NLD leaders repeated the same procedure once more, but the only effect was that even more people turned up the day after that. In the end they had to ration her appearances, and she started to give her speeches every Saturday at four o'clock in the afternoon. For many of the inhabitants of Rangoon this became almost their regular weekend outing. They brought food and drink with them and sat on blankets and waited until Aung San Suu Kyi's head became visible on the other side of the gate. She spoke for exactly one hour, mostly about political matters of course, about the SLORC, the imprisonment of NLD activists, and the basic principles behind a democratic system. However, after a time she placed a letterbox by the gate, where people could write questions that she later replied to and commented on during her weekend appearances. She spoke in an informal, almost easygoing tone, and she often joked with the crowds. The meetings were monitored by the security police, and Aung San Suu Kyi always finished her speech by calling on the crowds to be careful and to hurry on home. Her experience from the election campaign in 1989 made her wise to the fact that those who took part in her meetings always ran the risk of being arrested.

During a number of months in 1995, Aung San Suu Kyi was able to move about relatively freely, but that did not last long. Her last visit outside the capital was made early in the autumn of 1995. She traveled to a monastery on the Thamanya mountain, about eight hours' car journey from Rangoon. There she met Hsayadaw U Vinaya, one of Burma's most respected monks. After the massacres some years earlier, he had repudiated the junta and refused to accept the donations and benefits that the junta offered to the monasteries in order to acquire better karma for themselves after the bloody crackdowns on the monasteries following the elections in 1990. Aung San

Suu Kyi gave a detailed account of this visit in the book *Letters from Burma*, a collection of articles she wrote for a Japanese newspaper in the mid-1990s. She highlighted the monastery school among others, where 13 teachers gave tuition to 375 children from the district around the monastery, without any resources at all for schoolbooks or writing materials.

That journey became her last for a very long time. When she and the others in the NLD leadership were to attend a Karen new year's ceremony a few days before the new year, the junta explained that her freedom no longer meant that she could travel as she wanted in the country. On another occasion she was going to travel to Burma's second-largest city Mandalay in order to open a new NLD office there, but just before the train was about to leave, her carriage was uncoupled and left standing at the platform. Authorities placed blame on technical problems.

As soon as she left her home to visit friends or party activists in Rangoon, she was followed by a car full of security police and two police motorcycles. If she visited a restaurant in the evening, it sometimes happened that it had to shut down the day after, so her possibilities of any free movement among people were extremely limited.

A journalist inquired whether they were trying to break her down by means of surveillance. She replied, "If that is what they are trying to do, they will not succeed. Besides, it's almost touching to see how poorly they hide their surveillance. What's the point of a secret police if it's not secret?"

The same "secret" police continued simultaneously to arrest NLD supporters and to harass the meetings of the party. On Burma's day of independence Aung San Suu Kyi had invited people to a great celebration at 54 University Avenue; among the guests were two members of Moustache Brothers, a well-known group of comedians from Mandalay. When both of the comedians were about to leave the party, they were arrested by the police and sentenced to three years' hard labor in the Kachin state.

The junta had furthermore got hold of a new weapon in the battle against the democratic movement. In the spring of 1993, the junta leader Than Shwe founded the Union Solidarity and Development Association (USDA). The idea was to create a force in civil society that was loyal to the regime, in the same way that Golkar has been to the dictator Suharto in Indonesia or the Chinese communist party to Mao. The plan was simple: every NLD meeting would be disrupted by activists from USDA, which had the whole power apparatus at their disposal. The members were recruited more or less by force. School pupils were told that their school grades would deteriorate dramatically if they did not become members. Out in the rural areas, impoverished young people were recruited by being promised that their parents would not have to pay tax, or that they would avoid being conscripted into the army. In the villages, the USDA often took over the monopoly on violence previously held by the police force and sharpened the political surveillance. Its youth section developed into something that almost resembled an armed militia, in which the members were trained in the handling of weapons, the martial arts, and intelligence work, always in close cooperation with the security service. Their foremost assignment was to disrupt and sabotage the political meetings of the opposition.

At one meeting in the town of Inndaw in the autumn of 1996, the USDA's general secretary, U Win Sein, had made several incendiary attacks on Aung San Suu Kyi. He demanded of his followers that they should "exterminate" the causes of the country's internal political problems. "Do you understand what is meant by eradicated? Eradicated means to kill," he yelled through his loudspeaker system and added, "Dare you kill Daw Suu Kyi?"

Later the same day, she and the rest of the party leadership were attacked when their cars were about to leave from a building in Rangoon. About two hundred USDA activists came after them with clubs and cobblestones. The car windows were smashed, but Aung San Suu Kyi succeeded in getting away unscathed. It later turned out that everyone who had taken part in the attack had received five thousand kyat, barely one week's wages, from the USDA. After several more attacks by the USDA, among others against a Buddhist ceremony at which Suu Kyi was present, she warned the world of that organization:

> The world community must realize that the USDA is not an innocent social-welfare organization, as it claims to be, but an organization being used by the authorities as a gang of thugs. Their operations resemble those of the Nazi Brown Shirts. The SLORC sent people from this so-called social-welfare organization to beat up people taking part in a nonviolent, religious ceremony. I must say that that amounts to something very, very close to what the Brown Shirts used to do in Germany.

In the autumn of 1997, the SLORC changed its name to State Peace and Development Council (SPDC), and the propaganda intimated that it would mean a change politically as well. Some of the junta's members were picked out and accused of corruption, but just as it meant nothing when Burma changed its name to Myanmar, so in the same way this change meant nothing in practice. Bertil Lintner disclosed later that the junta had employed the American public relations firm Bain and Associates Inc., which had recommended a cosmetic rearrangement to quiet international criticism.

Rajsoomer Lallah pointed out that no improvements in human rights whatsoever had occurred during recent years. He had just taken over the role of the United Nations special envoy for human rights. In November 1998 United Nations secretary general Kofi Annan once more invited the SPDC to initiate a dialogue with the democratic opposition and the ethnic minorities. However, no dialogue came about this time either.

In the mid-1990s it also became apparent that the NLD had internal problems. First, there was hardly anything left of the organization that had been built up during the election campaign in 1989. Most of the party offices had been forced to close, several hundred leading activists were in prison, and the restrictions concerning Aung San Suu Kyi's freedom of movement prevented a rapid reconstruction of the party.

Second, the junta's arrests, torture, and harassment made several leading representatives defect from the party and openly reject Aung San Suu Kyi. The first to defect was Ma Thanegi, one of the women who had been in the NLD leadership group and who had walked behind Aung San Suu Kyi when the rifle was aimed at them in Danubyu during the election campaign in 1989. Ma Thanegi had spent three years in prison, and now she accused Aung San Suu Kyi of being too dogmatic, stubborn, and unwilling to really solve the country's problems. She wrote an article in *Far Eastern Economic Review* in which she encouraged the international community not to see Burma as a game between good and evil, black and white. There are always gray zones, she wrote, and the answers to a country's problems are never simple.

The core of her criticism was the sanctions. Influenced by the struggle against apartheid in South Africa, Aung San Suu Kyi had exhorted the world at large to direct economic sanctions at Burma. Her exhortation concerned trade and commerce, and investments in tourism. (In a country like Burma it is very difficult to travel as a tourist without the money one spends ending up in the pockets of the regime.) Ma Thanegi did not make these charges explicit, but between the lines one could read that she recommended foreign capital and investments to solve the country's problems. She also accused Aung San Suu Kyi of blocking a dialogue with the junta. Instead of initiating talks with the generals, she had chosen to put pressure on the junta and ask the world to desist from providing aid and economic support.

Her attack received much attention and was supported by the circle of businessmen who had found their way to Burma after the economic liberalization, as well as by several foreign diplomats in Rangoon, whose view was that the politics of isolation were a thing of the past.

However, the greatest loss of all for the NLD was still perhaps U Kyi Maung's defection. He had been one of Aung San Suu Kyi's closest collaborators and the chairman of the party during the election campaign. U Kyi Maung had earlier made an ambivalent statement that Suu Kyi was devoted, on the verge of being fanatical, and he had made it clear that he understood this to be a flaw. Rumors now had it that he defected in protest against her leadership. Later on, twenty-five of the parliamentarians who had been elected from the NLD in 1990 wrote an open letter in which they accused Aung San Suu Kyi of blocking any meaningful dialogue with the junta.

Was there any truth in their criticism?

On the one hand, the answer is no. This criticism, which has been part of the political discourse since then, is bizarre. What can one really expect of a person who has spent so many years under house arrest and seen her own friends and colleagues die in the country's prisons? Furthermore, ever since she came forward as the leader of the democratic movement, she has wished for a dialogue with the junta. When she was released after her first house arrest, what she first requested was precisely talks, not any immediate and unconditional capitulation by the generals. It was the junta that refused to conduct talks with her. In one interview with *Asia Week* in 1999 she even opened up the possibility of carrying on talks with the junta at a lower level and that she herself did not necessarily need to be at the table. Several times in the 1990s she emphasized that she was not necessarily striving for any formal political position for herself. Even in that way she was seeking to emulate Gandhi.

That attitude can be called neither dogmatic nor inflexible, and the criticism against her must be seen as partly an effect of the junta's propaganda, and partly that of an increasing frustration in sections of the democratic movement over the fact that developments were standing, and remain standing, still.

Burma has gotten stuck at rock bottom, and in that situation there are many who hope for something, almost anything, that can kick-start the process of change.

On the other hand, it may be a problem that the democratic movement is so dependent on Aung San Suu Kyi, and that it is really impossible to criticize her without seeming to support the SPDC. There is probably also some truth to the accusation that she is intractably stubborn—which is good and bad—and that she made a number of statements after her first house arrest that may be perceived as both dogmatic and severe. "It's us or utter devastation," she said, for example, at a press conference a few weeks after her release. Several years later, during dinner at a restaurant in the Shan state, she revealed to a close friend that if there was anything that she regretted from those years in the 1990s, it was precisely those words. It was really U Tin Oo who had used them to describe the significance of the democratic movement for the future of Burma, and she had repeated them as a way of honoring her older party comrade. However, it was far too rhetorical, she admitted, and it was exploited time after time by the junta to stamp her as a person who would rather sacrifice Burma's economic development than her own political career.

The image of Aung San Suu Kyi is, in other words, more split than one might perceive at first glance. An image emerges of a person who is prepared to negotiate almost anything if only it leads to greater openness and democracy, but who also makes certain basic demands of her counterpart. The junta must release all political prisoners, allow the NLD to be active, and permit Aung San Suu Kyi herself freedom of movement.

When those demands—perfectly reasonable—are not met, she can be just as stubborn as her critics assert.

The junta was made to experience this, if nothing else, in the summer of 1998. For over two years they had refused to carry on any kind of meaningful talks and prevented her from leaving Rangoon. She had done all she could to restore the NLD organization in the capital, but she had also been harassed during that work. On May 27, members of the NLD gathered at a congress that had been hastily announced and at which they demanded that the junta should convene in August at the latest the parliament that had been elected in 1990. As usual the junta responded by arresting a few dozen of those who had been elected, in order to make an example of them.

In that situation, Aung San Suu Kyi decided to test the limits of her own freedom of movement. Twice during the summer of 1998 she attempted to leave Rangoon by car, but both times she was stopped by the police. On July 22 she made a third attempt. She got into a car along with an assistant and two chauffeurs. They drove west toward Bassein in the Irrawaddy Delta. After twenty miles they were stopped by armed police. Aung San Suu Kyi refused to turn back, however, and for six days the whole of her party slept in the car, watched by the police and international media. They had no food with them and only a limited amount of water, and the police saw to it that nobody could reach them with supplies. Later on the police decided that enough was enough. They jerked open the doors of the car and threw out the chauffeurs. Aung San Suu Kyi, who was lying asleep in the back, was pushed violently down into the seat, and then the car was driven back to University Avenue.

Aung San Suu Kyi was furious. "They kidnapped me. They even stole my car," she said via a spokesperson, and she promised to make a new attempt to leave the capital as soon as she had recovered her strength.

The moment was strategically chosen. While Aung San Suu Kyi was spending the nights in the backseat of a car on the outskirts of Rangoon, the ASEAN was holding a meeting in the capital city of the Philippines, Manila. The U.S. secretary of state, Madeleine Albright, was present at the meeting, and along with her colleagues from the ASEAN countries she put pressure on Burma's representatives to release Aung San Suu Kyi and initiate a dialogue with the democratic movement. The spokesperson for the SPDC, Hla Min, rejected the criticism with irritation and accused Suu Kyi of having consciously provoked the clash so that Madeleine Albright would have an excuse to attack Burma.

During the autumn, the NLD formed a committee to represent the popularly elected parliament, and the junta responded by once more increasing the pressure. Over a thousand NLD activists were imprisoned or forced to reject the party. Several popularly elected parliamentarians were arrested in so-called guesthouses, and the junta explained that they would stay there until they had been put through a "reforming education." If there had been any trust between Khin Nyunt and Aung San Suu Kyi in 1994, it had now definitely been demolished. In January 1999, the NLD handed in a summons in which the powerful chief of the security police was accused of undermining and sabotaging a political party that had every right to act freely according to Burmese legislation.

And at that exact moment, when the situation in Burma was at its most dramatic, something happened in Oxford that changed everything: Michael Aris was told that he had cancer.

Some very heavy years for the family had passed. While the boys had of course suffered severely from not having their mother for six years, they had never complained or for one moment criticized Suu Kyi for her decision to remain in Rangoon. Alexander was already in the process of leaving home when she was confined to house arrest, and he moved to the United States to study. Kim was just on his way into his teens and missing his mother. Michael had also been given a post as guest researcher at Harvard in 1990, and for two years Kim stayed at the home of Michael's sister, Lucinda Phillips, and her spouse, Adrienne. "The house was not the same without the restless, creative presence of Suu," he said much later on, when he had married and started a family, and was working in Oxford. "There were always friends coming and things happening, and we had some fantastic travels. Without her, I suppose we lived a simpler life."

The family traveled to Burma twice after her release in 1995, the first time in the summer and then around Christmas. After that Kim received permission to travel there twice by himself during the years that followed. He stayed with her for a couple of weeks at a time. Since the family had always been very strict about the boys' right to a private life, nothing has ever been written about these occasions. The only thing Suu Kyi has mentioned is an anecdote about how Kim taught her to listen to reggae and rock during one of his visits. When he first arrived, he walked around with a Walkman all day every day, with the music at full volume in his headphones. Suu Kyi became worried that he would injure his hearing so she allowed him to play his CDs on the stereo in the house. She, who had never listened to anything other than classical music, found herself liking Bob Marley as well as the Grateful Dead.

Michael Aris had not been given an entry visa since 1995, despite having applied several times. Life had carried on. He continued his work as a teacher and researcher and among other things been one of the people who founded a center for Tibetan studies at the University of Oxford. Just before Christmas Eve in 1998, he was informed that he had prostate cancer. In the days between Christmas and New Year's he called his friend Peter Carey. "I've got one piece of bad news and one piece of good news," he had said to Peter Carey. "The bad news is that I've got cancer. The good news is I'm going to beat it."

Then he received new test results showing that the illness had spread to his lungs and spine. He understood that he did not have much time left and immediately applied for a visa to Burma. He wanted to see his wife one last time. However, he was denied an entry visa even on this occasion. The medical system in Burma did not have the resources to take care of him, the junta explained in a statement, and they then suggested that Aung San Suu Kyi "who is in good health is free to travel to England to meet her dying husband who desperately wants to meet her." It must have been a terribly hard decision, but after having discussed the matter several times on the telephone they decided unanimously that she must stay. The junta wished for nothing better than to be rid of her. If she left the country, the generals would prevent her from returning, and the struggle of the past years would have been in vain. During the winter and spring, while Michael was in the hospital, they talked to each other every evening. The junta had still not allowed Suu Kyi to connect a telephone, so she had to go to the home of a foreign diplomat in Rangoon in order to receive Michael's calls. This worked until the junta understood what they were doing, and one evening the telephone line died as soon as they had said hello to each other. The diplomat has described how he saw Suu Kyi weep for the first time at that moment.

Alexander had moved to the United States to study, and he now returned temporarily to Oxford to be close to his father. He and Kim did not agree with their parents. They longed for their mother and they also wanted their parents to be together during the last period of Michael's life. "You can imagine how hard it was to deny them that," Suu Kyi said later.

A broad international campaign started to persuade the generals to change their decision. Bill Clinton, Kofi Annan, and even the pope, John Paul II, appealed to the junta to let Michael Aris enter Burma. But nothing helped. He died on his birthday: March 27, 1999.

"They were very similar to each other," says Debbie Stothard, who got to know Michael during the years she was working for Suu Kyi. Debbie had been on a visit to Europe in 1998 and he had invited her to Oxford.

Kim and Alexander with their mother during a visit to Rangoon after the first house arrest (1989). *Courtesy of Norstedts.*

"It was fascinating to see the house at 15 Park Town," she says. "He had decorated it almost as homage to Suu Kyi. Portraits of her hung everywhere and plaques and pictures from all the prizes she had received during the years." When they had talked for a few hours, Michael Aris insisted on driving her back to the railway station, so that she would be sure to arrive there safely.

"That was also typical," she says, laughing. "I've traveled all over the world and would have been able to get myself to the station without any problem. But he had the same kind of human caring as Suu Kyi. She is always very concerned about her colleagues. She worries about their families, sees to it that they eat properly and makes tea for them when they need a break. He did the same kind of thing. They were like twins."

On their way to the station they passed through central Oxford, and Michael Aris pointed out places that Suu Kyi used to visit. "That was where my Suu used to go when the children were small," he said as they drove past a park. Or "that was where my Suu used to work," when they passed the Bodleian Library. It was as though he had carved out a sphere that was only theirs, against the background of the last years of public life. A map of common memories. Ann Pasternak Slater has perhaps captured something of the relationship between them in her essay on Suu Kyi. At the end of her text she quotes the poet W. B. Yeats: "How many loved your moments of glad grace, / And loved your beauty with love false and true. / But one man loved the pilgrim soul in you."

"It's my belief that it was the distance that killed him," says Peter Carey. "It was very heavy for him not to be able to meet Suu, at the same time as he had to take care of everything at home in England. He was a clever Tibetologist, he wrote books and looked after the children, while being a public person. He really had no private life to call his own after 1988, but I never heard him complain. He did all this first and foremost because he was fond of Suu."

13

The Murder Attempt

The tug-of-war between Aung San Suu Kyi and the junta continued into 2000, until Suu Kyi decided to test the limits once more. She got into a car, just as she had done two years earlier, this time along with her party colleague, the almost eighty-year-old U Tin Oo. Fourteen youths from the NLD, who were living in an annex on the grounds of Lake Inya, drove first in a Toyota pickup truck. When they came to Dala on the other side of the Rangoon River, the road was blocked by two military trucks, and just as in 1998, Aung San Suu Kyi refused to turn back.

"The soldiers got very frustrated," says Maung, one of the young students who sat in the back of the pickup truck in front of Suu Kyi's car. I met him in Rangoon in 2010. "The chauffeur locked the steering wheel so that they wouldn't be able to roll the car off the road and they didn't know what to do to make her turn around. They sat on the hood and rocked the car so that it moved a couple of centimeters. In the end the car was quite simply lifted off the road by a group of soldiers."

There they remained for nine days.

"The first four days were extremely exhausting," says Maung. "We only had some biscuits to eat and barely any water. Those of us who had traveled in the pickup truck had to take turns in sleeping, and most of us just lay down on the ground outside the car with a jacket as our pillow. However, we had decided to endure it. Daw Suu Kyi was almost sixty years old and U Tin Oo was almost eighty. If they could manage it then so could we."

After four days they received permission to leave the cars and buy food and drink in the village nearby. They rigged up a piece of cloth outside Suu Kyi's car to protect her from the worst of the midday sun. The junta's propaganda apparatus then started to present it all as an "excursion" or a "tea party." In order to reinforce this impression, the military brought in loudspeakers that played "Material Girl" by Madonna at top volume.

"They don't even know what music I like," said Aung San Suu Kyi later, with a laugh, when she recounted the incident.

The United States and the European Union condemned the junta's action and demanded that Suu Kyi be allowed to travel freely and meet her party comrades in other parts of the country. The junta gave their standard reply that the restrictions were in place for her own security. In an official statement they explained that the population in Dala did not approve of the sanctions against Burma and that their "anger" might lead to violence against Aung San Suu Kyi and her party. The only people who were surprised by that statement were probably the villagers in Dala.

It ended in the usual way. After nine days, a group of two hundred soldiers arrived. They forced Aung San Suu Kyi into an ambulance and drove her back to Rangoon. As soon as she was free again, she booked a ticket for the train to Mandalay, but then the security police intervened straight away. They carried her away from the train, and a few hours later the news was out all over the whole world: Aung San Suu Kyi had once again been confined to house arrest.

They really did not know how to deal with her. The plan had been to keep her away from public life, by means of house arrest or other restrictions, for such a long time that she would be forgotten, or in any case lose her popularity. However, at the beginning of the 2000s this had mainly ended up in a deadlock. The national convention had been put on ice in 1996. The NLD had opted out, and several of the ethnic minorities were deeply critical of the junta's attempts to steer the convention and marginalize their demands for a federal constitution. The junta had also received severe criticism for the regulations applied to the convention. Those who criticized the formation of the process could be sentenced to twenty years in prison, which meant that the delegates did not even dare to express any views from the rostrum about the working methods of the convention.

The truces that Khin Nyunt had negotiated with the ethnic minorities were still in force, but none of the groups had laid down their arms. The conflict might blow up again at any time. For example, the Kachin Independence Army and the regime's troops clashed several times after the election in 2010, and as I write this the new government has declared a will to find a long-term solution, but all the guns are still there and the long-sought political solution seems possible but still very far away.

In the beginning of the new millennium the country's economy was in a state of stagnation. After Burma became a member of ASEAN in the summer of 1997, the junta hoped for rapid economic development to stay in power. However, Burma was still just as corrupt and hard to work with as ever for foreign companies, and the financial crisis of the 1990s had furthermore struck in Southeast Asia just a few months after its membership became valid. The countries that had been expected to function as the junta's locomotive were now compelled to deal with their own problems with unemployment and galloping poverty. As the millennium approached, a third of all the children in Burma were suffering from chronic malnutrition.

Yet the junta still tried to keep up a façade. The newspapers were filled with examples of success and photos of generals who inaugurated new building projects. The propaganda went so far that the security police tried to convince the political prisoners the country was actually on the right track now. When NLD activist Zin Linn was released just before Christmas in 1997, after seven years in the Insein prison, he was picked up by a security agent who drove him around Rangoon, showing him new hotels, roads, and bridges. "Can't you see the enormous economic development that the SPDC has provided for the country?" asked the agent. "How can you be against this? Don't you want things to go well for Burma?"

When Aung San Suu Kyi had the same question put to her by Australian journalist Roger Mitton, she replied,

> But isn't putting up bridges and building roads the job of any government? If you are going to talk like that then we'll have to start making a list of all the bridges and the roads and the railways lines that were

put up by the colonial government. If you are going to say that good government is one which builds bridges and lays down roads and railways, then we'd have to favor the colonial government as a very good government. But I doubt that the regime would accept such a definition. . . . This is just normal work that any government would be expected to do and I would not think that this is a justification for a military regime to keep clinging to power.

The junta's propaganda did not mention anything about unemployment, of course, which was assessed by certain people as being over 50 percent. Or the enormous social problems following in the tracks of drug abuse, or the growing HIV epidemic that harvested thousands of deaths every year.

During the years around the turn of the millennium, reports also began to flow in about the junta's ever more brutal assaults against the ethnic minorities. The junta had increased the pressure against the guerrilla groups that had chosen not to sign the truce. At the beginning of 1995, the town of Manerplaw was attacked, being then the center for several of the resistance groups. Manerplaw fell into the hands of the junta, and the region that had been controlled by the Karen people shrank to a tiny strip of land on the border with Thailand.

In order to finish off the remains of guerrilla resistance, the junta then applied a so-called four cut strategy, which means that their aim was to cut off the opposing army's access to information, weapons, supplies, and new recruits. And the only way to do this was to attack the civilian population. In April 1998, Amnesty International released a report showing that the junta had forcibly moved over 300,000 people from the Shan state in eastern Burma. The government troops had entered the villages, burned down the huts, killed the cattle, and forced the population to go with them to new settlements in central Burma. This displacement created a wave of refugees who took themselves over the border to Thailand, but hundreds of thousands of people also became domestic refugees inside Burma. And those who tried to return to their former villages were shot to death by Tatmadaw. The number of forcibly moved and dispossessed refugees has multiplied many times over since then.

Later that year, Amnesty International published two reports showing that the situation was just as much of an emergency in the Karen and Karenni states. Another report from the organization Shan Women's Action Network revealed that the regime's troops had used rape systematically as part of their warfare. In an interview in *Bangkok Post* Naang Yord, a middle-aged woman from the Shan people, describes how all the inhabitants of her village had been forcibly moved to central Burma. The earth there was dry and barren, and they had no way of making a living. Along with her daughter and her niece, Naang Yord had crept back to her old home village to salvage the rice harvest. But a Burmese military patrol caught sight of them and the nightmare began.

"They put a sheet of plastic over my head," said Naang Yord, "and then took turns raping me. I couldn't see what they did to my two girls, but I heard them panting desperately a little way away. After that I heard two gunshots."

The soldiers disappeared from there, and Naang Yord was able to free herself. The first thing she saw when she tore off the plastic sheeting was her niece's body, lying nearby. She had been shot in the ankle, probably because she had tried to crawl away from the soldiers. The second time they had shot her in the head. The journalist Vasana Chunvarakorn from *Bangkok Post* met Naang Yord and other women who had had similar experiences in sheltered accommodation in Thailand. Their pain permeated every word in her article: "Those who listen to the survivors' stories have to push their imaginations to a terrifying limit. The women's weak voices are heard only as a whisper. They have scars on their foreheads, ankles, and wrists. Their skin seems to give off a scent of dejection, with distinct traces of suppressed rage. Can anyone really handle what they have experienced?"

After several months into her second house arrest, Aung San Suu Kyi realized once again that the junta had changed their tone. Khin Nyunt met her a number of times, and according to one of her close colleagues at that time, she and the hard-boiled head of security reached an understanding. It would be wrong to assert that Suu Kyi trusted Khin Nyunt—he had previously shown that negotiations might only be a strategy for status quo, not a meeting to reach compromises—but the feeling she received was still that he was searching for a way forward.

The continued economic crisis certainly played a part. The regime could not even provide a living for its own population. At the beginning of the

2000s there periodically existed famine in parts of the country, and the state authorities were so dysfunctional that they were not able to pay the wages of the ordinary soldiers in the army, while at the same time the officers continued to assemble large fortunes. Even as late as in the beginning of 2010, they received a wage that is the equivalent of not more than five dollars a week. This explains some of the assaults against the ethnic minorities—plundering was and is a way for the soldiers in Tatmadaw to survive. Reports have even come in about them selling ammunition and weapons on the black market for a little extra money.

During the early 2000s, the external pressure had also increased, if only marginally. The United States had introduced a ban on new investments in Burma, and harder sanctions by the European Union were being discussed, although not against any of the goods that meant anything for Burma's exports. The United Nations working committee UN entity International Labour Organization (ILO) had aimed sharp criticism against Burma because the country systematically made use of forced labor. The ILO calculated that about 800,000 people were being forced to work without pay on roadwork, building schools, and as porters in the army. When the junta had received such criticism previously, they had waved it away and claimed that it was an Asian tradition to provide free labor for one's government. However, this time the ILO exhorted all its member organizations, states, and companies, as well as unions, to stop dealing with Burma if the situation was not improved.

In December 1999, the United Nations General Assembly adopted yet another resolution (54/186) demanding that Burma should live up to the United Nations' basic principles on human rights. This document was unusually direct in tone for a diplomatic product. It demanded that the junta start a tripartite dialogue with Aung San Suu Kyi and representatives for the ethnic minorities. The 1990 elections should be respected and the power should successively be channeled over to a government based on the election results. The resolution demanded an immediate stop of the assaults against the ethnic minorities, as well as the exploitation of forced labor and child soldiers.

Another explanation for the new willingness to negotiate was that Kofi Annan had appointed the Malaysian Razali Ismail as the United Nations special envoy to Burma in April 2000. Razali had worked as a diplomat for decades. He had been Malaysia's ambassador in India and led a number of his country's delegations at ASEAN and the United Nations. During a period in the 1990s he was also the chairman of the United Nations General Assembly. Malaysia's government has always had good relations with Burma's military junta.

Razali seems to have convinced Khin Nyunt of the need for a dialogue, and a person close to Aung San Suu Kyi says that she and Khin Nyunt were in agreement about an advanced plan of their course, which among others meant that the NLD would retake its seats in the national convention. While the talks were going on, a total of 244 NLD activists were released from the prisons, of which 54 were parliamentarians from the elections in 1990.

However, most Burma experts were nonetheless skeptical of the junta's ambitions.

"SPDC talked with Suu Kyi to buy time," said Aung Zaw, the editor in chief of the Thailand-based magazine *The Irrawaddy*. "Time to buy more weapons and time to give the Burmese people more false expectations that there will be political reforms."

On May 6, 2002, Aung San Suu Kyi was released. In the television broadcasts of her first day of freedom she looked worn and tired out. She was being led through crowds of people on her way to the NLD head office. On one occasion she seemed close to falling down. However, just as was the case after her first house arrest, she recovered and was soon able to take charge of the task of restoring the democratic movement.

A government spokesperson affirmed that she was now "free to practice her political duties, even the ones connected to her party, NLD. Today we turn a page and write a new chapter for the people of Myanmar and for our relations with the international community. There is no way back."

Mass media all over the world immediately cabled out the news that the political deadlock in Burma was on its way to being resolved. "This is the first decisive step SPDC has taken in years," said Dr. Zar Ni, a Burmese exile and the founder of the organization Free Burma Coalition.

Clearly, not everybody was as positive, however. Aung Din, who had been in prison for five years because he had been one of the leaders of the student revolt in 1988, pointed out that the junta had as of yet not made any concessions that decreased their own power. Some political prisoners had been released, but they could be imprisoned again whenever it pleased the junta. "Besides, there are more than 2,000 political prisoners in Burma's prisons. They must be released too," noted Aung Din in *The Irrawaddy*.

One thing had, however, really been changed: for the first time since 1989, Aung San Suu Kyi was free to move around outside Rangoon. And there was no lack of work to do. The formidable party apparatus that the NLD had set up before the elections in 1990, the network of offices and activists that had constituted the basis of the party's election victory, had systematically been pulled to pieces by the military junta. The number of offices had been greatly reduced, the leadership had been held in prison or under house arrest, and the activists had been harassed by the USDA and the military security service. Aung San Suu Kyi therefore did as she had done during the election campaign thirteen years earlier: she set out on the road. Within the course of a few months she had visited dozens of NLD offices in the vicinity of Mandalay and Pegu, in the Karen state, the Mon state, and the Irrawaddy Delta.

It now became apparent that her popularity had not diminished. The foreign diplomats who had claimed that she had played out her part as a political role model had been wrong. Even profoundly so.

All over Burma, Suu Kyi was met by rejoicing crowds of people. In many places tens of thousands of people came to listen to her, and in several ways it began to resemble the mass movement that had made the junta so nervous during the election campaign in 1989.

A Swedish diplomat stationed in Bangkok met her after her release. He was received on the ground floor of the house on University Avenue in an eight-sided room with benches placed around the walls. Everything was decorated with traditional Burmese fabrics. At one end of the room, for some strange reason, stood a set of drums. After her second house arrest, her home had once again become a meeting place for those active in the party. When the diplomat asked Suu Kyi about the drums, she explained that the young people in the party enjoyed playing them.

The diplomat describes how Aung San Suu Kyi was full of energy and hopes for the future. He had with him an invitation to Sweden from the Swedish foreign minister Anna Lindh, and Suu Kyi seemed sincerely interested in making the journey. For the first time since 1989, she believed in the possibility of leaving the country without its implying lifelong banishment. They met once again in 2002 and talked about humanitarian aid to Burma, among other things. On several occasions during the 1990s, Suu Kyi had exhorted the world at large not to give humanitarian aid as long as the donor countries were not completely certain that the aid was really reaching those who needed it most. The gross corruption in the country meant that officers and civil servants often lined their own pockets with aid money. Now Suu Kyi was no longer as negative. She had made a number of study visits to projects aimed at reducing the spread of HIV and she had seen that aid could be elicited. She also encouraged Sweden and other countries to accept exchange students from Burma. She said that it did not matter if children and supporters of the junta were those who traveled. They would in any case acquire a broader view of life through living abroad, and that would be good for everybody.

However, she was of the opinion that sanctions against Burma could still be useful. The United States and the European Union ought not to ease up on them without marked concessions on the part of the junta, and a basic demand was that the two thousand political prisoners in the country be released from prison.

She did fundamentally distrust the junta's talk about political liberty, of course. Such promises had been given previously, and as soon as pressure on political changes had become too great, restrictions had been reintroduced.

This time it was the junta's "popular" base, the USDA, that was to be the means of silencing the opposition. At every meeting, the NLD was surrounded by hundreds of perpetrators of violence, often criminals who had been released from prisons on the condition that they put themselves at the disposal of the USDA. They usually yelled slogans in support of the regime and jeered at Aung San Suu Kyi in the same way that the state-owned mass media did, calling her a spy and a whore who had married a foreigner. Their aim was to provoke a violent counterreaction from the followers of the NLD.

The SPDC had simultaneously closed the door in the face of further dialogue. During the second half of 2002, Aung San Suu Kyi waited for an invitation to real political negotiations, but no such invitation ever arrived.

There is much to indicate that the unclear behavior of the junta was dependent on an internal conflict. Despite their unscrupulous, extremely brutal methods, Khin Nyunt was a pragmatic politician. He understood that the military regime was going to fall, the question was only when and how. Would the transition to another system take place in a peaceful manner or would it be like Romania? Would the people hang their oppressors from the nearest lamppost? Nobody knew what the plan looked like, and perhaps Khin Nyunt was doing a double-cross in the same way as the others. It was possible that he felt more unsure of his power since his protector, the old dictator Ne Win, had been humiliated and publicly dragged through the mud. In Burma there were many who had assumed that it was he who was ruling the country from the wings, even a long time after he had formally resigned in 1988. However, in March 2002 the junta had sent out information that Ne Win had been confined to house arrest and that several of his relatives had been arrested, accused of planning a coup against the junta. Ne Win died in December 2002, still under house arrest, and the state-owned newspapers did not even mention that he had passed away.

It is unclear what kind of relationship Khin Nyunt had with Ne Win at that time, but it is conceivable that he was actually searching for an exit strategy through talks with Suu Kyi. Both of the other top names in the junta, Than Shwe and Maung Aye, were of a quite different opinion. Basically they still thought that the democratic movement should be combated by means of violence and that Aung San Suu Kyi should be kept in isolation.

On the afternoon of May 29, 2003, Khin Nyunt had a meeting with a foreign diplomat. When they had been talking for a few minutes, Khin Nyunt suddenly received a call on his cell phone. He cast a glance at the display and then he accepted the call.

"His face got very pale," the diplomat told me when I met him at a small café in central Bangkok, "and when he had put down the receiver he sat in silence for at least a minute. After that he excused himself and left the room."

Khin Nyunt had just been informed that Aung San Suu Kyi was about to be murdered.

On the night before May 30, Suu Kyi and her party had spent the night at the home of an NLD supporter in the town of Monywa, some miles to the west of Mandalay. They were on a tour in central Burma and had a couple of stopovers left until it was time to return to Rangoon. Only a few days before her departure, Suu Kyi had had a conversation with a close acquaintance. He had complained about the NLD's lack of a real political program. If they were to take the new political liberty seriously, then they must formulate their ideas more clearly when it came to educational policy, social policy, and other areas where they were critical of the junta's policies. "You are right," Suu Kyi had replied. When she returned from her journey, she was intending to gather a group and draw up the guidelines for a more explicit political program.

On the morning of May 30, she inaugurated a new NLD office in Monywa and then met a group of young people who were going to form a local youth section. The time was about ten a.m. when their five loaded trucks left Monywa to continue on northward. In the first vehicle sat a chauffeur, Aung San Suu Kyi, and some NLD activists from the local party section. In the fourth vehicle sat a group of young people from the NLD who were also acting as her bodyguards. U Tin Oo, the aged vice chairman of the party, traveled in a minibus last of all and behind him snaked a long caravan of supporters who had chosen to accompany them northward from Monywa.

After some miles they arrived at a village where the whole party stopped to inaugurate yet another NLD office and to meet yet another group of young people. This was the shape the tour had taken. The interest in Suu Kyi and the NLD was so great that they would have been able to start any number of local sections. All that was lacking was time.

At half past eight in the evening, Suu Kyi's caravan only had a couple of miles left to Depayin, where they planned to stop for the night. Darkness had fallen. The road twisted and turned northward, barely six feet wide, badly worn, and wet after the day's rain. When they passed the little hamlet of Kyee, they were met by thousands of people who had all gathered to catch a glimpse of Aung San Suu Kyi. By a white stone sign marking the border of the hamlet, they were stopped by two monks who had taken up their position in the middle of the road. One of the bodyguards in the fourth truck leaped out to find out what they wanted.

"We have been waiting for a long time. Ask Daw Aung San Suu Kyi to give a speech," said one of the monks. The bodyguard explained that they did not have time to stop in Kyee since people were waiting for them in Depayin.

At that moment four small trucks drove up behind the caravan. In the back of the trucks stood mercenaries from the USDA yelling the slogan: "Relying on external forces, axe handles; people with negative views, we don't want!"

The people standing along the road yelled back: "We the people, in turn, don't want you!"

That sufficed as a provocation. The men jumped down from the trucks and started to strike out wildly around them with pointed iron bars and bamboo rods. One of the trucks accelerated and drove right into the crowd of people. People were gripped by panic and ran in every direction. The mercenaries beat their way forward through the crowds toward Aung San Suu Kyi's truck. Meanwhile at least three thousand USDA supporters approached from the sides. Everyone understood that this was not one of the USDA's ordinary provocations. This was well directed, and the attackers were so numerous that nobody could escape. Wunna Maung had been in one of the lorries in Aung San Suu Kyi's caravan and saw the bloodbath firsthand.

"They beat women . . . after pulling off their blouses and sarongs," he has said in a report about the incident published by the organization ALT-SEAN. "When the victims covered in blood fell to the ground, I saw the attackers jumped on to them and wrapped their hair around their hands and pounded their heads against stone surface of the road, with all their force."

While the dirty asphalt was being stained red with blood, the attackers yelled that the women were "racial criminals" who were intending to marry Kala (a Burmese word used disparagingly for Indians and Westerners). Another witness was fifty-year-old U Khin Saw:

> I saw how people were brutally mishandled. I heard how dying people whimpered in pain, screamed in agony and called out for help. . . . It was as though all hell was let loose. I saw how the attackers knocked people down with all their strength and how they hacked at them with sharpened iron bars. . . . They struck until their victims were no longer alive.

The young people from the NLD, most of them students in their twenties, formed a ring around Aung San Suu Kyi's truck to protect her, but the attackers were too many. Several of the students were gravely injured. The photographers Tin Maung Oo and Ko Thin Toe died on the spot from hard blows to the head. When the assailants had reached the truck, they struck indiscriminately against the windows, doors, and roof. Suu Kyi's chauffeur realized what was at stake and stepped on the accelerator as hard as he could, and the car shot off through the chaos. A few miles farther on, they were stopped by a group of agents from the security service, who dragged Aung San Suu Kyi out of the backseat and carried her away. U Tin Oo, who had been sitting in the last vehicle in convoy, was given a hard blow to the head and carried away by the USDA forces.

Nobody has been able to prove it, but there is evidence that speaks for the fact that the agents who Suu Kyi met had been sent out by Khin Nyunt and that their assignment was to take her away from the massacre. About seventy people were killed at Depayin, but according to the media controlled by the junta, the number of fatalities was only four, and they claimed that the violence had started because Aung San Suu Kyi's caravan of trucks had driven right into a group of "peaceful government supporters" who were demonstrating by the roadside.

One of those who were injured during the attack was the thirty-six-year-old NLD activist Ko Chit San. In the report about the massacre he tells that he found himself still at that place when about eighty policemen with shields and batons suddenly turned up, barely an hour after the massacre:

About eighty policemen, holding shields and wooden clubs, came to [one area of killing after the massacre was over]. . . . Two officers got out of the cars and checked the killing field. Hiding under cover of night, I witnessed that the eighty policemen threw the bodies of the dead and injured, as if they were garbage, into the trucks. I could clearly see in the lights of trucks that had been to that area before and others that got there later, although I could not discriminate between who was who. The two Helix pickup trucks left at the scene were pushed down into the rice field and then they set them up as if they had overturned. The other two Helix pickup trucks were set up to look like they had had a head-on collision. Then they took pictures of them with video and still cameras, for the record. After that, I left that area so that I could find a venue to hide for a night.

For several days it was feared that Aung San Suu Kyi had been killed or seriously injured. Nobody knew where she had disappeared to. The state-owned media cabled out a fantastic story about an international conspiracy against her and that she needed to be protected against a group of professional murderers who had been sent to Burma. "We don't know the target for the assassins, but we will be blamed if anything happens to her," said the foreign minister, Win Aung. The junta leader Than Shwe wrote a letter to his colleagues in ASEAN, in which he claimed that the NLD had planned to create anarchy in the country just in time for Aung San Suu Kyi's birthday on July 19. The letter was intended to excuse the massive campaign that now began to suppress the democratic movement yet again. Within a few days the junta had shut down all the NLD offices and made it clear that they would not tolerate any political mass meetings. There is a law in Burma that says that more than five people may not gather in the same place without permission from the authorities. This law, a remnant from the British colonial era, has been used diligently through the years, but during periods of greater openness the police had not placed that much importance on it. Now it was being applied slavishly.

At first the junta refused to say where they were keeping Suu Kyi prisoner, and there were rumors that she was dead and that the junta did not dare to tell the truth for fear of the people's revenge. However, after a number of weeks it emerged that she had been thrown into the Insein prison. There she remained until September, when she was diagnosed with an illness that compelled her to undergo a gynecological operation. When she was discharged from the hospital she was taken to her home on University Avenue for a third period of house arrest.

The noose had once again been tightened, and this time it would be over four years before the population in Burma would catch a glimpse of Aung San Suu Kyi.

14

The Saffron Revolution

A 1947 black DeSoto picked me up from outside the hotel. The car was in perfect condition, with shiny chrome work on the instrument panel.

"It's my father's," said the chauffeur, a young man who, to judge by his appearance, could have found a place in any reggae band. "He has always taken good care of this car, as though it was a child. Mostly so as not to have to buy a new one. We could never have afforded that."

It was January 2010, and I had traveled to Burma to interview some of Aung San Suu Kyi's colleagues. Darkness was about to fall as we slowly glided along the road. There was a scent of incense and spicy food from the outdoor food stalls in the streets. Rangoon is and as far as I know has always been full of street trade. People sit on blankets and cheap mats and sell everything from dried fish to two-month-old issues of magazines like *Time* or *New Statesman*. There are crowds everywhere. Children playing or working in their parents' street stall, women in their eighties with their two or three remaining teeth red from betel nut juice.

Central Rangoon has not changed much since the 1950s. The blocks in the harbor district consist of long, narrow lanes lined with turquoise, white, and blue three-story houses that could just as well have been taken out of an early novel by Graham Greene. The style is colonial and decadent. The façades are stained by soot and damp. The plaster has fallen off and the windows are so shabby that one wonders how the panes can remain in the frames. It is as though somebody had moved one of the most charming suburbs of Paris to the tropics and then allowed it to rot for half a century.

We passed some young men who wanted to exchange dollars on the black market.

"Change money? Good rate for you!"

Nobody in Burma believes any longer in the domestic economy, and the inflation is brutal, so dollars have become the most desirable currency. When I first traveled to Burma in the mid-1990s, one received 250 kyat for a dollar on the black market. Nowadays it's four times that amount.

We are on our way to a teahouse to meet Zaw Zaw, a former member of the NLD who now calls himself an activist.

A meeting with Aung San Suu Kyi was out of the question. She had not been allowed to meet any journalists since May 2003. The fact is that she had not met many people at all during the most recent, long period of isolation. She had been visited by her doctor, her two housekeepers, on a few occasions one of her party comrades, and on even fewer occasions by UN representatives.

Razali Ismail was given permission to meet her a few times during the autumn and winter of 2003–2004. On the first occasion, Suu Kyi had written down a list of names of the young NLD activists who had been at Depayin. She wanted Razali to check that they were safe or—if they had been arrested—that they were being treated well by the authorities.

"It was tragic," says Debbie Stothard, who later received the list from Razali. "Who was going to tell her that several of the young people had been killed at Depayin?"

Beginning in the spring of 2004, no further visits were permitted. Razali was blocked from entering the country, and in January 2006 he resigned from the post of the United Nations special envoy in protest against the junta's unwillingness to cooperate. He was replaced by Ibrahim Gambari, a Nigerian politician who did not have any particular previous knowledge about Burma and who, up until his resignation in 2009, did not succeed in finding any cracks in the junta's façade.

For Gen. Khin Nyunt, the third party in what could have been a meaningful dialogue, the period after Depayin was a political roller coaster with regard to power. Khin Nyunt has always been a survivor, and despite the obvious conflicts with Than Shwe, he was appointed prime minister in August 2004. By then he had continued to be in favor of talks with Suu Kyi, though he didn't take part in them himself. After her release in 2010, Aung San Suu Kyi mentioned that there had also been a short period of dialogue following the Depayin massacre.

"I can say that real discussions took place when I met with Col. Tin Hlaing, Maj. Gen. Kyaw Win, and Brig. Gen. Than Htun after the Depayin incident," she said in an interview with the magazine *The Irrawaddy*. "I think they did the best they could. Whenever I spoke with them, I always noticed that they raised good points. That's why I never thought that I was always right. I always felt friendly toward them. Perhaps they felt the same about me. However, what we discussed has never actually been implemented."

Khin Nyunt's first measure as new prime minister was to launch a "roadmap to democracy." In practice, it would be a rehash of the plan he had already launched in the 1990s. First he reconvened the national convention, whose assignment was still to draw up a new constitution. After that the junta promised yet again that elections would be held.

Parallel to this, the economic liberalization would continue, but now more and more members of the junta began to question the deep dependence on China that had developed during the 1990s. India and other countries in Asia were competing to capture market shares for themselves, not least in the growing oil and gas industry. Than Shwe and the junta's second-in-command, Maung Aye, considered that Khin Nyunt, who himself came from a Chinese background, was far too concerned about having good relations with the rulers in Beijing.

It is impossible to know whether it was his desire to open the economy for Chinese businessmen, his contacts with Razali, or perhaps his willingness to compromise in the relations with Suu Kyi that was the decisive factor, but in the middle of October 2004, Khin Nyunt was dismissed as prime minister. The coup was made public in a press release that announced that Khin Nyunt had resigned "for health reasons." He disappeared without a trace, and several months later information leaked out that he had been taken to a top-security prison in the Coco Islands in the Indian Ocean. Over two thousand of his most loyal colleagues in the military security service were simultaneously sacked or imprisoned.

When I traveled to Burma in 2005 to do research for my book *Granatklockorna i Myitkyina* ("The Grenade Bells in Myitkyina"), I met several political activists who pointed out with grim humor that the security apparatus since Khin Nyunt's fall from power had become "harder but more stupid."

"That is still true, but only partly," Zaw Zaw pointed out, when we had seated ourselves on the small plastic chairs and each ordered a cup of green China tea. "Than Shwe has intensified surveillance, so people are more frightened nowadays. The organization USDA has started to function more and more as a security service and the control has become extra hard after the great protests in 2007. The people from USDA are also being made into village chiefs and the organization is to be provided with offices in all towns and villages. USDA is on its way to becoming the new totalitarian power center in Burma."

Zaw Zaw was earlier active in the youth section of the NLD. When Aung San Suu Kyi was freed at the end of the 1990s, he lived in one of her houses on University Avenue, along with a group of other young people from the NLD. To stop the young people from organizing themselves politically, the junta had closed all the universities in 1996, and they were not reopened until four years later. The idea was to avoid a new student revolt, but the effect was partly the direct opposite. A whole generation of academics became unemployed and now had more time to get involved in the democratic movement. Later on Zaw Zaw continued with his involvement and was a driving force in building up new NLD sections during Aung San Suu Kyi's tours in the countryside in 2002 and 2003.

Zaw Zaw now told me that he was tired of it all. Not of Aung San Suu Kyi—she still has strong support (and since her release I'm pretty sure Zaw Zaw and his friends have even greater confidence in her work)—but of the others in the NLD leadership.

"They are old and afraid and don't dare to do anything," he says while taking a gulp of tea. "When the monks' protests started in September 2007, everyone was waiting for the NLD to take the lead. But it didn't happen. Instead they encouraged people to take things easy and not to demonstrate.

The uprising therefore lacked political leadership, and it became easier for the junta to quell the demonstrations."

Zaw Zaw had an intense gaze and an ironic smile, and during our conversation I caught myself thinking about Aung San. This must have been how the young nationalists worked during the 1930s. One hundred percent focused on the task at hand. Tired of the "oldies" in the movement.

For those who have been following the developments in Burma through the years, the demonstrations in 2007 came partly as a surprise. It was obvious that the population in Burma hated the regime and that poverty had increased the dissatisfaction. But there was not much to indicate that so many people were ready once again to confront the junta openly. Nineteen years had passed since the gigantic protests in 1988, and Aung San Suu Kyi had effectively been kept out of the public eye since 2003.

This in turn meant that the international interest in Burma had faded. A rapid review of the international English-language newspapers shows that the number of news articles about Burma decreased dramatically during the years 2003–2007. The ethnic cleansing and the assaults along the borders of Burma are not newsworthy enough for the Western press.

It was as though the human rights campaign that had started with such intensity in the 1990s had lost its thunder at the same time. Burma showed in a brutal and concrete way that the promises of a perpetually expanding democratic world did not necessarily have to be kept. The optimism among Burma's exile groups also diminished in the 2000s. Many activists had spent almost twenty years away from their home country, without meeting their families or their childhood friends, without seeing any clear result of the campaign for democracy at home. When I traveled along the border between Thailand and Burma in 1998, most of the people I met believed that the junta would fall within a year or two. "Next year in Rangoon," said one student who had fled after the elections in 1990, when we said good-bye to each other in the border town of Mae Sot. But the following year, everything was just as usual in Burma. The oppression just as severe. The poverty just as immense. This does not mean that the work of the exile groups had been in vain all these years. Quite the opposite. By educating young people along the border, establishing a dialogue between the ethnic groups, developing medical care, and discussing basic political issues, they are creating a popular base that will increase the chances of success for democracy in Burma when the day arrives for developments to take such a turn.

However, the junta did not fall. Burma did not become a new South Africa, at least not with the aid of some "quick fix." Perhaps it was a result of the restlessness of our times and our demands for rapid results. When the Burma campaigns did not achieve any results, many young Western activists moved onto the next thing.

The decrease in interest resulted most of all from the attack against the United States on September 11, 2001, and on the ensuing war on terrorism. For a number of years, the international discourse was almost entirely about fundamentalist Islam, the brutal methods used in the war on terrorism, and the West's own violations of human rights. The United States invaded Iraq in March 2003, just two months before the junta in Burma decided once again to strangle the democratic movement.

The junta did all they could to link their own fight to stay in power to the war on terrorism. The members of the democratic movement were more and more often called terrorists, and the state-owned newspapers carried continual reminders about the groups that were still at war with the junta. In particular, the population in the Muslim-dominated regions in the Arakan states to the west of Rangoon was badly affected. The Burmese government army commenced harsh attacks against the guerrillas from the Muslim Rohyinga people, who were fighting against Tatmadaw. The Rohyinga people, who had been living in the Arakan state for hundreds of years, were called Muslim extremists and "infiltrators from Bangladesh." The populations of hundreds of villages were driven away with violence and were replaced by Bamar who were forcibly moved from other parts of the country.

On a few occasions, smallish explosive charges were detonated in Rangoon, but they were probably primed by Christian Karen groups that had tired of jungle warfare and chosen terrorism as a method. At the end of the 1990s, a Karen group calling itself God's Army had occupied Burma's embassy in Bangkok for a few days, and on another occasion its members held several hundred patients hostage in a hospital in the town of Ratchanaburi. These incidents received tremendous international attention when it turned out that God's Army was led by Jonny and Luther Hto, twins who were then only eleven years old. Their followers believed that they had magic powers, among other invulnerabilities, and in all of the photos that were published of them each had a cigarette in the corner of his mouth.

However, God's Army was crushed within a few months and there was no more "terrorism" in Burma.

The junta did not receive any support either from the United States or the European Union when it came to their purported problems. Yet the junta was able to benefit from the change in the international climate that the war on terrorism brought with it. The world was once more deeply affected by the logic of the Cold War. This meant partly that Burma fell off the world's radar since there was no way of linking the "little" conflict in Burma to the "big" conflict against radical Islamism. Countries like Russia and China could furthermore use the terrorism card when they argued for Burma's case in the United Nations or other international contexts.

The lines of conflict after 2001 have also created a new kind of affinity between those countries that were lumped together by the United States during the Bush regime as "the axis of evil." Burma, Iran, North Korea, Eritrea, and other similar countries have realized that they can become stronger through cooperation. In their resistance to democratic reforms, they have found a solidarity that should really be impossible for regimes whose identity is based on nationalism and on fear of the rest of the world.

In this way one can say that the junta had succeeded with their strategy. They were no longer the focal point for the international floodlights, and by isolating Aung San Suu Kyi they had strangled the domestic opposition. Foreign diplomats in Rangoon and groups that wanted to see increased trade with Burma even started to say that the world must accept the military rule, cooperate with the junta, and stop relying on Aung San Suu Kyi. Almost twenty years had passed since the elections in 1990, despite everything. How long should the results actually be valid? Had the junta not actually consolidated their popular support?

It was this that made the monks' saffron revolution so hopeful. It reminded the whole world of what was at stake in Burma.

Although it did not really start with the monks at all.

In the autumn of 2004, several of the student leaders who had been in the vanguard of the demonstrations in 1988 were released, among others

Min Ko Naing and Ko Ko Gyi. Most of them had been in prison for almost sixteen years. When I visited Burma in the spring of 2005 I met some of them. The meeting took place under extremely hush-hush circumstances. It was the middle of the night and we sat on the floor of a candlelit apartment in central Rangoon. The security police were spying on the student leaders who had been released, round the clock, so I had arrived there two hours before the others so that nobody would take note of my arrival. They told me about life in prison, how one copes with years of isolation, and how it feels to lose a major part of one's life.

"We were prepared for things to take that turn," they said. "We had seen how earlier generations of activists had sacrificed their lives or been thrown into prison."

One of them said that every day during his imprisonment, he thought about his day as though he had still been at liberty. When breakfast was pushed in to him through a hatch in the door, he thought about the kitchen back at his parents' home. How they used to sit drinking tea and eating rice together. In the evenings he fantasized about get-togethers with relatives and student friends, their conversations, laughter and arguments. Every day.

And in the same way as Aung San Suu Kyi during her periods of house arrest, they had meditated every day for at least an hour. It was a way of clearing their thoughts and focusing on the aspects of their existence that they were able to influence.

They told me how the strip lighting in the cells was on all day and night in order to break them down mentally, and how they were mishandled during the long interrogations with the security service. I asked whether they were intending to get involved once more? Did they dare to risk their liberty yet again? They contemplated the answer.

"We must first find out which possibilities we have. Just at present we are under such tight control and we don't know what the opposition movement looks like."

In February 2007, information leaked out that small groups of activists had carried out public protests in Rangoon. They gathered in groups of five to ten persons, handed out leaflets, and protested against the unemployment and poverty in the country. The United Nations had classified Burma as one of the twenty poorest countries in the world, and late in the year 2006 inflation increased exponentially. The price of rice, eggs, and cooking oil rose to such high levels that many people could no longer afford to buy even these most basic of daily groceries.

Events began to resemble those in 1988, and this impression was reinforced by the name 88 Generation Students, chosen by the group leading the gradually expanding protest movement. Those whom I had met in Rangoon two years previously were part of this movement. Their movement grew during the spring and summer, and when the junta decided on August 15 to abolish state subventions of oil and gas, they saw their chance. The decision to abolish subventions was taken after the World Bank and the IMF had recommended precisely such measures. However, nobody had counted on the junta's abolishing them altogether, and the decision was as usual made completely without warning. The prices doubled several times over, and people were suddenly forced to spend their total incomes on fuel and transport. 88 Generation Students decided to carry out a larger demonstration on August 19. About four hundred people assembled in central Rangoon, but at that point the junta struck immediately. The leaders of 88 Generation Students were thrown into prison, and the activists who had already been in prison for over fifteen years were given prison sentences of up to sixty-five years.

It was in this situation, when 88 Generation Students had been silenced, that the orange-robed monks took over, and a whole world dressed in orange to support their struggle.

On September 5 the soldiers crushed a peaceful demonstration in the little town of Pakokku. Three monks were injured, and the day after, a group of young monks took a number of civil servants hostage in a building near the monastery. They demanded an apology for the unnecessary violence of the previous day, but the military refused and the protest escalated step by step to become the most extensive popular protest since 1988. When the demonstrations were at their peak, over a hundred thousand people had dared to go out onto the streets. The monks marked their attitude toward the military in the same way they had after the elections in 1990: if they passed officers or members of their families they turned their begging bowls upside down and refused to accept alms—a tremendous insult to every faithful Buddhist.

The most emotional moment of the protests was when a group of monks wandered along University Avenue in order to honor Aung San Suu Kyi. When they arrived at the barricades outside her house, one saw how the soldiers hesitated. Would they let the monks through? Would it give them bad karma if they stopped them? An officer pulled out a communications radio, and on a few shaky sequences taken by an onlooker one can see how he nods, puts down the receiver, and gives the order to let the monks pass. Suu Kyi met them at the gates to her home. They prayed together and people standing beyond the barricades claim that she was weeping. She had been able to show herself in public for the first time in several years. And for the first time in several years the monks revealed who they understood to be the rightful leader of the country. It was as though the whole of Burma had been given an electric shock. The Burmese journalist Myint Swe described how the simple fact that she once again appeared in public brought new energy to the democracy movement.

The junta realized that the situation was beginning to get out of hand. To avoid risking anything, the junta leader Than Shwe sent his entire family abroad. They chartered a plane from the air company Air Bagan and flew to Vientiane, the capital of Laos.

However, they really did not need to worry. The military had learned its lesson since the demonstrations twenty years ago, and the whole security apparatus had been trimmed to handle exactly the same type of situation as the monks' protests in 2007. On September 25, the junta threatened the demonstrators with violent reprisals. Soldiers and military vehicles were stationed at the Shwedagon Pagoda, and the next day they attacked a demonstration procession with about seven hundred participants. They fired tear gas grenades and advanced into the crowd of people while striking wildly about with batons and rifle butts. The same afternoon, photos were cabled out from Burma showing monks continuing to demonstrate. Some of them, still dressed in their orange robes, had put on gas masks as protection against the soldiers' attack.

On September 27, reports came in that many members of the army refused to participate in the assaults on the demonstrators. The British newspaper *The Guardian* published information that a group of officers had openly given their support to the protest movement, and a rumor said that four hundred soldiers at a regiment outside Mandalay had been arrested because they refused to obey orders. It is unclear if the information was really true, but in order to avoid disruption within the army, the junta leader Than Shwe personally took command of the troops.

That was the last day of extensive protests. In the morning, the junta struck out against the monks. Those who were not arrested were compelled to remain inside the monasteries that were surrounded by heavily armed soldiers. By the Sule Pagoda in central Rangoon, a large demonstration was repulsed and several people were killed when the army opened fire. One of them was Japanese photographer Kenji Nagai, who was shot to death when he was about to take photographs of the soldiers' excessive violence. A hidden camera from the radio station Democratic Voice of Burma caught the whole incident on film. It is a macabre and tragic sight when Kenji Nagai raises his camera, adjusts the focus, and then falls headlong backward, hit by a bullet from a machine gun. He dies a few seconds later on the warm, damp asphalt by the Sule Pagoda. Later, when the crowds of people had been dispelled, a soldier went up to him and took the camera from his dead body so as to get rid of all the evidence.

After September 27, things became routine again. The protests faded when people no longer dared to go out onto the streets, and the military was slowly able to regain control.

The teahouse where Zaw Zaw and I are sitting is by coincidence situated just a stone's throw from the Secretariat, the redbrick building where Aung San was murdered in 1947. Aung San's spirit hovers over the democratic movement, in the same way that Aung San Suu Kyi is present in our conversations the whole time, directly or indirectly. In a whisper, Zaw Zaw describes how the Lady followed the protests in 2007, full of hope and expectation. "She realized that it would perhaps not lead to any dramatic changes, but that it was important that people dared to demonstrate openly. It created a completely new generation of democratic activists."

Zaw Zaw was himself out in the streets every day during those autumn days in 2007. He organized the students and activists who walked side by side with the monks to protect them against police and military harassment. During our conversation, he tells me about the violence that confronted the demonstrators when the junta decided to suppress the revolt. Zaw Zaw was walking in a demonstration in one of Rangoon's northern suburbs, near the Insein prison, where the military did not have to worry about foreign journalists. On the morning of September 27, the soldiers started firing tear gas at the procession of demonstrators. After that they opened fire with live ammunition.

"One of my best friends got a bullet in his head," said Zaw Zaw, and for the first time during our conversation at the teashop he looked uncertain. His gaze started to wander, and he smoothed back his dark, long hair and took a deep breath before continuing: "It was as though the whole of the back of his head had exploded. I couldn't sleep that night. Hid in a cellar. Then the adrenaline took over and the day after I was back in the demonstrations again."

Zaw Zaw marched along the streets together with the orange-robed monks. They clapped their hands twice, then took a step forward. *Clap, clap.* One more step. *Clap, clap.* One more step.

A quiet, slowly advancing procession against violence.

15

All These Anniversaries

There are plenty of tragic anniversaries in Burma. They have greatly increased in number during the decades marking the struggle for democracy. Aung San's death on July 19, 1947. The massacres at Rangoon University on July 7, 1962. The popular uprising on August 8, 1988. Aung San Suu Kyi's speech on August 26 of the same year. The SLORC's seizure of power on September 18. Suu Kyi's house arrest on May 30, 2003. The crushing of the monks' protests on September 25, 2007. Hurricane Nargis in May 2008. To name but a few.

Sometimes it's good to think about all the years Aung San Suu Kyi has been either isolated or under strict surveillance by the junta and compare what's happened in your own life during the same period. When she was arrested the first time in July 1989 I was a twenty-one-year-old student in the city of Gothenburg, Sweden. I still had a year of classes and examinations before I would graduate. After that I have worked as radio journalist, press secretary for a union in Sweden, editor of three magazines, book publisher, and writer of a column in a newspaper. I have had three kids, married, and divorced. I have become middle aged and published five books.

Society has changed dramatically. The Berlin Wall has fallen, computers and information technology have become permanently enmeshed in our lives. Both Bill Clinton and George W. Bush had two terms as U.S. president;

the attacks of 9/11 led to the war on terrorism; China, India, and Brazil have risen to possibly become new superpowers one day; and the people of Tunisia and Egypt have forced their dictators to leave the country.

In Burma, very little has changed during the same period, and Aung San Suu Kyi has been under house arrest for most of the time.

The decisive question is when all these tragic anniversaries and all these developments, for better or worse, in the surrounding world will become too much for the military to cope with. When will the protests and the activists' enormous personal sacrifices finally have an effect? All dictatorships fall, of course, but Burma's generals have developed a huge capacity for riding out all the storms and hanging on to their power. They know exactly how to pit countries and interests against each other, with the only end being to preserve military rule. And while this oppression continues, the anniversaries will just become more and more numerous.

The international community has not discovered any working solution for breaking the deadlock. The United Nations' and other international actors' operations have mainly had the aim of calling on the junta to engage in dialogue with the opposition. Time after time they have demanded that Aung San Suu Kyi be released, that a dialogue should start, and that the rights of the ethnic minorities must be respected. During my interview with Aung San Suu Kyi, she was still searching for someone to talk to: "We have to wait and see what the new parliament and the new government will do, and then we have to find out whether they are interested in a dialogue or not. We are always open for that."

And maybe, hopefully, that is what we see now, as I write this. With the ongoing talks between Suu Kyi and president Thein Sein, that would be a true breakthrough. But as so many Burmese exiled activists state: so far very little has changed the fundamental political structure in Burma. The military can intervene as soon as it thinks the changes have gone too far. As soon as it feels its own power base erode under its feet.

The failure of the international community to be the catalyzer of real change is so far complete. Razali made some minor progress in 2002 and 2003, but it stagnated. After the saffron revolution in 2007, the former United Nations envoy Ibrahim Gambari traveled to Thailand, where he yet again demanded talks among the junta, Aung San Suu Kyi, and the ethnic minorities. At that time he had a world that was more critical than ever backing him up. The United States and the European Union had introduced new sanctions against the trade in precious stones and timber, among other commodities, as well as against yet another group of junta members and their families. Russia and China had agreed to discuss Burma at the Security Council. The United Nations demanded in a resolution that the conflict in Burma should be settled in a peaceful manner, without brutality on the part of the military. However, China and Russia, in parity with ASEAN's member countries, basically claimed that the violations in Burma were a domestic matter that had nothing to do with other governments.

From 1990 until today the United Nations has had nine different envoys who have made a total of forty-one visits to Burma. Each time the visit has been preceded by speculations about a breakthrough, each time the envoy has demanded a dialogue. And each time this effort has resulted in nothing at all. And even if there now seem to be some real efforts to open up Burma and actually change the politics of all those years of military junta rule, it's still a fact that the UN had very little to do with it.

Not even repeated reports of murder, torture, and rape have had any effect.

In September 2005, Nobel Prize winners Václav Havel and Desmond Tutu presented the report "Threat to the Peace" about the crisis in Burma. The report states that the situation in Burma is worse than in other cases in which the United Nations has chosen to intervene. The civil war and the attacks against the ethnic minorities are two such deciding factors, as is also the humanitarian crisis: the millions of refugees in neighboring countries, the drugs from the golden triangle, the spread of HIV that always follows in the tracks of heroin use, the democratically elected government that was never allowed to take over back in 1990. These factors would each on its own motivate a sharper reaction on the part of the United Nations, wrote Havel and Tutu. But nothing has happened. The United Nations has not taken seriously its responsibility to protect the civilian population.

During my travels in Burma, at least before the last year's development in the country, I have met many activists as well as "ordinary" Burmese, who have quite simply stopped believing in the United Nations or any other international organization as a factor of change. "We no longer count on any help from outside the country," said one young NLD activist whom I met the day after my meeting with Zaw Zaw. "There were such hopes after 1988, those who fled to the border after the massacres counted on receiving military support, perhaps from the USA, but it didn't happen that way. And since then nothing has worked. A new popular uprising is necessary to overthrow the junta. We have to work underground and organize our opposition."

The situation among the ethnic minorities is particularly desperate, which became clearer than ever in the aftermath of the election in November 2010. Ethnic minorities like Kachin, Karen, and Shan had warned the surrounding world of the threat of a new war. They had seen the junta gather massive amounts of soldiers in the border areas, and the ethnic minority leaders thought their resistance to the fake election was the reason. The junta would take their revenge, trying once and for all to take control of the border areas.

The war restarted a couple of days after the election. The Tatmadaw attacked Karen villages in eastern Burma, and around fifteen thousand refugees immediately crossed the border into Thailand. Fighting also broke out in the Shan state and elsewhere, and later the war with the KIA was restarted after fifteen years of cease-fire.

During my travels in the Kachin states in 2005, I met many young people who in all seriousness hoped that the United States would invade Burma, just as it had done in Iraq. They were fed up with the whole situation. Tired of decades of war and living in a country where their own future would be decided by a xenophobic regime with little or no understanding of world developments.

As a matter of fact the junta have used the fear of an invasion in their propaganda. When they moved their administrative capital from Rangoon to the brand-new town of Naypyidaw in central Burma, Than Shwe said that the move had been made to "avoid an attack by the ocean." All the Burma experts in the world scratched their heads and wondered in surprise what threat he was speaking about.

There is no military threat against Burma. At least no external military threat. And the guerrilla armies have been active since 1948 without any success in their ambition to overthrow the central government.

The idea to invade would probably never enter the minds of Washington officials, since there are not a sufficient number of oil wells or security policy interests at risk. However, in November 2011, when Hillary Clinton made the first official U.S. trip to Burma since the 1950s, it also become clear that the new political landscape, despite all the understandable skepticism about the military's real intent, has opened a new dialogue between the United States and the regime in the new, strange capital of Naypyidaw.

In any case, a military invasion, no matter the political development, would make the conflict in Iraq seem like a walk in the park. The military controls an army of 400,000 men, and they have still not succeeded in gaining control of the mountains in the last fifty years. Dozens of armies would not recognize an occupying power. The drug cartels in the mountains would give their support to the generals in Burma. The reality of the situation is that the country is in an eternal state of war. It has never existed in practice, since the military have never recognized the rights of the ethnic groups to independence within the framework of a federal state.

After the protests in the autumn of 2007, the United States and the European Union demanded yet again that a dialogue should be held between the junta and Aung San Suu Kyi, and they introduced new sanctions aimed at the junta members and their families. But they did not dare to aim the sanctions against the oil or gas industries this time either.

The Burma issue also came up in the Security Council of the United Nations, and for the first time China and Russia did not use their vetos. Meanwhile, the junta carried on developing their "roadmap to democracy" and forced the adoption of the new constitution.

As the situation in Burma was relatively stable in the two years following Hurricane Nargis and because they managed to keep Aung San Suu Kyi under house arrest after John Yettaw's swim in May 2009, the junta felt it safe to move on with the election.

This decision was probably also based on the fact that the international community was ready to reconsider its relations with Burma. To start with, their attitude toward humanitarian aid changed after Hurricane Nargis. Most countries had approached Burma with great caution up until then, but after the catastrophe the people's needs were so enormous that that attitude was no longer perceived as reasonable.

The increased foreign presence was the most evident change between my trips to Burma in 2010–2011 and my previous visits. It is obvious that more and more foreign companies are to be found there. Now cafés and restaurants have even appeared where aid workers and other Westerners gather for lunch and dinner. The prices are of course higher than at other places.

When the American John Yettaw went for a swim, despite its total madness, he succeeded in focusing the spotlight on the junta's violations. Mass media all over the world reported on the sentences against Aung San Suu Kyi and her staff. Photographs of the demonstrating monks once more filled TV screens, and politicians across the globe demanded—for which time in a row?—a dialogue with the opposition. However, when United Nations secretary general Ban Ki-Moon was to visit Burma a few weeks after Yettaw's swim, he was not even permitted to meet Aung San Suu Kyi, despite the fact that he had made that request to the junta. Than Shwe explained that it would not look very good if the head of the United Nations were to meet a person who was prosecuted for a crime.

Perhaps the only positive effect of Yettaw's action was that it made the junta appear yet again as unreasonable, brutal, and almost medieval in their view of the legal system.

The swim also coincided with the process whereby several countries were on their way to further reconsidering their policies toward Burma. With President Barack Obama at the helm, the United States decided to redirect its policies. Economic sanctions and political isolation had been the basic attitude of the United States since 1988. Now Obama wanted to initiate a dialogue with the junta, the same promise that he had given to a number of the regimes that his predecessor, President Bush, had refused to speak to. The sanctions would remain in place as long as the junta did not make any concessions or release Aung San Suu Kyi, but the talks implied a marked change, and the European Union announced that it was considering a similar change, even though it's sometimes hard to see any clear message from the EU.

Unfortunately, some of the foreign diplomats and business people in Rangoon took this new message of dialogue and the election in November

2010 as an excuse for advocating a more dramatic change in policy. They wanted the international community not only to open up diplomatic channels to Burmese counterparts but also to dismantle the sanctions, and as bizarre as it might seem given that the election was such a farce, they also saw the election process as a true step toward more openness and democracy in Burma. Many people make this mistake, and a few weeks after the elections the magazine *The Irrawaddy* provided some of the more hilarious examples:

Priscilla Clapp, a senior American analyst and former diplomat associated with the Asia Society, believed that since seventy senior officers and many junior ones retired from active service in order to run for election, that would pave the way for a new and more reform-minded generation of army commanders to take over. No such thing has happened.

David Lipman, the Bangkok-based European Union ambassador, called the election "the only game in town," implying that the international community should play along with the junta or not play at all.

A British expert, Dr. Marie Lall of Chatham House, was extolling the virtues of the politics of "collaboration" advanced by EU-funded local NGOs such as Myanmar Egress, who later reached some international notoriety by being critical of the release of Aung San Suu Kyi. They claimed her release had made their own social work more complicated.

Lall hoped the National Unity Party, made up of former generals, was "not only set to beat the [junta backed Union Solidarity and Development Party] in many constituencies, giving it real power at a national level, it is also likely to take a different stand to the current regime on many issues, starting with land-owning rights for the peasants." She concluded, "The elections are the first step out of the impasse between the military and the wider population."

NUP got 5.6 percent of the seats in the new parliament. The junta didn't accept any competition, not even from a party basically loyal to a continued military rule.

Those who recommended closer cooperation with the junta placed their hope in a group that is often called the Third Force. This is a loosely defined group of politicians and exiled Burmese who assert that they have taken up a position between the military and the NLD.

The "policymakers" also proclaimed the death of the National League for Democracy and questioned the relevance of Aung San Suu Kyi.

The junta couldn't have been happier, since they have always tried to marginalize Aung San Suu Kyi politically. The laws that were adopted in view of the election in 2010 meant not only that she herself was denied the possibility of running as a candidate, but also that the NLD would be banned as a party if Aung San Suu Kyi remained a member of the party's leadership. If they kicked her out, their members would be allowed to run as candidates. If they refused to stand in protest against the rules, then they would also be banned.

The junta had trapped the NLD in a position where its members would be losers whatever they chose to do. The party decided to boycott the election and was therefore disbanded as a working political party.

After NLD's decision to boycott the election, a group of NLD activists decided to form a party of its own, National Democratic Front, with Dr. Than Nyein as its chairman. The party got only 1.5 percent of the seats in the elections, and when the authorities asked NDF to sign a document admitting defeat, the party leadership refused.

"I don't accept the election results because this election was absolutely not free and fair," said Than Nyein. "According to the election law, after the result is announced, the loser has to sign a document that he or she is defeated. But any candidate from my party did not or won't sign that. Now we are going to file a complaint against the election results to the Election Committee."

Even the regime's own announcements show clearly that the election was flawed. Right after the election the state-run media stated that 102.9 percent of a constituency in Pegu Division north of the old capital Rangoon had turned out to vote. They later corrected this number. The "correct" should have been 99.57 percent. In a township in western Rakhine state, 104.28 percent of the electorate were said to have voted. USDP even "won" in two constituencies in Kachin state where the elections had been canceled.

In other words: both the process leading up to the election and the outcome spoke volumes against those who had put their hopes in the junta's goodwill to actually use the election as the starting point for wider reform.

Basically, the democratic opposition in Burma considers the new constitution to be unfair. The ethnic minorities are also very skeptical of, not to
say hostile to, the new constitution. It doesn't give them any of the independence in regional member states that they have been wishing for since
the 1940s. On the contrary, the new constitution establishes that the most
decisive political issues will be controlled by the central government.

The point is that both the constitution and the election are parts of a plan
the junta have been working on for two decades. When the national convention was appointed in 1993, this was exactly its officials' final goal. Now,
over twenty years after the great demonstrations in 1988 and Suu Kyi's
entrance onto the political stage, they have succeeded in tailoring a political
solution that will make it possible for them to remain in power and still, on
the surface, appear to have changed the system.

After her release Aung San Suu Kyi was asked by the magazine *The
Irrawaddy* what she thought about the diplomats who had put some faith
in the election process. "Well," she said with one of her trademark laughs,
"perhaps this was a good lesson for them." Interviewed by *Financial Times*,
she elaborated, "Sometimes I think that a parody of democracy could be
more dangerous than a blatant dictatorship, because that gives people an
opportunity to avoid doing anything about it."

No political power in Burma nor any diplomat or foreign politician can
deny the fact that Aung San Suu Kyi is the natural leading figure of the democratic movement and Burma's most supremely popular politician. Any
doubts about this should have been removed after the release of Suu Kyi.
Every oppositional force, even the politicians who had decided to run in
the election, made it clear that she is still the legitimate leader of the democracy movement.

On the other hand, one could say that Aung San Suu Kyi has adopted a
new attitude toward the political environment after the elections. Burma is
still controlled by the military, but it's also different from what it was in 2003
when she was put under house arrest. The change in attitude from the international community and the fact that the democracy movement was split
before the election creates a different political landscape. In one of the first
interviews after her release, she also mentioned the changes in people's abil-
ities to communicate. She had noticed it in the speech she held outside the

NLD office the day after her release. "The first thing I noticed was that there were many more young people in the crowd that welcomed me. Many of them were using cell phones. They were taking photographs with their phones, which I had never experienced before. There was no such thing ten years ago, but it has become quite widespread these days. I think there are more communication lines than before. It is important."

These changes were probably the reason for her to talk even more than usual about compromises and the need to "listen to all parts of the Burmese society as well as to the international community."

The junta have often used talks with Suu Kyi as a method for propitiating the world at large, and as soon as they have gotten their way internationally they have once again closed the door in the face of the democratic movement. Still, there is possibly something new and more hopeful in the changes we have seen during the summer and fall of 2011. In the talks between Suu Kyi and the regime, in the release of some political prisoners, in the fact that NLD can work openly and reorganize itself as a political force. NLD is once again allowed to work as a political party, and in November 2011 it got permission to run for a few open seats in parliament. Even Aung San Suu Kyi was allowed to run as a candidate, something that had been completely out of the question for the previous rulers of Burma.

So on one hand changes seem to be happening. Now more than ever. In the late summer of 2011 Suu Kyi herself described the situation as the most positive change in any Asian country since the 1980s. On the other hand, many of these changes happened in Burma before without any real difference, and before the opposite is proved, one must unfortunately assume that the same will happen this time too. The situation among the ethnic minorities is a problem of certain importance. The intensified fighting between the regime's troops and a number of ethnic guerrillas shows that the problem in Burma is not only focused around the conflict between democracy and dictatorship. It was the ethnic issue that brought down the democracy in the 1950s, and it will be the most important problem for any future government to solve, to make sure that the same isn't repeated.

I believe that it is somewhere here, in the futile efforts from the international community and the ongoing problems in Burma, one can find the explanation for why Aung San Suu Kyi has remained such a powerful global symbol for democracy and human rights. If hopes of a more open world carried her into the limelight, then it is the opposite that has kept her there.

She has been a reminder of the failure.

The world became freer after the fall of the Berlin Wall but that liberty was relative. China opened up economically, and investors and diplomats have flocked around the centers of expansion and development on the Chinese east coast. However, there has been no question of any political reforms. The communist party has retained its power monopoly. Dissidents and independent journalists are persecuted and imprisoned. China's rapid development has established a completely new global system and Burma's military junta have wanted to surf on the waves of its success.

Aung San Suu Kyi has always emphasized in her political commentaries that there is a link between politics and economy. She has argued for economic sanctions for reasons of morality but also because that is one of the few powerful weapons left if one does not believe in military violence. However, sanctions only work if most countries agree on the politics of isolation. Over and above this, countries and international organizations have leaned on diplomacy and political leverage, but neither of these has been effective in the case of Burma.

Asked about it in the early days of February 2011, Suu Kyi repeated the same message she has been delivering for the past twenty years. "The best way is coordination," she says. "A coordinated approach to the Burma problem. Unfortunately the coordination is quite poor. As you probably know not even the EU has a coordinated view on how to handle the situation."

But even though Aung San Suu Kyi is critical of the present lack of coordination, she is still hopeful, in the same way she always is, whether with regard to politics or personal matters. She always seems to be blatantly realistic about the present and unbelievably hopeful about the future. It's just a question of being persistent. "One has to see that coordination is achieved by a lot of hard work," she says. "It just doesn't happen automatically."

What is fascinating about Aung San Suu Kyi is that she still believes that cooperation and dialogue—nonviolence—are effective methods. Her personal background is almost tailor-made for the discourse on human rights that has been conducted since the fall of the Iron Curtain. She stands with both feet in the anticolonial struggle. She has been influenced by the American human rights movement, the anti-apartheid movement in South Africa, and Gandhi's theories on civil resistance.

She has worked for the United Nations and is the first to highlight the impact of that world organization. She knows that there are no roads to take other than the diplomatic and the political, despite the United Nations' obvious deficiencies and the inability of the international community to influence the regime in Burma in any meaningful way. And she knows that it may take time. She herself has often compared Burma with South Africa. It took thirty years to do away with apartheid. For many years the system seemed to be totally impenetrable. Then suddenly the change came.

In an interview with the magazine *Vogue* in 1995, after the first period of house arrest, she received the question of just how many years she was prepared to sacrifice for the sake of Burma becoming democratic. "That could take a long time," she replied. "It could take all my life."

It's a fascinating statement, but let's hope it doesn't take that long. Let's hope the failures of Burma are in its past and that Aung Sang Suu Kyi's name will remind us of success, besides the importance of personal courage and hope in the most desperate of times.

While I have been working on this book, many people have asked me how she can cope with making such enormous personal sacrifices? Why does she remain in Burma? It is over twenty years now since she was first confined to house arrest. Just consider your own life—what were you doing in the summer of 1989—and you will realize just how many anniversaries have passed.

Yet the question is wrongly put in a way, since it emanates from the idea that Aung San Suu Kyi's sacrifice is unique. However, the fact is that history is full of people who have made tremendous personal sacrifices for a greater cause. The Norwegian resistance fighters during the Second World War, the union activists in Latin America, the independence movements within the colonial system, political dissidents in China, refugees all over the world. The difference is perhaps that similar sacrifices have often received greater attention because they have been made by men.

In the interview with Alan Clements in the mid-1990s, Aung San Suu Kyi said that the greatest difference between herself and her father is the feeling of responsibility. Aung San felt even in his youth that he had a mission that was more important than his own person, and he spent the rest of his life taking responsibility for the calling that he understood he had been given. He literally sacrificed himself for a greater cause. When she was young, Aung San Suu Kyi never experienced the same "calling" to greater missions, but the sense of responsiblity had crept in gradually, and during a number of years in the 1980s she felt an ever greater restlessness. She "was looking for a mission" in her life. That was the reason she offered herself as a candidate when the democratic movement needed her. That was why she left the "little world" and took the great step out into the "big world."

Her family had already been separated from one another during certain periods. There was nothing to indicate that her house arrest would last for the better part of two decades. But when she had finally challenged the junta, when she had demanded to be thrown into prison, when she refused to leave the country, then there was no going back, that was impossible. She could not say one day that she was thinking of challenging the junta, then change her mind and travel back to England again. That would have demolished a good deal of her political capital inside Burma, even if she had remained a significant voice internationally. Such a decision would furthermore have been foreign to both her values and her highly principled stance.

"I missed my family, particularly my sons," she said after the first six-year period of house arrest. "I missed not having the chance to look after them—to be with them. But, I did not feel cut off from life. Basically, I felt that being under house arrest was just part of my job—I was doing my work."

Her family, the two sons and the marriage with Michael Aris, has always been an important part of the story of Aung San Suu Kyi. One of the most touching moments after her release in 2010 might have been when Aung San Suu Kyi met her youngest son, Kim Aris, at the international airport. It was a couple of days after her first speech. Kim had applied for a visa as soon as it became clear that the junta would actually release her. It was denied for several weeks, but Kim was waiting in Bangkok for an opening in the junta's policy. Ten days after his mother's release he finally got the papers and took the first flight to Rangoon, barely an hour's trip by plane over the Karen mountains in eastern Burma.

It had been more than ten years since they had last seen each other, and just before walking into the airport terminal, Aung San Suu Kyi said, "I'm very happy." Tears welled up in her eyes when they first looked at each other, and then she slipped her arm around his waist. The two posed briefly for photographers, and Kim Aris took off his green jacket and in front of the airport security and the public bared his right arm, where he had a tattoo of a red flag with a fighting peacock and a star—the symbol of the NLD.

His mother looked at it for a second and smiled. Later she declared she was grateful the junta gave him a visa. She also said she had been close to her son during all those years.

"I don't feel that I've been apart from him. I never felt apart from him."

SOURCES AND SUPPORT

To a great extent, this book builds on interviews with people who have met, worked with, and gotten to know Aung San Suu Kyi through the years. Many of them have asked that they remain anonymous—in certain cases because their participation would be dangerous for themselves, in other cases out of concern for Aung San Suu Kyi. I have let them remain anonymous, and in some cases I have changed names and places in order to avoid divulging their identities. I would, however, like to mention the following people by name: Debbie Stothard, Nyo Ohn Myint, Ann Pasternak Slater, Peter Carey, Jenny Tun-Aung, Moe Zaw Oo, Moe Myat Thu, Zin Linn, Lian Sakhong, Sein Win, Malavika Karlekar, Clas Örjan Spång, and Jan Nordlander. For reading and support during the time of writing, I would like to thank Annika Nordgren Christensen, Jonas Ljung, Bertil Lintner, and Martin Gemzell.

Regarding newspapers, I have systematically searched the digital archives first and foremost of the *Bangkok Post*, *The Nation* (Thailand), *The Irrawaddy*, *Far Eastern Economic Review*, the *Times of India*, *Washington Post*, Associated Press, *The Independent*, and *New York Times*.

An endless amount has been written about Aung San Suu Kyi, but as an effect of her isolation there are only a very few real biographies. I have benefited greatly from Justin Wintle's book *Perfect Hostage*, the most thorough of the biographies, especially the descriptions of Suu Kyi's childhood and time in Oxford. Barbara Victor's *The Lady* has also been an important source, as has Bertil Lintner's *Aung San Suu Kyi and Burma's Struggle for Democracy*. *Freedom from Fear*, the collection of texts that Michael Aris compiled in 1991, is still the most personal description of Suu Kyi. When it comes to her own words, Alan Clement's *The Voice of Hope* is the only really thorough text, along with her own articles in *Letters from Burma*.

During the years I have been writing about Burma, dozens of reports from Amnesty International, Human Rights Watch, and other human rights organizations have passed across my writing desk. Some of them are direct references in this book and I will refrain from including them all in the list of sources. Taken together I have mainly used the following written sources:

Ad hoc commission on the Depayin massacre. *The second preliminary report*. Euro-Burma office, 2004.

Aung San Suu Kyi. *Aung San of Burma: A Biographical Portrait*. University of Queensland Press, 1984.

————. *Freedom from Fear: And Other Writings*. Edited with an introduction by Michael Aris. Penguin, 1991.

————. *Letters from Burma*. Penguin, 1995.

————. *Let's Visit Burma*. Burke Books, 1985.

————. *The Voice of Hope: Conversations with Alan Clements*. Seven Stories Press, 1997.

Aung-Thwin, Michael. *Parochial Universalism, Democracy Jihad, and the Orientalist Image of Burma: The New Evangelism*. Pacific Affairs, 2001.

Bingham, June. *U Thant: The Search for Peace*. Knopf, 1966.

Chee, Soon Juan, Järnfjäril. *Om Aung San Suu Kyi och Burmas skitiga historia.* Silc förlag, 2006.

Clements, Alan. *The Next Killing Fields.* The Real Story Series, 1990.

Havel, Václav, and Desmond Tutu. *Threat to the Peace. A Call for the UN Security Council to Act in Burma.* UN, 2005.

Houtman, Gustaaf. *Mental Culture in Burmese Crisis Politics: Aung San Suu Kyi and the National League for Democracy.* Tokyo University of Foreign Studies, 1999.

Krarup Nielsen, Aage. *De gyllene pagodernas land.* Bonniers, 1959.

Lintner, Bertil. *Aung San Suu Kyi and Burma's Struggle for Democracy.* Asianetwork, 2007.

———. *Burma in Revolt: Opium and Insurgency since 1948.* Silkworm Books, 1999.

———. *Outrage: Burma's Struggle for Democracy.* Kiscadale Publications, 1990.

Maung Maung. *Burma and General Ne Win.* Religious Affairs Dept., Rangoon, 1969.

Maung Myint. *The International Response to the Democracy Movement in Burma since 1962.* Center for Pacific Asia Studies, Stockholms universitet, 2000.

Naw, Angelene. *Aung San and the Struggle for Burmese Independence.* Silkworm Books, 2001.

Sargent, Inge. *Twilight over Burma: My Life as a Shan Princess.* Silkworm Books, 1994.

Stewart, A. T. Q. *The Pagoda War: Lord Dufferin and the Fall of the Kingdom of Ava, 1885–86*. White Lotus, 1972.

Thant, Myint-U. *The River of Lost Footsteps: A Personal History of Burma*. Farrar, Straus and Giroux, 2007.

Tucker, Shelby. *Burma: The Curse of Independence*. Pluto Press, 2001.

Victor, Barbara. *The Lady: Aung San Suu Kyi, Nobel Laureate and Burma's Prisoner*. Faber and Faber, 1998.

Wintle, Justin. *Perfect Hostage: A Life of Aung San Suu Kyi*. Skyhorse, 2007.

ABOUT THE AUTHOR

Jesper Bengtsson is a journalist who has followed developments in Burma for more than a decade. He is the chairman of the Swedish section of the human rights organization Reporters sans frontières (Reporters Without Borders). The author of *Burma: A Journey in the Shadow of the Dictatorship* (2007), he has also written editorials for the Swedish newspaper *Aftonbladet*.